Typewriter Battalion

. . . .

TYPEWRITER
BATTALION

DRAMATIC FRONT-LINE DISPATCHES FROM WORLD WAR II

• • • • • • • • • • • •

EDITED BY JACK STENBUCK

INTRODUCTION BY
WALTER CRONKITE

• • • • • • • • • • • •

WILLIAM MORROW AND COMPANY, INC.
NEW YORK

LIBRARY OF CONGRESS CATALOGING-IN-PUBLICATION DATA
Typewriter battalion : dramatic front-line dispatches from World War
II / selected and edited by Jack Stenbuck.
p.   cm.
ISBN 0-688-14190-0
1. World War, 1939–1945.   2. World War, 1939–1945—Personal
narratives.   3. War correspondents—Biography.   I. Stenbuck, Jack.
D743.T97   1995
940.54'1—dc20   94-41260   CIP

Printed in the United States of America

First Edition

1 2 3 4 5 6 7 8 9 10

BOOK DESIGN BY FRITZ METSCH

To the memory of Ernie Pyle and the thirty-one other members of the American press who, like so many they accompanied into battle, gave up their lives on bombers, battleships, and invasion barges and in the front lines in order that the world might know the horror, tragedy, and full meaning of war and the price of freedom and liberty for which men fought.

Introduction

. . . .

WALTER CRONKITE

We all abhor war. And when government leaders presume that war is necessary, they are not only betraying a failure of policy but admitting that human beings have not advanced very far from the cave. Nowadays, as modern weapons assure mass slaughter once the shooting begins, it seems that people and nations would put as much effort into assuring peace as they eventually do in trying to win wars. All of this leaves the peacemakers with nothing more than clichés, such as the phrase "There is nothing glamorous about war."

Unfortunately, they are wrong. The unparalleled fraternity that men (and now, presumably women) find in battle, the heroism of those who lay down their lives for their buddies and for a cause, the thrill of the deadly chase where both the pursued and the pursuer know that one of them will not return from the field of combat— these are the stuff of high drama.

The drama is essentially tragic, but the tragedy is laced with all the expressions of human performance—bravery, cowardice, modesty, bravado, irony, humor. Many of the stories have been preserved in the retelling by surviving participants, and some have been captured in memoirs and reconstructed history. But the most reliable reports of how it really was can be found in the dispatches of the newspaper and broadcast reporters who accompanied the troops into action and to a large degree shared with them the dangers and the vicissitudes of combat.

Just as war itself is glamorous, nothing in the field of journalism is more glamorous than being a war correspondent. We all recognize the model of the newspaper reporter dashing from one scene of action to the next, press badge tucked into his hatband, notebook in hand. His mandatory costume reeks of wartime experience—the trench coat with its vestigial epaulets. I feel certain that every one of the people whose dispatches contributed to this book at some moment or other sensed, if only momentarily, the aura of romance about them. With some this recognition of their own special caché was far more pervasive than with others.

Collected here are the stories from the foxholes, from the bloody beaches, from the burning decks, from the crippled bombers, reported as they happened by those who truly were entitled to know what its government was doing in its name. This is never more necessary than during the times when citizens in our country are being sent out to kill and be killed to further national policy.

But if the press is to be present, it must also be prepared to observe the necessity of secrecy in many aspects of the military operation. And the military, on its part, also must understand that it must not censor for political reasons. This delicate balance was for the most part achieved in World War II. It was not achieved in Vietnam, where the lack of a formal relationship between the press and the military led to a totally adversarial experience. Then later in Granada, Panama, and the Persian Gulf, the military defied every precept of democracy by refusing the right of the press to be at the scene of the action.

This book might be taken by the new generation in the military and the press as a textbook on how effective battlefront reporting can be without endangering combat security. And it can give us hope that if there must be other wars in other places, at least the public will be permitted to know the truth and at least that part of our democracy will be preserved.

Contents

· · · · · · · · · · · ·

CONTENTS

About Jack Stenbuck

. . . .

Jack Stenbuck, our father, began this collection of great World War II correspondence before the war ended, probably in 1944. We discovered the *Typewriter Battalion* manuscript in April 1992, following our mother's death at age ninety-one in Los Angeles. Hannah was a saver, and in the closet of their Brentwood apartment, we discovered a treasure trove of original manuscripts by "Big Jack," among them this anthology. Dad, who had died in 1975, was a wonderfully fulfilled man as the result of a life chockablock with sparkling accomplishments within and without the newspaper field—his first and everlasting love. We can only guess how he became inspired to accumulate this remarkable outpouring of journalistic splendor, but we are convinced that it was his innate editorial sense that caused him to recognize that the work of these writers would be valuable long after the war had ended and the newspapers they appeared in had been thrown away.

Dad was born in 1900, a fraternal twin and one of five children of an immigrant family, the son of a tailor who migrated to Wisconsin. In 1916 he started a job as a five-dollar-a-week office boy on the Milwaukee *Sentinel*, to support his premed education at Milwaukee Normal. A year later, his college education on hold, he climbed a two-year ladder first as a reporter, then in subsequent jobs as sportswriter, copyreader, makeup editor, telegraph editor, assistant editor, and finally, at age nineteen, city editor. In 1921 he joined Hearst's *Wisconsin News*, and in 1926, motivated by the responsibility of a newly formed family and the advice of his publisher that "he who brings in the money makes the money," he abruptly made an overnight switch from editorial to circulation director. For twenty-two years of his thirty-year career with the Hearst newspapers, Dad was the consummate circulation director, first in Milwaukee, then in Detroit and Boston, and finally in New York, where he became leader of the flock as general circulation director of all the Hearst papers and a member of the company's editorial board. In 1942 he left the newspaper business and started what became the largest public relations firm in New England. During this time he launched a career as one of the nation's most prolific magazine contributors, with more than a hundred articles published in *Reader's Digest*, *Collier's*, *Redbook*, *Esquire*, *Coronet*, and other leading publications of the day. Dad spent his final years as a consultant to the Thompson Organization and the *Times*, of London, the Houston *Chronicle*, and the Hearst newspapers.

In his life our father was granted the exciting privilege of participating in and contributing to the "golden age" of American print journalism, the twenties, which roared out of World War I—spawning an "anything goes" society that welcomed flamboyance of the likes of a William Randolph Hearst and his expansive empire. Then suddenly the decade of the thirties—a shower of ice on the flappers' fires—took away the rampant optimism of the twenties and substituted despair. In the newspaper world the Great Depression forced failures, consolidations, and shrinking empires. It was a period when a newspaper had to do more than dispense the news in order to survive. Dad, among an early few, saw clearly that a newspaper, after all, had become a product, like Ivory soap and Coca-Cola, which, to survive and flourish, must adopt techniques of marketing and selling or become a historical statistic.

In those two decades of extreme contrast, our father honed the skills that nurtured a great journalistic career that years later, in 1969, brought forth the comment from the executive vice-president of a major news organization that "Everyone but everyone in the newspaper business has at least heard of Jack Stenbuck. Your reputation in the field is outstanding."

We hope that this tribute to the great journalists of World War II will also forever be a tribute to our father's journalistic abilities.

—NANCY ROSENFIELD and JEROME STENBUCK

Jerry wrote this tribute to our father. I didn't change a word; I felt it was perfect. But now I have a sad addendum. My beloved brother passed away in October 1994, eight months before the publication of this book.

For two full years we were involved in what we felt was a very sentimental journey, working to publish the manuscript we had so serendipitously discovered in our mother's apartment. We shared the love and pride for the project, which brought aging siblings even closer together. It caused us to reminisce frequently about our dad's colorful journalistic career, and the impact he had on the careers of succeeding generations of our family.

Jerry's frequent lament in his last few days was that he wouldn't be around to celebrate our ultimate accomplishment. I just know he is hugging "Big Jack" and saying, "See, Dad, Nancy and I did it for you!"

—NANCY ROSENFIELD
November 1994

Foreword

. . . .

Never in all history had the drama of war been painted as vividly and completely, at the very moment it was unfolding, as in World War II.

From the day Hitler unleashed his Wehrmacht hordes, an army of war correspondents—men and women—voluntarily courted untold hardship, danger, and even death itself alongside fighting men in every corner of the globe in order that the world might have, firsthand and without delay, the full story of this great holocaust.

No mission was too dangerous, no battlefield too remote. War correspondents rode flak-filled skies in bombers, sailed sub-infested seas in battleships, submarines, and other vessels of war, jumped with airborne troops by parachute, and stormed bloody beaches in riddled landing craft while enemy gunners reddened the waters around them with a withering fire.

From the desert wastes of El Alamein to the fogbound Aleutians, and from the volcanic slopes of Iwo Jima to the D day beaches on the coast of Normandy, they lived—and too often died—with the GIs, the men of the maquis, the little people of some bomb-blasted London or Coventry, the generals and admirals.

World War II was different from World War I, and so was its

coverage by the press. Whereas a handful of correspondents covered World War I, mainly from the comparative safety of headquarters in the rear, with an occasional conducted tour of a quiet frontline sector, World War II found hundreds of accredited American correspondents continuously sharing invasion and battlefield dangers with the men they wrote about.

In the Russo-Japanese War the world was many weeks in learning how the Russian fleet was sunk. In this war D day itself was almost as real within the hour to the farmer in Iowa, the lumberman in Oregon, or the ranch hand in Texas as it was to those who stormed ashore, as a result of the excellent on-the-spot dispatches from the correspondents who went along.

From Burma to London, and from Yugoslavia to Da Nang, there are simple graves that speak eloquently for their bravery and devotion to duty. In proportion to their numbers, the casualties they suffered in dead and wounded exceed those of the men in combat about whom they were writing.

They knew the dangers and the price and, like all men going into battle, knew paralyzing fear, yet they kept on going, often actually battling for a chance to share in the most hazardous missions for the sake of an eyewitness story. Frequently, at the point of utter exhaustion, they came back from these dangerous missions to race the clock amid the crash of bombs and to file stories that will live as masterpieces of splendid writing under deadline pressure.

There were some occasionally whose articles met unexpected delays in transit and who were among dead or wounded before the stories they had filed reached their destinations and appeared in print.

Unfortunately a single volume cannot do justice to them all. Undoubtedly some whose work merits special attention have, for one reason or another, been omitted from this collection. From the millions of words written on the war, it is obvious that no one group of articles can represent a unanimous selection of the very best.

Nevertheless, an attempt has been made here, in many cases after consultation with distinguished editors, to include a cross section of the best—stories chosen for the quality of their telling, the drama of events described, or their importance to the world's history.

I am indebted to the following executives and their newspapers and press associations who graciously granted me permission to include their correspondents' copyright material in this book:

I especially want to express my appreciation to Barry Faris, editor in chief, the International News Service; Lawrence Winship, managing editor, the Boston *Globe*; George Minot, managing editor, the Boston *Herald*; Paul S. Deland, managing editor, and Charles E. Gratke, foreign editor, the *Christian Science Monitor*; and Basil Walters, supervising editor, and Hal O'Flaherty, foreign editor, the Chicago *Daily News*. Without their encouragement and help in the beginning, the collection of this material would have been impossible.

I am also forever grateful to the following for their cooperation and permission to reprint material from their publications: The United Press International and Hugh Baille, general manager; the North American Newspaper Alliance and John M. Wheeler, president, and Henry M. Snevily, general manager; AP Newsfeatures and M. J. Wing, general editor; the New York *World-Telegram and Sun*, Lee B. Wood, editor; the Boston *Evening American* and Winn Brooks, managing editor; the Los Angeles *Times*, and Frank P. Haven, managing editor; the Chicago *Sun* and Frank Taylor, assistant publisher, and E. Z. Dimitman, executive editor; the New York *Herald Tribune* and George A. Cornish, managing editor; *The New York Times* and managing editors Edwin L. James and Turner Catledge; the Chicago *Tribune* and J. Loy Maloney, managing editor; the Boston *Traveler* and Harold F. Wheeler, managing editor; the Des Moines *Register Tribune* and W. W. Waymack, managing editor; the Detroit *News* and W. S. Gilmore, managing editor; the Milwaukee *Journal* and Waldo R. Arnold, managing editor; the Canadian Press and J. A. McNeil, general manager; the New York *Sun* and Keats Speed, executive editor; the Chicago *Times* and Russ Stewart, managing editor, and Irving Pflaum, foreign editor. Also, I am indebted to George Carlin, general manager of United Features Syndicate; Dick Thornburg, managing editor, the Scripps-Howard Newspaper Alliance, and Henry Holt and Company, Inc. for permission to use the Ernie Pyle story excerpted from his book *Brave Men*; and Helen Gurley Brown, editor, *Cosmopolitan* magazine.

Lastly, but no less gratefully and warmly, I embrace my former associates at the Hearst newspapers, W. R. Hearst, Jr., editor in chief; Frank Conniff, national editor; and Kingsbury Smith, publisher of the New York *Journal-American.*

—JACK STENBUCK
New York, 1945, and Los Angeles, 1974

I Saw the Sneak Attack

· · · · · · · · · · · ·

BY

JOSEPH C. HARSCH

STAFF CORRESPONDENT OF THE *CHRISTIAN SCIENCE MONITOR*

HONOLULU, Dec. 7, 1941—Planes with red balls under their wings came in through morning mist today and attacked America's great mid-Pacific naval base and island fortress here.

We have probably paid a heavy price, but we know where we stand.

There was no warning of any kind. The remnants of the tourist trade lay on the sands of Waikiki Beach long after the bombs began to fall, believing that it was a practice maneuver. Only when smoke piled into the sky from the bombs did the mass of the inhabitants grasp the fact that Japan had begun to wage war on the United States in one of the most daring surprise attacks of modern military history.

The scope of the attack and the results are military secrets.

Your correspondent was awakened by sounds made familiar by long months in Berlin.

I awoke my wife and asked her if she wanted to know what an air raid sounded like in Europe. This, I remarked, is a good imitation. We then proceeded to the beach for our morning swim, assuming with everyone else in the hotel that it was just another practice maneuver by the navy.

Off shore a freighter seemed to list. I thought it was just a practice turn to add realism to the maneuvers. Only when the radio began telling the people what had happened could one grasp the incredible fact that the Japanese naval forces had managed to strike their blows at the fortress of Oahu.

The city of Honolulu took it like a veteran. There was no hysteria.

The civilian defense organization went into action quickly and smoothly. The greatest problem was to keep the curious under cover. The people had been so conditioned by maneuvers and practices and the knowledge that this island would be one of Japan's first military objectives in the Pacific that they took it in their stride, once the idea penetrated that this was a real war and not just another practice.

The Honolulu Star Bulletin, the leading evening newspaper, was on the streets with an extra before noon and the familiar American newsboy cry rang through streets to the accompaniment of occasional explosions in the distance. The damage in the city itself is negligible.

The Japanese planes came in at low altitudes. Many people on the street saw the red ball under the wings distinctly. Several are known to have been brought down although the official report has not yet been released either on American or enemy losses.

The attack began at 7:55 o'clock in the morning. Throughout the day less than a dozen bombs fell on the residential part of the city of Honolulu and these apparently were more or less accidental. The brunt of the attack obviously was delivered carefully and deliberately at the striking power of the American forces based at Pearl Harbor and various air fields.

Eye witnesses living near Pearl Harbor, Hickam Field, Wheeler Field, Kaneohe Naval Air Base, and other smaller bases saw repeated attacks by bombers on each beginning with the start of the battle.

I was at a hotel about 15 miles east of Pearl Harbor. From that point I could see clouds of white smoke peppered with black bursts of anti-aircraft fire over the Pearl Harbor area throughout most of the morning, while out at sea great geysers of water jumped skyward around many ships dodging about on the horizon. Several merchantmen approached the harbor during the action and all were subjected sooner or later to some enemy attention.

Often the enemy planes were concealed above the cloud masses and the only evidence of their presence was the sound of motors and the heavy ground fire. The number of attacking planes was impossible to estimate, but the total sound effect was similar to that heard in Berlin during the heaviest raid this writer experienced there when American observers estimated that well over fifty planes were engaged.

That Berlin raid was of relatively short duration while this attack of the same intensity lasted off and on for most of the day, being heaviest until noon and dwindling off into short attacks, presumably by a few planes during the afternoon.

The enemy began sustaining losses from the outset. Civilians reaching the city from the Pearl Harbor area after the first attack reported seeing three Japanese planes downed from the first wave. Later reports from other parts of the island came in of other planes brought down at every major point attacked.

People along the Waikiki Beach area had grandstand seats. The curve of the shoreline made it possible to witness the panorama of the outer harbor, with a great column of smoke over Pearl Harbor rising to the cloud-studded sky. Hundreds of people spent the entire day along the beach, watching the sight, regardless of occasional falling shell fragments and nearby bombs.

The enemy planes were occasionally visible. During the morning I saw one flight of what appeared to be five two-engined medium bombers approaching the island from the southwest almost over my head. They met heavy anti-aircraft fire and swerved away to the sea again without completing the attack.

Those seeing the attack distant from the Waikiki grandstand found difficulty in appreciating the meaning of the dramatic spectacle. But those from the Pearl Harbor area were different. A naval wife who had taken her husband to Pearl Harbor just when the attack began arrived back at the hotel about 9 A.M. terribly shaken. She had driven back from the harbor area with Japanese planes flying, according to her estimate, less than 100 feet overhead spraying machine-gun fire along the road.

Her arrival was necessary to convince most of the hotel residents that this was really war. She had reached the main gate of the harbor just as the first wave of Japanese planes came in. She said the men at the main gate, even under the shock of surprise, stood their ground and never for one moment relaxed their routine inspection and challenge of every person entering the yard.

It has come. Underneath the feeling of shock, horror and resentment, there already is a widespread feeling of relief. At least the uncertainty is over. At least, the time for vacillation and controversy has ended.

. . . .

JOSEPH C. HARSCH

Joseph C. Harsch was born in Toledo, Ohio, on May 25, 1905. In 1929, after studying history at Williams College in Massachusetts and Cambridge University in England, he joined the *Christian Science Monitor*, where he worked until his retirement. He also served as a radio commentator for CBS and the BBC.

Harsch once claimed that if he were dropped blindfolded into any of the European capitals, he could recognize it by its smell. His radio broadcasts and *Monitor* stories were datelined from all over the world, most notably Berlin, New Zealand, Australia, Java, and Pearl Harbor at the time of the Japanese attack. His experience led him to write two books, *Pattern of Conquest* (1941), about Nazi Germany, and *The Curtain Isn't Iron* (1951).

Our Ghosts Haunt the Japs

· · · · · · · · · · · ·

BY

ROBERT J. CASEY

WAR CORRESPONDENT OF THE CHICAGO *DAILY NEWS*

WITH THE UNITED STATES PACIFIC FLEET AT SEA, March 4, 1942—
The war has been brought into Japanese waters by the "stop and
sock" section, the seagoing commandos of the Pacific fleet. This is
being written at no great distance from the Japanese coast, only a
thin whisper from the bulk of Japan's stay-at-home Navy, not too
far from Japan's vital supply line to the expanding racket in the
Southwest Pacific. If it is no surprise to you, well, it certainly was
to the Japs.

The last couple of weeks have been fairly disconserting for the
Son of Heaven in these parts. The great force, supposedly sunk in
bulk at Pearl Harbor and conversationally blasted piecemeal every
so often since, has tested the Japanese strength all across the Pacific
and has now come impudently to the door of Japan itself.

It smashed up, and this you know, Jap air attacks on the fleet,
south of the Gilbert Islands, with virtually 100 percent destruction
of the attacking force. It has recently made a more thorough desolation of Wake Island. And finally, it has blown up Minamitori
Shima, another naval base like all the rest except that it is in a
portion of the Pacific that the Mikado has long considered his private pond.

There was turmoil in the Japan-dominated portion of the ether that strange night. There were whispers of questing airplanes in the dark overhead. The short-waves crackled with messages whose uneasy tempo made it unnecessary to understand their text—with gravely considered ballyhoo in English, disclosing nervousness and fear in a too repetitious song of victory—:"eight unidentified planes were shot down in an attack on Minamitori Shima early today and the raiding force driven off not having damaged the island's unimportant installations. There were few casualties."

"Japanese airmen downed thirty-two United States bombers in an encounter south of Gilbert Island; all our aircraft returned safely. A United States carrier damaged severely or sunk."

"A raid in force by United States cruisers, destroyers and planes on Otorji Island, formerly Wake, was repulsed after brief fight. One cruiser was set afire, one destroyer sunk. There was no damage to Japanese installations or personnel." (All this, oddly enough, was true except for the distribution of losses.)

And there were little blats on the communication bands. You got the sense after awhile that out there not far away in the night many a big ship was streaking unceremoniously for home. You could envision the rest: Destroyer screens farflung and watchful lest we contrive—as usual—to sneak past patrols and this time drop some crumps on important ships—possibly battleships—that infested these waters.

The cause of all this commotion was just another of those smouldering fires on the island where Japan had set up an important base. But you did not need to understand the Japanese to comprehend the gist of the babble coming up from the horizons beyond the ashes. But this one was getting too close to the point where sheltered homefolks of Japan might be able to see it.

Another sign on the horizon, as possibly interpreted by the fairly intelligent high command, was that a war fleet, able to get to Marcus Island, obviously could get to Yokohama—and the same half-ton bomb that would uproot a power plant on Marcus would be definite bad news for a battleship. And if the home defense fleet was not safe at home, where was it safe?

Among odd fragments that came over the sizzling radios, there was mention of an air-raid alarm in Tokyo—the first air-raid alarm in the long, interesting history of Japan. And there would have been nothing significant in it except for the fact that the day before the bad news came to Marcus Island nobody would have bothered to twist the crank on the siren.

From then on watchers on the housetops of Tokyo might go on hoping for the best, but they never could be sure. Right then, the Japanese knew we were in position, should our commander figure the job was part of the strategy, to make the air raid alarm come true. It is not the amount of damage we have done in Minamitori Shima that counts in the psychological box score at the moment. It is what we could do if we wanted to, and to the household guards of Tokyo it will be a lasting puzzle why we haven't.

You won't find much about Marcus Island (or Minamitori Shima) in the encyclopedia or atlas, or, for that matter, in the Pilot book for the Northwest Pacific. It was discovered back in the '40s by a Frenchman and visited many years later by the U.S.S. Tuscarora. It is a small, high island that for a long time remained on the charts as "uninhabited." Like Wake, its change in status was due to the fact that Japan, stretching out farther and farther its spread of culture in the Western Pacific, needed a link between its mandated islands and the Ogasawara Islands, an archipelago adjacent to and almost part of Japan proper.

Marcus is about a thousand miles from Tokyo, which yesterday made it a comforting outpost for Japan and today makes it a possible base for bombing raids on important Japanese cities. As distances go in this war and in the Pacific, 1,000 miles are hardly worth mentioning.

Despite Japanese caginess about the movements of home fleets, it long has been known that the waters behind Marcus have been considered safe maneuvering ground. Marcus itself might be without fortifications or important defenses, but it was a listening post within striking distance of which no enemy could hope to get unnoticed and which, therefore, no enemy would ever approach.

So in the darkness of the morning of March 4, Tokyo time, we came abreast of Marcus and sped our airplanes on their way to the impossible.

With full knowledge of the odds against us, the dangers adding up rapidly on the decks of unnumbered, unknown ships, that might be lying over the edge of the horizon, with the possibility not too remote of a fight with a good quorum of the Jap fleet, you could not but invest the performance with color and pageantry and suspense. It must have had all those qualities and yet it had also all the routine, efficiency and repetitious glamour of a Friday afternoon in a steam laundry.

The planes took off in the false dawn just as they used to in what we called peace times. Their only novelty was wreaths of flaming blue vapor about the engines—and that, too, might be remembered as a peacetime phenomenon to anybody who had ever got up early enough to see it.

They circled the fleet and rose up through what critics used to label "a dramatic sky"—tumbling dark clouds with light finding its way around them to the sea—a full moon exploding through them every time a rift rode by on the gale. In a few minutes they were gone, a cloud of them a little blacker than other clouds.

Marcus, here we come.

For us, as for other ships in the force, the blasting of Marcus was strictly an aerial action. The island lay over there with numerous other mysteries, beyond the horizon. We could only take the word of strategists that it would not be worth our time or material to run in alongside and level it with a surface attack, and that its main importance is not as a fortress but as a bomber relay, filling station and listening post.

So as the planes went out of sight in the puzzle of cloud and moonlight, our part of the job was finished. The ships swung about to go somewhere else.

But it was an interesting feature of this expedition that we were never completely out of it even though few of us in this life may ever cast a jaundiced eye on Minamitori Shima. We kept no radio communications with the bombers, nor they with us, but they talked with each other and we eavesdropped—as presumably did the Japanese.

We heard the comment of the aviators as they dropped down from the cloudrack on the unsuspecting island—their poor opinion of it—their designation of hangars, tanks, warehouses, the radio station and other targets. One squadron commander reported, "I think some planes took off from your side. My vision was obstructed by haze," and the answer of another squadron commander, "No planes have taken off."

Then another bit of cross-talk in English from a jumble of Japanese. "They're rolling planes onto the field. Get them!" And the laconic answer of the pilot. "I am getting them"—more brief orders and a long silence.

We knew when we saw them coming back, a couple of hours after the take-off, that we had done pretty well and had not paid much for our impudence. The bombers were riding along in parade formation, a series of perfect V's. Had they taken a beating, we knew they would have dispensed with this review stuff and stragglers would have been streaking for home unescorted and obviously glad to get there.

For a few minutes we saw a perfect exhibition of close-order flying—class A movie stuff—and then, one by one, they peeled off to land at quick intervals. We counted them as they came down and checked the count with the observers and lookouts. Two planes were missing. One of the lost bombers came home slowly after the rest of the flight. Its wing tips had been damaged and something was wrong with the elevator controls, and it circled about in erratic flight that held thousands of men hypnotized. Finally, it got its wheels down and glided toward the carrier at a cockeyed angle. It came down in a perfect landing and the fleet breathed again.

Shortly after 10 o'clock word came to our crash detail to stand by to pick up the plane that would attempt to land in the water alongside us. There were more relays of information about this plane. It had taken a lot of ack-ack, some of it in the wings, some in the gas tank, and now was nearly out of fuel. The pilot had reported he thought he had enough to carry him in.

At 11 o'clock the crash details were dismissed and the gear packed away. There had been no further word from the missing pilot.

That then is our story of Marcus. We slipped past mobilizations of land planes that the indignant Japs sent out to strafe us; we avoided traps that probably were numerous right about that spot; and we got on with our interesting work. The sheer drama of the episode can much better be obtained from the Japanese. So far as you can judge from the radio, they appreciate it.

Wake Island, formerly Otori, formerly Wake—lies behind us, a bit of coral desert as useless, at the moment for war or other human enterprise, as it was before Pan-American Airways found it on an old chart and subdivided it.

It is as flat and empty as Wotje—which at the last writing was like a section of the lunar landscape—and mortuary plumes of smoke rise up from it into the blazing afternoon sun and jets of flame color its sky at night, just as in the Marshall Islands after the fleet passed by.

At least part of what is due the United States Marines, the defenders of Wake in its previous operations, has been collected—and if Japanese inspectors have got around to look at what is left of this historic island, they can guess some of the details of the probable next payment. That the line in the Pacific, through the Gilberts, the Marshalls and this forsaken archipelago of coral corpses, is now definitely wiped out must rate as a severe annoyance to the son of heaven.

That the United States is able to go right on catching Japan's heroes with their supposed naval and air strongholds as wide open as a First Ward clambake, must be a matter of even greater concern—at least, that is the thought that comes to you as you watch a fair-sized powder magazine blow up and a good chunk of airport installation roll over into a churning lagoon.

The shells scream past and Stukas dive and four-engined bombers plaster you with dynamite from somewhere up in the stratosphere, but the fleet comes in, destroys everything in sight and goes away again ad lib.

One suspects that the ad lib part of the program is what really concerns Japan. Military establishments can be repaired with time and energy and patriotic fervor. But there is little use in repairing them if the United States ghost fleet, which ought to be keeping quiet on the bottom of Pearl Harbor, can steam up as it pleases over the subs and under air patrols, make ashes of all the fine projects and kill off the current population.

So it was with the Marshalls and the Gilberts, and so today with Wake. Maybe you have heard that the fleet, taking the place in its turn, stopped in a few hours ago to plant such Japs as chanced to survive the experiment, in a pile of ashes and debris much deeper than the one they had contrived for themselves when the little garrison of Marines finally had capitulated. And if you ever hear the Japanese radio you will know that the Son of Heaven's enterprising colonists, who took over the premises under the new name of Otori Island, consider the matter serious indeed.

There is not much left here now to give aid and comfort to any invasion force on its way eastward, but it is obvious that there may be still less any time. It is perfectly feasible to repeat yesterday's performance until nothing is left of the island save its original dust and all the Jap tenants are one with the hard-working coral who built it.

The Japanese had gone to some trouble to take this little atoll as one of the first acts of their peculiar war policy.

Any time the smoke clouds part, you can see the wrecks of a cruiser and a couple of destroyers on the beach where the Marine artillerymen dissected them. They worked from Monday, Dec. 8 (Dec. 7 Honolulu time) until 5 P.M. Dec. 22 with a considerable naval force, shock troops and some two hundred airplanes to reduce a defense garrison of 378 Marines and seven sailors and a civil population of one thousand. They made the attack an important issue in their Pacific campaign and, so doing, made it important in the eyes of all America.

It was not sentiment, however, that brought the fleet here, any more than it was the lure of the Japs when they swarmed over it. Wake, equipped, supplied and manned in Jap hands, continued as a threat to the zones of United States' defense eastward. So, in line with the policy of eliminating these nuisances up to, and including Japanese waters, the fleet arrived off shore one morning and, as has been indicated, took the place apart. Here is the log:

A couple of hours before sunrise, somewhere not far from Wake, we got up and went to the wardroom for breakfast. The scene reminded you somewhat of a refectory in a bus station, with the freshly awakened drivers leisurely stoking coffee for the day's run. The waiters were the only anxious ones in the room.

They had to convert the premises into a hospital right away—at any rate, as soon as we gave them a chance.

Before getting into the war paint I took a look outside. There was a dark sky with scattered lumps of clouds. But it was not going to be any gray day. You could see that.

I went below, gathered a life jacket, a tin hat, an ear cotton gas mask, binoculars and a flashlight, and crawled up to the platform of the foremast above the sky control.

There was no moon, the ship stole seemingly without motion in vast, black water. A star that looked like Mars, and probably wasn't, blazed red near the horizon to the east. We were steering straight for the southern cross. The other units were not visible. In the shadowy corners of our decks nothing was moving. If you stepped sideways, you stumbled over the kids of the watch relief, still stealing a little sleep about their gun positions.

I heard one of the gunnery officers mumbling about lights ahead that turned out to be meteors masked by clouds and the plaint of somebody on the bridge that he was learning to navigate by braille.

At 6:30 o'clock the sky began to lighten and we turned east. There was a terrific wind and the sea promised to be the roughest we had met since leaving port—and the question was when that would be. It was virtually impossible to stand up on the searchlight platform. My tin hat was rising straight off my head and flopping down again uncomfortably and—for the unseen gunners on the platform below—dangerously.

7 A.M.—A salmon-pink glow was spreading out slowly ahead, but it was not a magnificent sunrise. There were banks of clouds on the horizon and ribbons of mist overhead—enough for dive bombers, if any. The wind was working up to hurricane velocity, literally blowing the ink out of the fountain pen. As always, it was cold. The seas were choppy and the ship was rolling at a loafing speed.

Through the lightening haze you could pick out some more of our ships closing in for the kill. There were no airplanes about at the moment, ours or theirs. Signs and portents were accumulating and without a crystal ball you knew that it was going to be a tough day, but a sunny and partly clouded, beautiful blue day, with a constant gale and a violent sea.

7:02 A.M.—Our planes began to warm up and you could hear the motor crescendo even over the screaming bedlam in the rigging. It is explainable how you can do this. You just pit one din against the other and your growing deafness sorts them out as individual plagues.

7:05 A.M.—The horizon was still empty and getting brighter.

7:08 A.M.—We began to drape our yard with flags. I kept smelling something like burned powder and marveled at it. You might call it prescience or a suspicion that we had run into a gas cloud left by one of the other ships. They could easily have let off a couple of salvos without our hearing them. This promised to be the kind of battle we used to see on the screen in the days of silent films—days of terrific activity and no sound at all, save the whirlwind of the ventilator.

7:10 A.M.—It was broad day now, though the sun, if any, was still behind a cloud bank on the horizon. You did not need to be a prophet to guess that the cloud bank would cause us trouble if the grandsons of heaven could get airplanes loose in it. You could make out the motley crew on the iron terrace below now—blue flash suit, denims, khaki coveralls, blue lifejackets, blue tin hats—hundreds of men now animate and alert, trying to balance themselves and their regalia against the wind.

7:13 A.M.—One of our planes went off as the ship rocked back in a jarring farewell. The catapult rolled back into place with a nostalgic imitation of the sound of a lawn mower.

7:18 A.M.—There was a flash of ack-ack in front of us. High up in the widening sky you could see the bright cross of a plane—it looked like a single seater flying boat—streaking across our bows to the ship immediately ahead in the column. We joined the hunt. Our heavy flak—with a detonation that shook the decks in your diaphragm, clutched at your throat and jarred your teeth—was weaving a dynamo fence across the sky, but nothing much came of it. The sky over and around us was filled with hearse-plumes rolling on their way with hurricane speed, a macabre hint to whatever air defense Wake might have. But the diver had dropped his bomb near one of our leading cans and slid out of sight in a low-hanging cloud cluster. We straightened into the column again—a thoughtfully wavering column.

7:31 A.M.—The Jap bomber, or another one just like it, popped out of the sun, high in the sky off starboard, and squarely above a group of our scout planes. The ack-ack went wild over him and the sky was muddled with cockeyed patterns of tracers.

The bomber dived almost vertically toward our planes, so abruptly that it looked for a moment as if it might have been hit. But suddenly it straightened out, threatening us or the ship next to us. The can on the outside of the formation threw up a string of flak and the Jap, incredibly changing his direction on a third time since his dive began, let go a bomb at the can. The can miraculously proceeded on its way through the descending glitter of the blast. Why, none can say.

In a minute there were several more flashes from the can, and the big ship leading the column. The mass of black muck from the ack-ack guns thickened overhead, and a Jap came staggering out of the mists. Like the other one, he may have been hit, but apparently he didn't know it. A 50-foot geyser of green water, with white pearl trimmings, went up alongside the column leader—a close one. We zigzagged into the shrieking gale and readjusted the cotton in our ears and for a moment our ack-ack was silent—for perhaps two minutes we got to appreciate the peaceful sound of nothing but the hurricane wind.

7:38 A.M.—Sickly yellow flashes began darting from the ships ahead of us. Our lookout picked up a plane from starboard and we went back to our mayhem while another diver rolled out of the sky, directly above. A bomb missed us and blew up like a spouting whale off port of the leader. This dive wasn't low and we saw the plane only for a moment as it turned into the sun. The ships had already swung at right angle—piling up white water in front and flattening peacocks' tails of green behind.

7:45—The planes apparently had gone away in perfect timing, like the curtain-raiser act in a variety show, because now, as we looked out to starboard, we got a glimpse of historic Wake, a grim, white coral graveyard, clinging to the horizon. At the same moment the ships rocked back with a blast of the main batteries and wreaths of yellow fumes wrapped us up.

7:47—This business looked as if it were going to be a repetition of the episode in the Gilberts and Marshalls. In the background fires were picking out a thin white line on this desolate reef. Almost before we could pick out our shells from those of the other ships in the general melee some dirty yellow flashes of guns going into action gave us more coordinates on Wake. A shell slapped over us and tossed up a 10-foot jet—small, maybe, but eminently worth attention.

Two land batteries were working on us—five inch, maybe six— we were not anxious to make certain. The range was pretty fair and the deflection somewhat off. Two fountains leaped up just short of the ship next in line. Then one between that and us. Our forward turrets leaned back and blasted.

7:50—Smoke puffs rolled and coalesced on Wake. We seemed to have landed a shell squarely in the lap of one of the batteries. However, there were others. You could see the yellow-red glare of their flashes against the black of spreading fires.

The Marines, manning their pom-pom batteries, which had not been firing since the planes went away, looked out upon this scene with eagerness and impatience. You sympathized with them even as the long guns knocked new chunks out of the Jap squatters' shacks and seemed likely to sink the whole island into the unseen lagoon.

7:55—A series of shots landed between us and the destroyer off starboard. Most of the bursts were short, but not enough. The destroyer seemed concerned only with our own troubles. Traveling at high speed, it seemed to submerge half the time.

The whole column of our ships was covered with green-yellow smoke. Something seemed to have smashed into the rigging of the ship ahead. A mess of gear was hanging down from the top foremast. Shells came screaming over us—three shells. Jets rose to starboard, 2,000 feet short. Came another flash from a land battery—over and short—four geysers—a queer bracket that didn't seem too close although it was still dangerous.

7:58—Whoever counts those things reported that five batteries were still working on us—the sea was chopped up with gushes and spatters. The scene, with flaming cannon, bursting shell and upflung geysers all over the blue sea, looked like nothing on earth except the thrilling cyclorama once exhibited in Chicago entitled: "Dewey at the Battle of Manila."

There was a new roar—five-inchers—which have the nastiest sound of all known artillery—began to go ad lib. And so did the eardrums despite the cotton packs.

8:05—Continuous noise. If you took your attention away from the clunks falling about the ship, you could count fifteen fires along the white line of reef. We were directly facing two islands in the Wake group, Wake and Peale. Wilkes, the third island, was somewhere in the smoke haze beyond the lagoon where our bombers were working.

Our shooting, it was apparent by this time, had improved since Wotje. It was no more accurate but more selective. A salvo here, and the explosion of burning oil. A couple of shells there—a seaplane dock went skyward. You could count the shells as they fell on the material sheds and wooden barracks easily visible through the glasses. You were glad of the unreality of the scene as the buildings disintegrated with whatever was in them.

8:10—Nobody seemed to pay particular attention to the land batteries while the gaunt ruins, marking the last stand of the Marines, were being battered apart. Two fountains leaped up short of us. Nobody was looking at them any longer. The sky control called something about splashes over—we were straddled again. But nobody paid any attention to that either.

8:13—A direct hit landed on the Wake oil storage. An orange ball unfolded, merging into a mass of black.

8:16—Another smash and another burst of orange flame. The land guns dropped one clunk almost on the deck of the can to our starboard. About this time we noticed that the dive bombers had not come back. It began to seem obvious that they had been caught grounded, rearming.

8:17—Another hit near the can.

8:18—Another hot orange puff on the island. All the guns on all the ships were firing and there was some contribution to the general turmoil from the Jap batteries still in action. In the midst of all this came the goonies, young albatrosses looking about for dynamited fish or riding the sticks left in the turbulent water by the shells.

8:20—Another red burst on Wake. We had been told that the Japs had brought in numerous tanks such as are used on American railroads for oil transportation. The fires multiplied; it seemed that we were picking them off in bunches, with a blaze from central points reaching out for any we had missed.

Through this dense veil, now and then, you would get an idea of the layout of the place—burned shells of the buildings the Japs had taken down ahead of us; white, almost silvery, squares of material storage and new barracks; one towered structure, identified by men who had been there before as a power house. There were no trees on this battered desolation, no color, no greenery of any sort; no cover from shells, and after awhile, no sign of human habitation.

8:21—A battery at the west end of the island fired one gun. A geyser rose short and far astern of us. A lance of flame started up through the black near the power house, with greenish sidebands that looked like burning dynamite.

At least one of the batteries seemed finished. The fire on the island was settling down to the routine of red and black gushes, almost in rhythm. Shore guns at the west end kept diligently at it and should be given points for perseverance. But shells were falling about us in a wider pattern and wilder. A battery commander over there probably noticed before we did that we were pulling away. Our stern turrets rumbled and shook the fantail of our last shots at the burning island. Then, save for the screaming wind that you had just about forgotten, there was silence.

You had a chance then to sit back and take inventory.

The action seemed finished save for a few odd ack-ack puffs tossed up against our spotters. The island, as the smoke drifted in shore, was fairly visible now. There seemed to be numerous square buildings, or pieces of them. The whole place looked something like a United States Army cantonment or construction camp, as indeed it was.

There was a large white building where Peale and Wake join—

we had not wasted a shell on it nor, for that matter, on many of the sheds that stuck out so brilliantly against the backdrop of smoke. In a while, probably, the fire would get to them. If it didn't, no matter.

At the ends of the island were piles of construction material, silvery tanks, machinery dumps with flames reaching out for them. You paused to wonder what would become of the plant that raised fresh vegetables in a water trough for Pan-American passengers. At the moment, there seemed only wonder if Wake was worth worrying about.

8:30—We were well away, looking back at the familiar smear of oil smoke on the horizon. Wake appeared to be another Wotje, another Jaluit, Molecap or Kwajalein.

8:37—Off to starboard, with startling suddenness, there was a burst high above the horizon. Clearing it for one brief instant and visible against the sky hurtled a big plane driving at full gun toward the sea, with a broad black arc behind it. A "Jap four-motored bomber," the lookout on the range finder called out. It was gone in a matter of seconds after it burst from the clouds, its grave marked by a tall, wavering cloud.

Another object—perhaps a wing, perhaps a smaller plane—fluttered down after it like a falling leaf and was gone before we could make out what it was. The range finder operator called out, "Crashed bomber sent down by one of our fighters that came upon him unseen in a cloud bank."

The Jap was headed straight for us when he came flaming out of the murk—he lit almost off our starboard bow. So we did not feel too sad about him as we watched his last private cloud waft over and join the billowing crepe in the sky over Wake. Our ship swung back into the zigzagging line and moved toward a sunnier, but no more satisfying, horizon.

It was some time afterward that the Jap radio mentioned our visit. We had been driven off, the announcer said, and somebody mentioned this to one of the officers who had been sweating over the guns.

"Driven off," he said. "Sure, we were driven off. And so was the Long Island hurricane. It didn't stay there, did it?"

. . . .

ROBERT J. CASEY

Robert J. Casey was a correspondent with the Chicago *Daily News* for twenty-seven years until his retirement in 1947. Before joining the *Daily News*, he served as a captain in the U.S. Army during World War I and was a reporter for the Des Moines *Register and Leader*.

Known for his adventurous character and colorful expense reports, Casey covered the French, British, and American armies throughout the world, including England, France, the Middle East, and the Mediterranean, and wrote more than twenty-eight books based on his experiences.

Casey died in 1962.

Flight from Java

· · · · · · · · · · · ·

BY
GEORGE WELLER
CHICAGO *DAILY NEWS* FOREIGN SERVICE

SOMEWHERE IN AUSTRALIA, March 14, 1942—For correspondents lucky enough to obtain transportation on [F]lying [F]ortresses, Java was hardly more than six hours from Australia and safety. But for any who stayed after the last American Navy units sailed on Sunday, March 1, and the last bombers departed at dusk the same day from Jogjakarta, Australia was much farther.

After being bombed in Soerabaja, bombed in Bandoeng, this correspondent on March 2, with William Dunn, of the Columbia Broadcasting System, and Frank J. Cuhl, of the Mutual Broadcasting System, the last remaining radio reporters, started for the southern Java port of Tjilatjap. De Witt Hancock, of the Associated Press, and William H. MacDougall, of the United Press, were the only Americans remaining and they planned to leave immediately in another car.

Our start was made amid a raid in which Jap Navy Zeros were attempting to destroy the eleven fighters and four bombers which alone remained as defenders of Java's western plateau, where the Netherland East Indies commander in chief, Lt. Gen. Hein Ter Poorten, once planned a Bataan-style stand. There were unashamed tears at our final handshakes with the men and women of the Dutch press bureau, headed by L. H. Rithman, the jovial and lovable director of that singularly honest and fearless government propaganda department.

In Tjilatjap's small cemetery lay, under walnut-colored wooden crosses, the bodies of American sailors who died defending Java. Others were there alive, the wounded with reddish scarifying marks from bomb blasts. Like ourselves, they were placed aboard a small Dutch Island steamer.

All day we waited in the tiny harbor expecting raids, but Jap fighters, based on Bali, were harassing the defenses around Rembang and only one alarm sounded and no bombs were dropped.

Naval physician Lt. Comdr. C. M. Wassell, of Little Rock, Ark., laid his bandaged, wounded charges out upon the steamer's bulkheads. One topic of conversation was our chances of piercing the Jap submarine blockade. At darkness we slipped out of the mine-dotted harbor, clouds obscuring the moon.

There were about 600 aboard, with cabins for less than 40. Many were officers fresh from the destruction of the Soerabaja naval base. About 90 percent of the passengers were Dutch navy people. Two were sailors I had interviewed at Java's easternmost end, Banjoe-wani, opposite Bali after they had spent two days and two nights in the water seven miles off Bali following the sinking of their destroyer.

Past minefields, a friendly thunderstorm took us in charge, convoying us under the cloak of darkness and rain through whatever submarines were waiting. We expected, even with the steamer's labored eight knots an hour, to be 100 miles at sea by daybreak. But dawn found us closer to Jap bombers.

The Dutch Admiralty having other last ships to send from the harbor the same night, one bearing enemy alien internees, spread them variously over the sea. Our ordered course lay straight along Java's shore directly toward the enemy base at Bali and about two miles from shore.

Out of the rising sun came the Jap bombers, the same distance off shore as ourselves to evade the listening posts. First came nine, then seven, then nine again. They were directly overhead, their motors humming incessantly. The day was blue and bright, but they had bigger prey than our ship in mind. Their missions were to bomb Tjilatjap.

We still pursued our creeping course along the shore. The captain knew the inadequacy of six lifeboats to carry 100 times as many people and did not dare to turn to sea. The passengers, fat with lifebelts, clogged the passageways, uncertain whether they would be bombed from above or below.

A burning sun beamed upon the greased lifeboat davits. I gave an unknown woman the journal of my 14 months of wartime evacuations with the request that, if her lifeboat reached the shore, she send it to the Chicago *Daily News*.

Nine returning bombers passed, parallel to the ship. Then, before the siren could even blurt the first peep of the quadruple, a signal meaning air attack, machine gun bullets and cannonshells came directly into the main saloon below the bridge. Sixty persons were instantly upon the floor, trying to crawl under benches. Somehow, I crawled into a B-deck passageway. Then came more hammering of steel and splintering of wood.

Whether we were being shelled by a submarine or attacked by an airplane was impossible to tell. I saw a curl of blue smoke arising beside one bulkhead door from an incendiary bullet.

"Stop pushing me," said the little Eurasian woman ahead of me on the jammed stairs. When she discovered I was attempting to lace her huge, mattresslike lifejacket, she grew quieter.

For an interval we arose. Then came again the terrible hammering and tearing of wood, running like a xylophone the full length of the ship. No motors could be heard, nothing but explosions. Each time the corridors were jammed with bodies. As we struggled downward, attacks began upon the sides of the ship, increasing our belief that we were being shelled from shore by the Japs who had already crossed the island. Then we were shelled and machine gunned from the seaward side.

Between attacks, we lay sweating and prone, some Malays and some whites, too, covering their eyes like the evil-fearing monkey curling into an embryonic ball.

I found the whole right shoulder of my bushjacket uniform

drenched with blood, which had soaked even my glass case. But I was not wounded. Three wounded lay in the corridors, but none whom I could recognize as having been beside me. Four times the death tattoo was played upon us. The rear-gunner got a bullet through his hat, another across his uniform.

For more than an hour after the last attack, all of us lay on the iron decks and in the darkness of closed compartments. Then slowly arose bodies dented with their own lifejackets, the cork of which was in some cases torn away.

There had been two Navy [Z]eros. One lifeboat was shot open. Hardly a ventilator, or stretch of canvas, but had been riddled. The Japs simply had shot all their ammunition at us.

But nothing could make us go faster than our eight knots. The sun was still high, it was hardly noon. We crept toward shore and entered the tiny harbor of Patjitan. There were no natives visible. The captain lowered the boats and asked all who wished to row ashore to leave. He said that we had only a "slight to perhaps 50-50 chance" of escaping. About 300 went ashore and were last seen trailing up a narrow path into country where the Jap spearhead was hardly twenty miles away.

Under cover of darkness, we again crept out to sea. Eleven days of sleeping upon open decks with lifebelts always entwined on one arm brought us, with our American wounded, to safety.

· · · · · · · · · · · ·

GEORGE WELLER

Soon after joining the staff of the Chicago *Daily News* in 1941, George Weller became a foreign correspondent and wrote hundreds of stories on Nazi Germany's infiltration of Europe. During this time he was captured by and escaped from both Germans and Chinese Communists several times, the longest detainment lasting more than two months. He filed groundbreaking reports on the collapse of Greece, the Battle of the Java Sea, life on a submarine off the coast of New Guinea (which earned him a Pulitzer Prize), and the withdrawal of German troops from the Mediterranean.

His postwar work covered even more of the globe, particularly the Near East and Asia. In addition to the Pulitzer Prize for reporting, he was the recipient of the George Polk Memorial Award and a Neiman fellowship. He also was the author of several books.

Weller was a native of Boston and was educated at Harvard, the University of Vienna in Austria, and the Max Reinhardt School of Theater in Schloss Schönbrunn.

MacArthur's Pledge—
"I Shall Return"

· · · · · · · · · · · ·

BY

BYRON DARNTON

NEW YORK TIMES

MELBOURNE, AUSTRALIA, Saturday, March 21, 1942—Melbourne organized a tumultuous welcome today for General Douglas MacArthur, Supreme Commander of the United Nations forces in the Southwest Pacific, who said yesterday in his first public statement since his arrival in Australia that he planned to organize an offensive that would drive the Japanese out of the Philippines.

(General MacArthur was greeted by cheering thousands in Melbourne, it was reported by the United Press, whose correspondent said that "never have I seen any man receive such acclaim.")

General MacArthur, who issued the statement at Adelaide before boarding a train for Melbourne, said:

"The President of the United States ordered me to break through the Japanese lines and proceed from Corregidor to Australia for the purpose, as I understand it, of organizing the American offensive against Japan. A primary purpose of this is relief of the Philippines. I came through and I shall return."

(On his arrival in Melbourne General MacArthur issued a statement in which he warned that modern war required careful preparation and "sufficient troops and sufficient material to meet the known strength of the potential enemy," the Associated Press reported.)

The lid was lifted to give General MacArthur an enthusiastic welcome after original plans to treat his arrival as a military secret had been abandoned in the eleventh hour. The news was broadcast by radio and published in the newspapers. The desire was to give the city, which had to hush hush the fact that United States soldiers were here until the ban was lifted two days ago, a chance to make a public demonstration of gratitude.

The plans were changed at the suggestion of General MacArthur, who is known not only as a brilliant military leader but also as a master of public relations. And there is no doubt that this city and all Australia want to show the Americans that they are most welcome.

Yesterday, even United States correspondents had been told at United States headquarters that they would not be allowed to cross the police lines when the new commander arrived. The secrecy was carried to such an extreme that mention of the general's name in any public place was frowned on, and the practice was to refer to him as "He," with a significant accent.

Last night Brig. General S. J. Chamberlain, who is chief of staff for Lieut. General George H. Brett, General MacArthur's predecessor as commander here and now his deputy, swept aside all folderol. Australian newspapers were hurriedly informed that they might publish the news and an Australian welcoming committee received permission to carry out its program.

A guard was assigned to stand at arms at the rail road station and a group of Australian and United States officials was assigned to serve as greeter. The Australians were headed by Francis M. Force, Deputy Prime Minister and Army Minister. Mr. Force said that the "presence of General MacArthur was an inspiration to all Australians."

· · · · · · · · · · ·

BYRON DARNTON

Byron Darnton, a *New York Times* foreign correspondent, was killed in New Guinea on October 18, 1942. He had been a former cable editor with the Associated Press. He was forty-four.

Japs Take Bataan

· · · · · · · · · · · ·

BY

BERT ANDREWS

NEW YORK *HERALD TRIBUNE*

WASHINGTON, April 9, 1942—The fate of the valiant defenders of
Bataan peninsula remained hidden tonight from an anxious nation,
but American and Filipino troops were believed, in the absence of
any word to the contrary, still to be fighting against the Japanese
from the island fortresses in Manila Bay.

War Department officials said no word had been received since
mid-morning to supplement a special communiqué issued at 5:15
A.M.—a communiqué which told of new onslaughts by the Japanese
and the toll taken among the defenders by short rations, disease and
lack of supplies, and which added: "This situation indicates the
probability that the defenses of Bataan have been overcome."

No one in authority at Washington would say what interpretation
should be placed on the word "overcome" as it pertained to the
36,853 men remaining of the land force which struggled gallantly
for three months and six days—the peninsula campaign began Jan.
3—against a foe estimated to number from 150,000 to 200,000.

These were the two chief possibilities:

That mass surrender may confront the men on Bataan while the
guns of the island fortresses roar new defiance.

That the Japanese may demand unconditional surrender of the

island fortresses as well, on pain of a no-quarter attack with tanks, artillery and planes against the peninsula fighters who have written a deathless page in American history.

The decision to be made on whatever demands the Japanese present rests with Lieutenant General Jonathan M. Wainwright.

Henry L. Stimson, Secretary of War, revealed that President Roosevelt had granted General Wainwright this power yesterday in a message which told him of the President's faith that any action he took would be "in the interest of the country and the splendid troops" he commanded.

This day of gloom began with the issuance of the special communiqué concerning the imminence of one of the worst single military disasters the United States has ever suffered.

General Wainwright had sent word that the Japanese had succeeded in enveloping the east flank of the American line—the flank held by the 2d Corps.

The 1st Corps was ordered to counter-attack "to relieve the situation." The communiqué added in unvarnished language, that the counter-drive failed "due to complete physical exhaustion of the troops."

The somber news came as no surprise to the President, since he had known of the gravity of the situation when he sent yesterday's instructions to General Wainwright.

Secretary Stimson summed up the immediate situation as follows:

"Our defense on Bataan has been overthrown. Corregidor is still fighting.

"A long and gallant defense has been worn down and overthrown.

"There is nothing but praise for the men who have so ably conducted an epic chapter in the history of the Philippines.

"The Philippines have now been united with us in battle as well as linked to the co-operation between the United States and the Philippines during the last forty years."

Secretary Stimson disclosed for the first time that tremendous efforts had been made since Jan. 11 to get supplies to the Philippines, directed from Australia by Brigadier General Patrick Jay Hurley, once Secretary of War in President Hoover's cabinet. The Secretary said, "For every ship that arrived we lost nearly two."

Secretary Stimson said that among the defenders of Bataan were the 31st Infantry Regiment, two tank battalions, air force ground crews who turned infantrymen when their planes were destroyed, and sailors and marines who reached Bataan when the Cavite naval base was abandoned.

Air personnel numbered 5000 men when the Japanese first attacked, Mr. Stimson said. At least 2000 of these and perhaps more, he said, took up rifles after their ships were destroyed. He observed that plane losses were extremely heavy on the first day of the attack.

. . . .

BERT ANDREWS

Bert Andrews was a director and chief Washington correspondent for the New York *Herald Tribune* from 1941 until his death in 1953. He was lauded as a tough and responsible newspaperman and author, best known for his voracious and unyielding investigative series on the State Department's employee dismissal policies, which earned him a Pulitzer Prize in 1948. He was also celebrated for his role in monitoring the investigation, headed by Richard M. Nixon, that led to the conviction of Alger Hiss on perjury charges. Andrews's controversial book *Washington Witch Hunt*, was banned from U.S. Information Service libraries during the McCarthy era.

At age fifty-two, Andrews died of a heart attack while covering President Eisenhower's summer activities in 1953.

The Fall of Corregidor

· · · · · · · · · · · ·

BY

LEE VAN ATTA

INTERNATIONAL NEWS SERVICE STAFF CORRESPONDENT

UNITED NATIONS HEADQUARTERS IN AUSTRALIA, May 6, 1942—
Lieut. Gen. Jonathan M. Wainwright, commander of American
forces in the Philippines, today surrendered Corregidor and three
other fortified islands in Manila Bay to the Japanese, a spokesman
for Gen. Douglas MacArthur announced.

American, British and Australian war correspondents were summoned shortly after 4 P.M. (3 A.M. New York time) to receive the
announcement of the fall of Corregidor, whose defenders battled
valiantly for five months against extremely heavy odds.

The end came after a ceaseless 27-day siege that began with the
fall of the Bataan Peninsula on April 9.

The Army spokesman said that prior to the start of the Japanese
drive down the Bataan Peninsula the garrison at Corregidor ex-
ceeded 3,000 men.

The number was greatly increased when many of the Bataan defenders took refuge on the island bastion just before the Japanese
over-ran Bataan.

In addition to surrendering Fort Mills on Corregidor, Lieut. Gen.
Wainwright ordered the capitulation of Forts Hughes, Drum and
Frank, situated on smaller nearby islands.

As an indication of the heavy punishment the Corregidor defenders sustained, the spokesman said that between Dec. 29 and the hour of surrender the island fortress has been subjected to more than 300 air attacks, some of them lasting 24 hours.

During that period, he said, approximately 200 Japanese planes were shot down or crashed during the Corregidor assaults and others were damaged.

Collapse of the bay forts will permit the Japanese use of port facilities at Manila for the first time since control of the former Philippines' capital fell into their hands.

While Americans and Filipinos manned the guns of the bay forts, no enemy vessel could pass into the dock area.

The communiqué announcing the fall of Corregidor said:

"Lieut. Gen. Wainwright has surrendered Corregidor and other fortified islands in Manila Harbor."

No reference was made to the terms of surrender.

Fall of the Manila Bay forts did not mean the collapse of resistance to the invader in other areas of the Philippines.

Fighting still continues in northern Luzon and on the islands of Cebu, Mindanao and Panay.

The capitulation of Corregidor and the other forts came after the Japanese had succeeded in skirting the three-mile stretch of water separating Corregidor from Bataan to launch land attacks against the defenders.

Back from the Hell at Dieppe

. . . .

BY

ROSS MUNRO

CANADIAN PRESS WAR CORRESPONDENT

WITH THE CANADIAN RAIDING FORCE AT DIEPPE, Sept. 1, 1942—For eight raging hours, under intense Nazi fire from dawn into a sweltering afternoon, I watched Canadian troops fight the blazing, bloody battle of Dieppe.

I saw them go through this biggest of the war's raiding operations in wild scenes that crowded helter-skelter one upon another in crazy sequence.

There was a furious attack by German E-boats while the Canadians moved in on Dieppe's beaches, landing by dawn's half-light.

When the Canadian battalions stormed through the flashing inferno of Nazi defenses, belching guns of huge tanks rolling into the fight, I spent the grimmest 20 minutes of my life with one unit when a rain of German machine-gun fire wounded half the men in our boat and only a miracle saved us from annihilation.

A few hours later there was the spine-chilling experience of a dive-bombing attack by seven Stukas, the dreaded Nazi aircraft that spotted out the small assault landing craft waiting off-shore to re-embark the fighting men.

Our boat was thrown about like a toy by their seven screeching bombs that plunged into the water around us and exploded in gigantic cascades. There was the lashing fire of machine-gunning from other Nazi aircraft and the thunder of anti-aircraft fire that sent them hustling off. Over our heads in the blue, cloud-flecked sky were fought the greatest air engagements since the Battle of Britain, dogfights carried on to the dizzy accompaniment of planes exploding in the air diving down flaming, some plummeting into the sea from thousands of feet.

Hour after hour, guns of the supporting warships growled salvos at targets ashore where by now our tanks also were in violent action.

Unearthly noises rumbled up and down the French coast, shrouded ten miles in smoke screens covering the fleet.

There was heroism at sea and in the skies in these hours, but the hell-spot was ashore, where the Canadians fought at close quarters with the Nazis. They fought to the end, where they had to, and showed courage and daring. They attacked the Dieppe arsenal of the coastal defense. They left Dieppe silent and afire, its ruins and its dead under a shroud of smoke.

The operation against Dieppe started from a British port in the evening. I boarded a ship which also carried the Royal Regiment of Toronto. It was seven o'clock and only then were we told that Dieppe was our destination.

The Royals took it coolly enough. They had been trained with the rest of the force for several months on Combined Operations for just such a job.

Maps, mosaics and photographs of Dieppe were issued and, as the boat put to sea with the other ships of the raiding fleet; the troops were briefed in their tasks.

It was a muggy night but the sky was clear. The sea was calm. It was Combined Operations weather.

Below deck the men sat around cleaning weapons, fusing grenades and loading the magazines of Stens, tommy-guns and Brens.

In darkness formed the flotilla, shadowy tank landing craft that looked like oil tankers, a score of small assault boats, destroyers, gunboats, motor launches and torpedo boats.

A few officers in the raiding party drank a beer with the ship's captain and chatted about everything but the operation. We had a snack of bully beef, bread and butter, and tea, and then went over the side into assault craft.

After leaving the mother ships, our flotilla of little craft took positions in line astern. The Royals were to land at Puits, one mile east of Dieppe, and establish themselves in that flanking area.

Just as we were pushing away from the mother ship, an old British tar whispered to us: "Cheerio laddies, the best of luck, give the ——s a ballicking."

It was pleasant in the open assault boats. Nobody seemed particularly nervous about the coming darkness, though it was to be the Canadians' first time in action.

I made myself think in terms of maneuvers, exercises in which I had taken part with these men in preparation for this night.

I had about convinced myself that this was another of those familiar exercises when at 4:10 A.M., about 50 minutes before we were due to hit the beach, a flare arched over the Channel.

Tracer bullets followed quickly, long green and red streaks marking their path. They were too close for comfort.

"E-boats," announced a sailor.

The atmosphere suddenly became tense. Wide-awake men tightened their grip on their weapons. A sailor hoisted a Lewis gun into place and cocked it.

Our boats slipped steadily through the quiet waters. The motor was hardly audible.

Then the E-boats appeared, close by off to one side. They opened up with lead that bounced bright red off one or two of our boats. Fire now came from several angles. It was the first time most of us ever had been under direct enemy fire. We flattened against the armorplating of our craft. The E-boats kept up a running attack for twenty minutes and the night became alive with streaking tracers. It occurred to me it was awkward to be travelling towards the Germans with other Germans hanging onto our heels.

But the Royal Navy took care of our unwanted travelling companions. Destroyers popped up with a barrage that sent the E-boats scurrying off like sea rats.

Aircraft drummed overhead by this time, heading for the south.

They were the first of the bombers for Dieppe, and in a few minutes great crumps shook the French channel shore as they unloaded their bombs on the port.

Nazi anti-aircraft defenses barked at the skies and a haphazard pattern of tracer and flak criss-crossed a horizon showing the first streaks of dawn.

They made a brilliant chandelier over Dieppe. Two searchlights probed for bombers dodging anti-aircraft fire. Other bombers went in, squadron after squadron.

Flashes of bomb explosions in the town to which we had crept within two miles revealed a concrete jetty at the harbor entrance. Anti-aircraft fire was heaviest from the cliff-tops on either side of the town.

Over on our right I could see another fleet of raiding craft bearing men of the Essex Scottish, the Royal Hamilton Light Infantry and the Calgary Tank Regiment to the main beach in front of Dieppe.

There was a great roar as concentrations of high explosive and smoke bombs landed on the east headland by the harbor with a blinding flash that seemed half a mile long. Black smoke bellowed out and turned white as it curled along over the sea to conceal our landing from the shore defenses.

Crouched low, the Royals gave their webbing last-minute hitches. Faces were taut, jaws firm. We knew this wouldn't be any party.

We could see destroyers and gunboats creeping up behind the attack flotillas racing for the main beach. The flame and peal of artillery told us that the naval bombardment of the town had opened. The navy kept up its torrent of shells into Dieppe as we sped for shore.

Already some of the Royals were landing at Puits as we headed for the beach at the base of a slope leading from the shore into a break between the cliffs.

To one side, fighter planes hopped in at sea level to blast with cannon and machine-gun fire the hotels and buildings full of Germans on the Dieppe esplanade.

Dawn was breaking. The battle of Dieppe got hotter.

We were to land in a matter of minutes. Through smoke layers

I looked up at the white cliffs growing higher before us. Anti-aircraft guns up there clattered unceasingly. Machine-guns drilled down bullets that clanged against the armor of our boat.

By the time our boat touched the beach the din was in crescendo. I peered out at the slope lying just in front of us and it was startling to see it was dotted with the fallen forms of men in battle-dress. The Royals ahead of us had been cut down as they stormed the slope. It came home to me only then that every one of these men had gone down under the bullets of the enemy at the top of the incline.

Vicious bursts of yellow tracers from the German machine-guns made a veritable curtain about our boats. The Royals beside me fired back with everything they had. One Canadian blasted away with an anti-tank rifle.

The Germans held a couple of fortified houses near the top of the slope and occupied some strong pillboxes. From their high level they were able to pour fire into some boats, ours among them.

Several bursts from machine-guns struck men in the middle of our craft. The boat's ramp was lowered to permit the men with me to get ashore, but German fire caught those who tried to make it.

The remainder crouched inside, protected by armor and pouring return fire at the Nazis. The Canadians' shooting was dead-on and half a dozen men in steel helmets and field-grey uniforms toppled from windows to the ground.

Other Germans made the mistake of trying to change their positions, only to be caught when sighted by Royal sharpshooters armed with Brens.

Caught by this unexpectedly intense Nazi fire, the Canadians fought a heroic battle from those craft that were still nosed up on the beach.

I lay behind a flimsy bit of armor plating and heavy calibre bullets cut through it a couple of feet above my head.

An officer sitting next to me was firing a Sten gun. He got off a magazine and a half, killed at least one Nazi, and then was hit in the head. He fell forward, bleeding profusely. A sailor next to him was wounded in the neck and another got a bullet through his shoulder. Those around the injured tied them up with field dressing. The fire was murderous now and the Canadians' fire-power was being reduced by casualties.

There were eight to ten in our boat who had been hit and a landing here seemed impossible. The naval officer with us decided to try to get the boat off the beach. On maneuvers there were times when it was difficult to do it quickly, but by a miracle it slid off and we eased away from the hellish fire with nerve-wracking slowness.

The Nazis pegged away at us for half a mile out. That attempted landing was one of the fiercest and grimmest events in the whole raid and the only spot where the landing was temporarily repulsed.

I will forever remember the scene in that craft: wounded lying about being attended by medical orderlies oblivious to the fire; the heroism of the Royals as they fought back and strove as desperately as any men could to get on the beach and relieve their comrades still fighting ashore; the contempt of these men for danger and their fortitude when they were hit. I never even heard one man cry out.

During the whole raid there were no stauncher fighters than these fighting soldiers.

Off Dieppe the raid flotilla re-massed after putting the troops ashore. Our wounded were sent to the hospital ship and I transferred at sea to another assault landing craft and then another and another.

They were floating about doing jobs at the different beaches.

At one stage, fifteen soldiers and I tried to get onto one of the beaches near Dieppe, but German cliff-side machine-gun posts, which later were wiped out, plastered us without hitting anyone and we turned back out of range.

Finally, we got ashore for a few minutes right in front of the Dieppe esplanade. The smoke screen was so thick, though, that one could not see much of the town and we took off again. The area in front of the town looked like a First Great War battleground, with broken buildings gutted or burning in all sections.

By 10 A.M. the Canadians, many of their actions led by tanks, seemed to have the town fairly well under control and to have stabilized the situation on the beaches.

Then, fifty minutes later, the Nazis sprang their one heavy attack by air. For 45 minutes Stukas, Dorniers, Heinkels and fighters swept up from the south and attacked the fleet whose terrific bombardment I had been watching from an assault craft just off the main Dieppe beach.

Earlier the enemy had sent over aircraft in fours and fives, but they had been unable to cope with the Royal Air Force and had resorted only to minor machine-gunning and inaccurate bombing.

But the big attack was a real one. German pilots, flying anywhere from 200 to 2,000 feet, showered bombs over the British ships, at the same time sweeping them with machine-gun fire. The sky was splotched with hundreds of black and white puffs from exploding shells and the thundering of the ships' guns was deafening.

Sometimes, the Nazis picked peculiar targets. At one time even their Stukas were dive-bombing our little craft, which this time carried only one naval officer, four ratings and this lone correspondent. Their bombs came crashing down on either side of our bouncing craft, making the sea look as if it had been churned by a tornado. Once we almost capsized, but we ended up with only a bashed stern and a shattered bow.

We had just picked ourselves up from the deck when a fighter zoomed in and gave us a hail of gunfire. But they added only more scars to our steady but still seaworthy craft.

The plane was one which had succeeded in avoiding squadrons of British planes which hovered overhead throughout the operation, picking off German machines attempting to get in close. Seven German machines crashed into the sea within the limited view we had of the complete scene.

One Dornier attempting to attack the destroyer was raked by fire before it could release its bombs. It exploded at about 300 feet. Small bits of debris were all falling into the sea.

Every little while a lone German would sweep on an isolated assault craft whose crew would reply with everything aboard. Sailors would pop off with Tommy guns and Lewis guns from hip level and some even used rifles. And they succeeded in bringing down some of those diving Nazis.

At noon, final re-embarkation of the troops was under way and the force was taken off the main beach.

With another smoke screen blanketing the raided town, the fleet turned for England. No German aircraft marred the departure and the navy gave some coastal installations another bump with its heavy guns for good measure.

Through the afternoon I sailed north in a craft to which the Stukas had taken such a liking. It was just an ordinary assault landing craft, 30 feet long and looking like a floating packing box. This is the way hundreds of raiders started back to England, but the sea stayed reasonably smooth.

I lay in the sun and slept and woke to see the white cliffs of England in the mist ahead.

British planes—fighters and bombers—were swarming south to France again in a steady stream with more packages for the Germans.

. . . .

ROSS MUNRO

After graduating from University of Toronto in 1936, Ross (Robert) Munro served as a second lieutenant with the Canadian Militia until 1940. The third generation of the Munro family to embark on a career in journalism, Munro worked as a reporter and editor for the Canadian Press and served as its war and European correspondent from 1940 to 1947. After the war he worked in the Ottawa bureau of Southam News Services, then joined the Vancouver *Province*. He became the paper's editor in chief in 1955. From 1959 to his retirement twenty years later, Munro was publisher of several Canadian newspapers, including the Winnipeg *Tribune*, the *Canadian* magazine, the Edmonton *Journal*, and the *Gazette* in Montreal. He simultaneously served as president of the Canadian Press during the years 1974 to 1976 and 1978 and 1979.

Munro was the author of *Gauntlet to Overlord*, published in 1945.

"The Witch" over Greece

. . . .

BY

HENRY T. GORRELL

UNITED PRESS STAFF CORRESPONDENT

AT A U.S. ARMY AIR FORCE BASE IN THE MIDDLE EAST, Oct. 3 1942—
I rode "The Witch" over Greece today with Americans from nine
states as they blasted two Axis ships and shot down two German
Messerschmitts before our bullet-riddled bomber sped home with
three wounded crewmen aboard.

Though the enemy drew American blood over Navarino Bay of
southwest Greece, they paid for it, and heavily.

Driven frantic by an avalanche of thousand-pound bombs from
two waves of American four-motored Liberators, the Germans at
Navarino Bay sent up Messerschmitt fighters to drive us away.

Our gunners blasted them to pieces in the sky when the German
pilots, their planes in flames, tried suicidal dives at our bombers.
Four out of five attackers were downed.

I rode the last bomber in our squadron, named "The Witch." We
roughly retraced the route over Greece over which in 1941 I retreated with the British Expeditionary Force before the crushing
German invasion.

The other two bombers in our group were called the "Snow
White" and "Jersey Jerks." We were all carrying bombs for Hitler.

"The Witch" got the worst of the ack-ack and the air fighting, because we were the last plane over the target.

Three of our men were wounded and "The Witch" was perforated with bullets and cannon shells.

The Huns appeared rather sore about the whole affair. In broken English, embroidered with considerable cursing, the Nazi flight leader attacking our ships shouted to the commander of our squadron, Maj. John Kane, Shreveport, La., to "get the hell off the air."

Our radio was interfering with his control of the German fighters. That struck the crew of "The Witch" as pretty funny.

But to start at the beginning. We were to bomb Navarino in two waves in a daylight attack. At the base the pilots and crews were briefed and warned that the opposition probably would be heavy.

It was a nice day for the long trip across the Mediterranean and the only disappointment was that a little dog named Duchess, mascot of the "Jersey Jerks," couldn't make the flight because there are no oxygen masks for dogs.

I got acquainted with the crew of "The Witch" as we flew in formation hour after hour toward Navarino. There was pilot First Lieut. Glade Jorgensen, blond, husky and square-jawed, from Fork, Utah, a professional trombone player back home. The co-pilot was First Lieut. Robert T. Goldberg, of Blooming Prairie, Minn. Both had been on nine previous missions in the Mediterranean area and this was their second against Axis shipping at Navarino.

Jorgensen's ancestors were from Denmark and Goldberg's parents had gone to America from Norway. Then there was the navigator, a husky fellow named Vlahakes, whose parents were natives of Greece.

"The folks won't mind this," he said, "because we are not bombing the Greek people but only enemy ships."

The only married crew member was Second Lieut. Henry M. Sparger, bombardier, Mt. Airy, N.C., lanky and slow talking, but quick on the bomb trigger. The radio operator was Staff Sgt. Joseph T. Byrne, of La Crosse, Wis., a short, stubby fellow who has a little goatee something like Little Abner's pa in the comic strip. Byrne was in a hurry to complete the mission, for he wanted to listen to the World Series.

The others were Staff Sgt. Donald S. Allen, gunner, New York City; a gunner named Frost; Tech. Sgt. Marvin L. Breeding, armored gunner, Dallas, Tex.; and Tech. Sgt. Joseph E. Farmer, St. Charles, Va.

I looked out the window at the other bombers and as we skimmed over the water our planes looked like monster sea gulls gracefully flying toward Greece. The sea had looked differently a year and a half ago when I was on a ship headed for Crete and German planes dive-bombed us all the way. This was my revenge and the song, "The Yanks are Coming," kept running through my mind.

As we approached Navarino we began to climb to the level where the oxygen masks were necessary and Jorgensen ordered everyone to adjust life jackets and put on parachutes. We climbed several hundred feet a minute in perfect formation. At 10,000 feet Jorgensen ordered oxygen masks turned on. Then he asked the leading bomber to advise when the bombs would be dropped so I could take photographs.

I thought how simple everything was, but remembered that was because these fellows were so business like and efficient. The top gunner whirled the turret and fired a practice burst. A red hot shell case clipped my ear and made me jump.

We now were almost to the target and Jorgensen banked so he could see the ships in the harbor. They appeared like pencils thousands of feet below. The ack-ack began to burst around us in black puffs and the first bombers were dropping their eggs.

A moment later we were over the target and bombardier Sparger turned loose the bombs right on the mark. I looked down and saw one of the ships heave apart in a tremendous explosion followed by fire.

Then the fighting started, and within a matter of seconds three German fighters were diving on our tail. That brought action from Jorgensen. Looking out the window, I saw earth, sky, planes above, planes below, all mixed with ack-ack puffs as our pilot twisted, turned, sideslipped and performed various acrobatics to get away.

But it was hard to shake the fighters. We were the last bomber in formation and the Jerries had glued their sights on us. Someone shouted: "There he is, for God's sake open fire." The oxygen masks were cumbersome, but we couldn't take them off. A machine gun started clicking and shell cases flew all over the place. I looked at Jorgensen and thought he was hit, but it was only a muscular contraction as bullets whizzed past.

One of the gunners shouted that he had knocked down a Messerschmitt and Frost got a second one. Over the telephone I heard Frost tell Jorgensen: "I got him, sir. There he goes on fire."

But that wasn't the end. The German pilot, attempting a suicidal collision, came straight toward our plane. Frost gave him another burst and the Messerschmitt crumpled apart in the air.

"That got him for sure, sir," Frost said. Then he added: "I've been shot, sir."

Jorgensen asked if he was hurt badly.

"Yes, sir. I'm afraid I am. I'm bleeding pretty badly."

We were dropping now and soon we could remove our oxygen masks. Jorgensen turned the Liberator over the co-pilot and we went to Frost's aid. He was lying on his back, bleeding. The tail gunner remained in his revolving turret watching for enemy fighters.

Sgt. Breeding cut off Frost's trouser leg, stripped off the blood-soaked sock and applied a tourniquet to his leg. My fingers were numb from the cold and the first aid kit was flaked with frost. Iodine swabs were frozen solid. Frost smiled and asked for a cigarette.

When he was fixed as comfortably as possible, Breeding asked Jorgensen to look at his leg. "I think I was hit too," he said. Breeding had a flesh wound in the ankle and Jorgensen applied iodine and bandaged it as best he could.

"The Witch" was badly banged up. Her sides looked like sieves. Byrne radioed to have medical aid ready. It was sunset but several hours of flying remained ahead. Jorgensen tried to get more speed but the superchargers were shot away, the automatic steering device was ruined, hydraulics damaged, an aileron knocked off and the self-sealing gas tank had been hit once. The engineer said he believed we had a flat tire.

I tried to cheer up Frost by saying he probably would get to go home.

"No soap," he said, laughing, "all the girls have married."

The weather turned bad and we rocked along in thunder and lightning. The engineer remained worried about the tire, but Jorgensen was confident he could set "The Witch" down even if the tire was flat.

The searchlights caught us as we reached the base and we flashed recognition signals. Jorgensen set "The Witch" down perfectly. Physicians took Frost in hand and he will recover soon.

"I guess we are living on borrowed time," said Goldberg. "It could have been a darned sight worse."

. . . .

HENRY T. GORRELL

Henry T. Gorrell was a fifteen-year reporter for the United Press and a veteran of two wars: the Spanish Civil War and World War II. He was captured by Spanish rebel forces in 1936 and in 1943 was awarded the Air Medal by President Roosevelt for "extreme gallantry" in saving an injured crewman's life while under heavy attack by the German forces. In addition, he was commended by the Headliners' Club for his reports on the war in Greece and won the Sigma Delta Chi Award, along with Ernie Pyle, for battlefront coverage.

Gorrell retired from the United Press in 1945 to become editor and publisher of the monthly *Veteran's Report*. He died in 1958 at age forty-six.

Fourth Battle of the Solomons

· · · · · · · · · · · ·

BY

IRA WOLFERT

NORTH AMERICAN NEWSPAPER ALLIANCE

FROM A BASE IN THE GUADALCANAL SECTOR, Oct. 27, 1942—The fourth Battle of the Solomons, which gave Admiral Halsey his baptism of fire as Commander of the South Pacific Force, was actually a development of the third and followed hard upon its heels. The week of lull in between was an uneasy lull, the Jap remaining in touch with us. At least he kept trying to touch us with his high explosives encased in bombs and shells and succeeded as often as he failed.

This Fourth Battle was typical of all the battles the Jap has fought to regain the Solomons and, for that reason among others, will be described here in detail.

The battle was fought over an area of 250,000 square miles, the bulk of it covered with water, and lasted five days and five nights. These days were as fierce, bloody and uncertain as all days of pitched battle are.

As far as this reporter can determine with his limited knowledge and the limited view he was able to get from a fast-moving seat in the arena itself, this battle was a work of considerable art on our part in strategy and tactics. Certainly it had in it all the chaos and tragedy and exultant soarings above tragedy of all works of great art.

Our side wrote the story. The Jap supplied terrible chapters in it, but we were in charge almost all the way through and in charge of the ending. The ending of the battle was that the Jap failed to achieve his objective.

I had no idea until I got here that a war was going on in this sector—the only serious-minded war the Japs are fighting anywhere in the world at present—and that shots were being exchanged daily and men were being killed and wounded daily. And that, for instance, the handful of [F]lying [F]ortresses engaged in this area have had exactly one day since July 31 when no enemy contact was made and no job of bloodying him up or getting bloodied up was done and that our Navy has been in action during the same period with the same, if not greater, intensity. I had no idea of this because the press, where I am accustomed to getting my impressions of what is going on in the world, was not allowed any means of telling the story.

And to tell the truth about it, this dispatch is being written by a reporter who has a story to tell and feels that telling the story would be useful to his country's effort to win the war and can't think of anything to do under the existing circumstances but tell it, even though he will have to trust to luck to get it to where it can be heard at a time when people will still be interested in hearing it.

This morning, in the midst of a widespread storm which will last several days, the Jap fleet broke off the engagement with ours and withdrew to its bristling fortresses in the north where we are not yet prepared to follow. The Japanese land forces on Guadalcanal, who had been trying to drive the Marines and Army infantry out of their way with everything they had including fourteen-ton tanks and bayonets and had succeeded in making something like a break-through, have now retired to positions where there is no point in our paying the cost of following them.

There is no point in following them because they are now relatively harmless without reinforcements and will die peacefully of starvation, as a cohesive army at any rate, if their sea lines of communications are kept broken. The Jap land forces lost nine tanks in the battle and approximately twenty-one times as many men as we did and have retreated to territory that we have no use for.

It must be remembered that the fight for Guadalcanal is not for the 100-mile island, but for the air facilities on the one tip of it and the sea roads leading there. Those air facilities are useful to the Jap as a base for operations southward and to us as a base for operations northward.

In addition to all their other difficulties, both sides raced the weather. Nature entered the arena with a front of its own, a black and storming pile of weather which is known even technically as a front. This front, like something created by Thomas Hardy, began advancing upon the battle area as the Jap fleet steamed out for action.

Meteorologists, or, as they are called here, weather officers, charted it anxiously. It had a long way to go, but it sent speeding out ahead of it scouts, points, screens and spearheads in the shape of squalls and cloudbursts, nature's main force following on behind.

The men, standing up tall to this eruption of nature, used it to conceal their maneuverings at first. But on the fifth day in the early hours of the present morning, Tuesday Oct. 27 (Monday, Oct. 26 in New York), nature's front took charge of the arena and set it boiling with a fury of its own. Admiral Halsey is known to his men here as a "rough brush." But not even a rough brush can sweep such a storm as this one out of men's eyes and in the blackened day that is now following the black night nobody, not even the tallest man, can see anything it would be useful to kill.

At the moment this is written, the various American staffs engaged in the battle are trying to add up thousands of eyewitness reports and determine how roughly the Jap was handled in his fourth effort to throw us out of Guadalcanal. When they have arrived at the score, they will radio the news home and a communiqué will be given out, which you will have read long before you can read this.

For reasons which are not only irritating but seem unnecessary, the Navy denies the press here any access to rapid communications and so handicaps it seriously in its war job of helping wake up our people to the fact that we are not going to start to fight when we get ready, but are fighting now, bloodily and desperately.

I don't know whether this dispatch will reach you in a week or two or three months or even whether it ever will reach you, but I

do know, having been on the mainland and out of the war as recently as last September, that people cannot be stirred by facts as
old as these will be by the time they reach print and cannot get any
sense of continuing pressure on their emotions, unless there is daily
communication between them and the battlefield.

We hold the ground and continue to hold it against ceaseless
pressure by the Jap. In the sense that the Jap has not pushed us
back and that we have denied the Jap a base there, we have won a
whole series of battles for Guadalcanal thus far. But we have not
yet won a victory there. For, while the Jap no longer has a base
there, neither have we been able to make a base out of it, Guadalcanal is not a base at all, but a battlefield.

We are winning in the Solomons in another sense too. The Guadalcanal area has become a kind of Verdun. A maw into which the
Jap is pouring his power and giving us a chance to blunt it. This is
not a nickel-and-dime operation for the Jap. In the last five days
here, he has lost something like about 300 planes. That's not a
filibustering expedition. That's a battle.

In the whole Solomons operation thus far, the Jap has lost about
fifteen times as much in ships, planes and trained men—the best
men he has—as in the Battle of Midway where he was denied de-
cisively access to the Western Pacific. In a war against a producing
unit as inferior as Japan's is believed to be, attrition is a weighty
factor. The Jap is throwing planes from his factories into battle. One
of the prisoners taken here recently is a 12-year-old boy who shipped
as a sailor on a patrol vessel. That might mean anything you make
it mean, but it can also mean that the Jap's manpower is beginning
to spread thin over the immense area he has conquered.

Intelligence here has not yet coordinated all its information and
interpreted the thousands of photographs made of the five-day battle. So the extent of the damage suffered by the Jap cannot yet, as
of today, be estimated with any accuracy. However, all that is information will be given you in a communiqué from the Navy Department, which, no doubt, you will have read and forgotten before
you can read this.

Jap losses were much greater than ours. There is a conclusive
reason for believing this, but I am not allowed to cite it. Damage

has been done to two Jap carriers, one Jap battleship, three of their heavy cruisers. Nobody has had time to count up the destroyers yet, they being only $4,000,000 or $5,000,000 engines of destruction and therefore comparatively unimportant.

What is believed to be the best and biggest carrier the Japs have is known to have suffered four direct hits with heavy bombs. Naval gunfire, in revenge for U.S. Navy Torpedo Squadron 8, which sank a Jap carrier at Midway and came out with one survivor, wiped out a whole squadron of Japanese torpedo planes before one of them could get close enough to the target to release a torpedo. Japanese Imperial Marines and infantry left at least 2,000 of their dead behind for us to bury at Guadalcanal.

However, this is not the kind of information this dispatch intends to communicate. What is desired is to tell you something of what the battle was about and how it was fought and to communicate at least some hints of the desperation with which the best young men of America have fought.

The Fourth Battle of the Solomons was a naval battle, but like most of the engagements in this prolonged and by all odds most curious war between navies in history, surface vessels did not figure in it vitally except as defenders of the pivots from which blows were swung. Airplanes were the striking weapons, carriers the pivots from which the strike was launched and another of the pivots was the land of the Northeast edge of Guadalcanal where the Japs and our forces slashed and blasted at each other over treacherous terrain with tanks, artillery, and finally, bayonets.

In the Third Battle of the Solomons, which ended a week ago, the Japs had forced a landing on Guadalcanal of troops and supplies. They had come in with five transports and a protecting screen of warships. Our planes had vaulted over this screen and sunk three of the transports, but at least two had got through. Then, apparently to spare their surface vessels further punishment and give their newly landed forces a chance to pull themselves together, the screen of Jap warships withdrew, one of the battleships in the force limping awkwardly.

The landing had been made very close to our positions, either because the Japs have no communications through the 100-miles of jungle and 8,000-foot mountains from the northern end of the island (which is theirs) or because they actually intended at the time to fight from their ships as we did when we occupied the island.

After the landing, the Jap foot forces and tanks withdrew from contact with our troops and the nervous business of sending out feelers in small squads and larger patrols began and endured for exactly a week. How nervous this business was is indicated by a marine I spoke to in the hospital here. He was on sentry duty on the beach. The duty seemed long to him and after a few minutes of it he began to sing to keep himself company. On the third or fourth bar, as he remembers, of "St. Louis Blues" he was shot in the foot by a Jap sniper and had to remain silent until his relief crawled up and found him. "If I had hollered out," he said, "the other fellows would have come to help me and they'd have got it." This happened on Wednesday evening, Oct. 21, during the "lull" deep in American territory.

Then two powerful Jap task forces put to sea and began to converge on Guadalcanal. One force came down from the Northwest, from the bases in Bougainville, Rabaul, and perhaps Yap. The other force, spread over several hundred miles, came down from the Northeast, apparently from Jap bases in the Carolinas, the Gilberts and Marshalls. At the same time, the Jap land forces on Guadalcanal began to move.

The objective of ths concerted move was easy to detect—the reduction of Guadalcanal. But their tactic, which had to be read by our staff officers from the flickering impressions received by aviators hurtling through the fog of war and the spearheads of weather nature's front was throwing out, was more difficult to interpret.

This reporter has not been made privy to staff deliberations, but he saw the lights burning and the faces paling with thought. And, from a portion of the information available to the staffs and from subsequent events, a guess can be made that the Japs were intending to use their carriers to give air support to their land forces and break down our own fleet, so that their surface ships could come in close and give artillery support to the same land forces with their big guns.

Apparently, too, the task force coming down from the Northwest was only making a feint, even though a very forceful one, while the task force coming down from the Northeast was the business. Anyway, this was the task force we elected to hit hardest, jabbing with the left hand and throwing Sunday punches with the right hand. And our staff seems to have come to the right decision because the Japs failed of their objective.

The first intimation we here had that a full-scale battle was in the making was when the Japs stepped up the tempo of their pepperings of the area. On Friday, Oct. 23, the air raids on the airport at Guadalcanal began to take on the lead-based complexion of a blitz.

In one raid there, sixteen Jap bombers came over with a support of twenty Zeroes. Grumman fighter planes (and, naturally, their youthful pilots) shot down all twenty of the Zeroes and got one bomber certainly, three probably, without losing a single plane or pilot. On the same day, two Jap destroyers sneaked in close in broad daylight, threw shells at our men and ran away safely. This need not be taken as any reflection on the alertness of our forces. Those fellows are fighting for their lives and are alert. But when [one is] fighting surface ships and bombers with fighter planes, the problem is of gasoline and the Japs, who are no slouches at timing, got in such blows as they did when our planes were on the ground being refueled.

Throughout Saturday, Oct. 24, weather was flocking in on the battle area and piling up and the Japs played a vast cat-and-mouse game with our forces, they hiding under the weather, we scuttling and beetling through it in an effort to locate them and determine what they were up to. The day was given over to the land fighting on Guadalcanal and to clashes between searching planes who shot each other down when cornered or when stumbling on an easy kill.

Sunday was a day which did not seem at all like Sunday here. Early in the morning, First Lieut. Mario Sesso, flying an Army Flying Fortress (he can't decide whether to call his plane "The Bronx Bomber" or "The Bronx Bird") on a search mission, happened through a break in the clouds below which a sizable Jap force lay.

The whole battlefield began instantly to twitch with radio messages and in a very little while to erupt with the full, awful force of war, continuing then without intermission until the Japs decided they could afford no more and withdrew.

Finding an enemy fleet is a hazardous occupation for an aviator. He not only has to find it, but stay with it while it is trying to knock him down. The PBY pilot who tipped off the Midway explosion summed up his whole enterprise by radioing his superiors the position of the Jap ships and their number and nature and direction and then added poignantly, "Please notify my next of kin." Incidentally he was over-pessimistic, for he lived through his experience.

The final, most violent phase of the battle hit first at the bull shoulders of the flying fortress Lt. Sesso was flying. A swarm of Zeroes came buzzing after him to shoot him down so that he could not continue to radio back the course changes the Jap ships were making to throw off pursuit.

Lt. Sesso played hide-and-seek with the Zeroes in the clouds, but he had to come out every so often to keep an eye on the ships. The first time he came out, a Zero was right in front of his nose and facing him. His bombardier, Sgt. Eldon M. Elliot, of Idalia, Col., flying his first combat mission and doomed to die young, fired into the Zero at the same moment the Zero fired into the fort. The bullets blew up the Zero and it shucked out its dead pilot and fell in pieces. One of the Zero's bullets hit Sgt. Elliot in the heart and he was dead before he could fall backwards into his chair. In the next hour, Lt. Sesso saw two more Zeroes fall away from him smoking. They are counted as probables because he had not the time to watch them hit the sea.

The business of finding enemy surface forces and sticking with them until your side could come up in strength and do some good went on continually during the days and nights of the Fourth Battle of the Solomons.

The Jap forces, as they entered the arena, and ours, too, split up into something like little floating pillboxes, separated and deployed in what they hoped would be an impregnable manner. They kept shifting position continually while edging in the general direction of their objective and each new position had to be discovered and attacked.

The last convoy of Jap ships was discovered at midnight Monday

night by a Navy plane piloted by Lt. D. L. ("Jake") Jackson of Free-
port, L.I. After lingering on the scene for an hour to give his support
a chance to start on up after him, Lt. Jackson made a torpedo run on
the carrier in this force. Torpedo planes are thought to have a mod-
est chance of survival only when a concerted attack is made on all
quarters of a ship at once in combination with dive bombers, all together dividing the fire of the ship so that the attack may be pressed
home and some of the attackers can remain alive through it.

Lt. Jackson, a blonde, soft-voiced young man with a soft skin all
pinked over by youth, and his crew understood this very well, but
they elected to make the run all by themselves anyway. They had
been in battle for five days by then.

Torpedo runs have to be made at suicidally low speeds because
aerial torpedoes are delicate instruments and flop over when
dropped too fast or from too high an altitude. Lt. Jackson made his
run at 120 miles an hour about thirty feet over the water. He gave
the enemy a square shake at a target for a very, very long time.
Every gun in the force was fired at him. The big cannons were fired
into the water to throw up splashes and wreck him. His entended
victim kept making violent turns to evade him. But he continued
steadily through the maelstrom, dropped his torpedo when about
400 feet away from his target, saw the torpedo land with a soft
squish in the black water and proceed correctly on its way and, as
he turned, heard the noise which told him his torpedo had arrived
at its proper destination.

Japanese and American search planes swarmed over the whole
250,000 square miles of battle area. They were threads, twitching
and curling and connecting the various centers of battle on the sea.

In the meantime, land fighting was proceeding as dolorously for
the Japanese as sea fighting. Their Imperial Marines and Infantry
were working their way forward slowly. Small fleets of planes would
dart in from the sea to help them. Occasionally, a few Jap warships
would break away from the furious banging our Navy was subjecting
them to and come close enough to Guadalcanal to help their troops
with big guns.

Well, that, roughly and on the surface, is what the battle looked
like—a corner of it given over to "better ole" land fighting between

men on foot or on armored wheels; relatively small patches of sea lashed volcanically by bombs, shells and bullets; the whole stitched together by search planes, patrol boats and submarines and buttressed by land and sea bases for services of supply and maintenance. And into this whole churned-up segment of the world, nature poured its own fury of winds and rains.

Only hints of the battle-rage with which our young men fought can be given by a single reporter.

The Navy vessel which took revenge for Torpedo Squadron 8 (wiped out by the Japs at Midway) was subjected at the time of its moment of triumph to a concerted attack from a squadron of dive bombers. The Japs were out to kill. Their torpedo planes came in on all quarters and blew up in the distance like human bombs throwing themselves against barbed wire. Their dive bombers dove on all quarters. Some of these blew up in mid-air with their own bombs, but most plummeted blazing straight down into the sea falling like a rain of fire all around the ship. The Japs scored no hits at all in that attack, but they came back. They came back again and again.

A Navy dive-bomber squadron out to get a Jap carrier was under the desperate assaults of a great mass of Zeroes for the last twenty minutes of its approach to the target. Our rear gunners shot down fifteen Zeroes in this approach, killing expensively armoured Japs at a rate of one every eighty seconds. The Zeroes were of varsity caliber. They were off the best existing carrier the Japs are known to have. They realized that if our squadron landed its wallop, they would die anyway, having no place to land, so when our bombers peeled off for their dive, the Zeroes followed them right on down into the withering fire from their own carrier. Our tail gunners kept shooting at Jap planes all through the dive while reporting altitude to the pilots (so that they wouldn't dive too low and hit the sea). Eighty per cent of the planes in this squadron got direct hits on the carrier. The carrier shot down more of its own planes than it did of ours for the simple reason that there were more of theirs in the line of fire.

Navy Lt. Atwell, piloting one of those awkward, clumsy PBYs, supposed to be useful only for search, made a dive-bombing attack on a Jap heavy cruiser at an angle of between 50 and 60 degrees.

This the Navy rates as true dive-bombing, calling the kind of dives the Germans make glide-bombing.

Lt. Atwell, an enlisted man up from the ranks and out to show why, scored one direct hit on the cruiser just aft of the smokestack, which is the place to hit those babies and destroy them. He came so close as he dropped down on his target that the debris from the bursting ship riddled his plane, splashes from near misses filled the whole tail of his plane with water and the concussions from his own bombs blew up a flashlight one of the crew happened to be holding in his hands. This small, strange explosion, probably caused by the air pressure inside the flashlight being greater than the air pressure outside, caused the only wounds suffered by Americans in the attack.

A striking force of Army Flying Fortresses was sent out after a heavy cruiser. They attacked in two formations, one close behind the other. As they began their bombing runs, their intended victim started turning in a 360-degree circle. They found him in a placid sea and his wake gushed out behind him like a squeal of terror from an animal running faster than its own sound.

The Jap had almost completed a full circle when the first formation dropped its bombs. The tall gunners in this formation were beginning to fill their mouths with curses because only one bomb made a direct hit and that one landed on the bow. "I already had the words in my mouth and could taste them there," one of them said. But before any words could be uttered, the second formation hit and bombs raked the cruiser from bow to stern. The heavy ship seemed to leap up into the air and then settle into a yielding cushion of sea, belching infernoes of flame from every wound. When the Fortresses landed here, about two hours later, the men went to mess with the look in their eyes of those who have seen an incredible sight.

Jap land fighting was both good and bad. Their army was bad, their Imperial Marines very good at everything except the bayonet. During these bloody days, Japanese infantry made charges that were pathetic. The tiny figure of a Japanese officer would rise up from the torn earth far away and wave a sword. Clusters of little men all huddled together would rise up after him and come forward, stooping over into our machine gun bullets and falling down dead or wounded in them.

The Imperial Marines were as good as anything our fellows have ever seen. These were the troops who broke through and got there and put up a tough fight about getting out of there. They used modern infantry tactics and filtered forward in their charges, keeping widely dispersed and flitting from cover to cover. In that way, numbers of them evaded our machine gun and rifle fire and grenades, but those who did had to face bayonets in the end and either ran away or concluded their lives that way.

Now that the battle is over, the situation has returned for the fourth time to its status quo ante. The Japs hang over Guadalcanal in the north all the way from east to west like Swords of Damocles. They will range and pepper and harass and do everything they can to make the island a battlefield instead of a base.

. . . .

IRA WOLFERT

Ira Wolfert was born and raised in New York City, working as a cabdriver to get through the Columbia School of Journalism. After graduating, he worked for a year at the New York *Post*, until joining the North American News Alliance in 1932. While in Asia as a correspondent, he covered the invasion of the Solomon Islands, which earned him a 1943 Pulitzer Prize for international reporting and on which his first book, *Battle for the Solomons*, was based. In addition, he covered the war in France (including the battle at Normandy), Belgium, and Germany.

After the war Wolfert went to Hollywood. He wrote the screenplay for the motion picture *An American Guerrilla in the Philippines*, based on a true story. Although screenwriting was lucrative, Wolfert fancied being a novelist instead. His list of books include *Tucker's People*, about the numbers racket in a New York slum, and *An Act of Love*, about a Navy flier.

General Clark's Fiction-like Adventure

BY
ROBERT G. NIXON
INTERNATIONAL NEWS SERVICE STAFF CORRESPONDENT

ALLIED HEADQUARTERS IN FRENCH NORTH AFRICA, Nov. 12, 1942—
A dramatic exploit rivaling the best of fiction, in which Maj. Gen.
Mark W. Clark and a group of other American officers made a secret
trip to Africa more than two weeks ago to make final arrangements
for the invasion, was disclosed for the first time today.

The story was told by Commander-in-Chief Lieut. Gen. Eisenhower. He himself likened the mission to the historic "Message to
García."

General Clark was to confer with high French Army officers and
to make the arrangements which to a great extent delivered French
North Africa into United States hands.

[In Washington, the War Department disclosed that Clark's secret conference in North Africa was held with representatives of
Gen. Henri Giraud, the famous French general who had escaped
from Germany.

["In this conference Clark opened negotiations which brought
about the collaboration of Giraud with the United Nations," the
War Department said.]

The adventurous and hazardous trip was undertaken just two
weeks before the occupation. It started on a rainy night in the Lon-

don blackout, when Clark and his men were taken to a secret airdrome and a plane took Clark to Washington for consultation.

"Almost every type of transportation except donkey back was used," Eisenhower said.

Planes, submarines, ships and motor trips were used, with frequent changes made, before Clark arrived at a lonely house somewhere in North Africa where he obtained complete plans of all French military installations in Morocco and Algeria.

He learned also of all the troop dispositions, who would be friendly and who could be depended upon. He was told the number, type and equipment of troops, and even arranged that two airfields outside of Algiers be delivered over to the American Air Force the moment landings began.

"It was every bit another 'message to García' exploit," Gen. Eisenhower said.

"Clark and his men volunteered for the job, gleefully, and they went there and risked their lives many times. They accomplished the job completely, got military and political information regarding the line-up of Frenchmen and friends in high position, and passed information on our plans to them so they could know what was to be done.

"They came back with so much that the success of this campaign must be attributed to this valuable assistance."

Clark's group included Brig. Gen. Lyman L. Lemnitzer of Honesdale, Pa., Col. Archelaus L. Hamblen of Maine, Col. Julius C. Holmes of Washington, D.C., Capt. Jerauld Wright, U.S.N., Washington, and British Commandos Captains C. J. Courtney, R. T. Livingstone and Lieut. J. D. Foot.

They left London in the dead of night in an automobile whose windows were shielded. Dressed in civilian clothes, they went first to Scotland in a black-out train, then took a plane before transferring to ships, a motor launch and a submarine at sea.

They lost all their clothing during one transfer and had to drape themselves in window curtains.

They dropped 150,000 gold francs ($18,000), carried in case bribes should be needed, into the sea and on one occasion nearly drowned.

General Clark, who shares an office with Eisenhower, took up the story.

"A few weeks ago," he said, "some sources in North Africa sensed that something was coming and suggested a conference with an American general in Algiers for negotiations.

"Our War Department received the offer favorably and I was picked. I used planes, ships, submarines, canoes and automobiles—everything but mules."

Clark told how he and his aides, when arriving at the selected spot, waited for a certain light which was the all clear signal.

"When we arrived at the house," he said, "it was filled with French military officers in uniform, although they, too, had made the journey in civilian clothes.

"We conferred all day and night until we had gathered all the information we wanted.

"Meanwhile, Arab servants had become suspicious. They went to the Axis-controlled Vichy police and reported that a conference of French and American officers was underway.

"Then we heard that the police were en route. I never saw such excitement in my life. Maps disappeared like lightning. French generals and other high officers changed from uniforms to civilian clothes in nothing flat. The last view I had of one general was going out the window.

"They went in all directions.

"The Americans and British rushed to the wine-cellar where we spent an uncomfortable two hours. Meanwhile the police search mingling with protestations of French officers made what was going on upstairs sound like a riot."

Clark told how he crouched in the cellar, pistol in hand and 15,000 francs in bribe money still in his pocket.

"If the police came down, I was undecided whether to shoot them or bribe them," he said.

The police finally departed, having satisfied themselves there was no one in the house. So the officers decided it was time to go. They gathered their maps and papers and kept them intact although they lost all their clothing and almost everything else when two small boats upset while they were crossing a nearby stretch of water.

While they were in the cellar, Clark disclosed, one of the British Commandos felt an explosive cough coming up. He turned to Clark and whispered:

"I'm afraid if I hold this cough back any longer I'm going to choke to death."

"I'm afraid you won't get a chance to choke," Clark told him.

In retrospect, the expedition had all the aspects of a mystery novel, a thriller and a drama of intrigue combined.

Out of all the huge expanses of North Africa, one pin-point of a house was selected for the meeting and to this Clark and his men made their way, guided by a dim light.

In broken English and broken French the members of the party and the occupants of the house exchanged greetings, passwords and credentials.

The owner told how he had sent his wife away for a vacation and then got rid of the servants by telling them they would not be needed.

Suspicious, some of the latter lingered and it was this which almost proved Clark's undoing.

After leaving the house, the party crept into the woods, where they hid during the day and moved only at night. The water crossing was almost a disaster.

"We lost almost all our clothes and I lost $18,000 in gold," Clark said. "I wonder if Morgenthau will get after me for that."

It was only after further trials and tribulations that the shivering, poorly-clothed expedition reached the unnamed spot where a transport was awaiting them. They arrived back in London just eight days after the start.

. . . .

ROBERT G. NIXON

Formerly of Atlanta, Georgia, Robert Gray Nixon, Sr., moved to Washington, D.C., to join the staff of the International News Service as State Department reporter. He was assigned to the London office of the INS in 1938. The following year he was injured by a piece of shrapnel that pierced through his helmet during an air raid at the beginning of World War II. After the war Nixon became the White House reporter and was elected president of the White House Correspondents' Association in 1949.

He left journalism to work for a Washington public relations firm, from which he retired in 1963. He died of cancer in 1981 at age seventy-five.

You Who Fell at Buna
Can Sleep Easily Now

· · · · · · · · · · · ·

BY

ROBERT J. DOYLE

MILWAUKEE *JOURNAL* STAFF WAR CORRESPONDENT

WITH THE AMERICAN FORCE AT SAIDOR, NEW GUINEA—Jan. 5, 1943—You have been dead more than a year now—you under the straight rows of small white crosses behind the busy port of Buna.

Many of you died with despair in your hearts, wondering how your country and your buddies could win this terrible war. You died with understandable doubt about whether we could win even at Buna. The United States army, as you knew it in that tropical Valley Forge, suffered many losses from Jap pillboxes and disease, beating against the Jap fortifications for nearly two months at the stinking little base of Buna, thousands of miles from Japan.

You were just a fighting soldier, not a general, but your common sense told you that the war could not be won that way. So you wondered, as you gave your life, if your sacrifice was in vain. Perhaps you know now, in death, as you are watching us, that it was not.

Buna had to be taken to remove the threat to our first big base at Port Moresby while we waited for the ships, planes and machines which are winning now. You and your young buddies of the 32nd division were all we had in New Guinea then to help the Aussie infantry on Kokoda trail.

So you marched with heavy packs through the jungles and

swamps, and many of you were exhausted and sick before you reached the enemy. But you fought them, often flushed with fever, throwing yourselves against the machine guns in grass covered pill-boxes.

I'll never forget watching you one afternoon plodding through a small coconut grove in the blinding rain, going to the front. Besides your packs and rifles, you carried mortars on your backs and a mortar shell in each hand. You lay in mud and rain the night before, rolled in your shelter half, and you were to spend countless more nights in water filled foxholes, alert at every sound.

No wonder you doubted whether we could win that way.

Well, fellows—you under the white crosses with whom we talked, joked and cursed—things have changed so much you would not believe it. We can hardly believe it. Those ships, planes and machines are arriving here now and Buna is an important base, thanks to you.

We hope you were watching when your buddies took Saidor last Sunday morning. It was a place like Buna—an overgrown grass airstrip and a couple of scraggly little native villages by the sea. It took seven weeks and hundreds of American and Australian lives to get Buna. Saidor fell in four hours without the loss of one American life. It's true that there were few Japs at Saidor, but that doesn't make much difference. The way your buddies went in there they would have taken it from a thousand Japs in short order.

They could come in from in front this time instead of wallowing around in jungles and swamps behind the Japs. Compared with Buna, it looked as though we had the whole United States navy and air force with us.

Remember our "fleet" at Buna—a few fishing boats and native canoes? You should see the ships we have now. Warships sat off shore pouring salvoes while fast assault boats carried the first waves of the Red Arrow infantry to the beach. Then came landing craft, lowering ramps to the beach and unloading a whole company in a matter of seconds. Then came the big ships which dropped their bows open on to the beach, and bulldozers smashed into the jungle, followed by jeeps, trucks, tanks and howitzers.

Remember our brave little air force, fighting against big odds?

We have so many planes now that the Japs are afraid to come out in the daytime. They will sneak around at night and drop bombs, but we've got real antiaircraft guns now, instead of the .50 caliber machine guns we first had at Buna.

Remember your old packs, shelter halves and heavy mosquito nets? Now the boys have light new jungle equipment—covered jungle hammocks keep them off the wet ground. New light carbines give them more firepower and tractors drag big artillery right through the jungle. Amphibious jeeps and ducks drive right into the ocean and plow through the waves like barges.

You thought we would have to fight the Japs inch by inch all the way through thousands of miles of jungle clear to the north end of New Guinea. Now we have enough sea and air power to leave the jungle and jump hundreds of miles behind the Jap front line, as we did at Saidor. A few more jumps like that, with pauses to build air bases, could take us to the end of New Guinea and over to the Philippines.

No, you Wisconsin and Michigan boys under those white crosses at Buna did not die in vain. You and the Aussies at Buna and Milne bay and the marines at Guadalcanal finally stopped the Japs. They caught us with our pants down, but you stopped them and started driving them back.

The echo of the hand grenade you threw at that pillbox with your last ounce of strength did not die. It grew louder and louder, to the thunderous roar of the bombs and shells which are now pounding the Japs in New Guinea, New Britain, the Solomons, the Marshalls, at Wake and in Burma, Java, Borneo and China.

Shadows of great formations of American bombers flicker over your graves and angry warships churn up waves which lap on Buna beach. Your comrades of the Red Arrow division are thinking of you as they carry the battle forward at Saidor.

· · · · · · · · · · ·

ROBERT J. DOYLE

Doyle was thirty-one when he and a companion were killed while traveling in central Java in 1950. Born in Chicago, Doyle attended Northwestern University, where he was an editor of the school's daily paper. After serving in the Navy the final year of World War II, Doyle studied Asian history and politics at Columbia and Chinese language at Yale. He joined *Time* magazine in 1947 and was Shanghai bureau chief during the revolution. He was Hong Kong bureau chief at the time of his death.

1,500 Miles of Heat, Rain, and Heat

· · · · · · · · · · · ·

BY

CHESTER MORRISON

CHICAGO *SUN* FOREIGN SERVICE

CAIRO, Feb. 6, 1945—Winston Churchill, referring to it as "the Battle of El Alamein, or more properly the Battle of Egypt," mentioned the "fierce battle which lasted for eleven days."

When the war is over and the campaign to which he referred is nicely embalmed in military textbooks, perhaps it will turn out as the Eleven-Day Battle. Its outcome certainly was decided in those eleven days, if not a month before when the enemy was stopped cold in the Battle of Hemeimat, a blow from which he never recovered. The textbooks will undoubtedly give credit to two men—Gen. Sir Bernard Montgomery for his masterly pursuit of the enemy and Field Marshal Erwin Rommel for his almost letter-perfect withdrawal.

This chapter of Egypt's history began Oct. 23, with a devastating barrage of several hundred guns of all calibers spaced along the thirty-mile front from El Alamein inland, with the heaviest fire spotted along the twelve-mile stretch toward the coast. On our side, every detail was perfect. Montgomery informed every man, from brigadier to truck driver, where and when the blow would be struck and every man knew his part.

The guns had been brought up during the preceding month;

thousands of men had been brought in, and hundreds of tanks and hundreds of planes. And just before the zero hour, when the tanks were already clanking up in the darkness along the desert tracks laid out across the sand for that specific purpose, came a sudden shift in wind.

For more than a week before the attack the wind blew steadily from the west, but that one night it suddenly reversed its direction and on the wings of an east wind the enemy heard the first warning that his number was up. He heard the tanks coming, for perhaps three or four hours, so he knew the attack was mounted. What he did not know was the tremendous power of that attack which, as Prime Minister Churchill said, "drove Rommel from Cirenaica and from Libya and finally to withdrawal into Tunisia." And now Churchill says "the enemy is 1,500 miles from Cairo and the Eighth Army will follow Rommel wherever he goes."

Following him has been a rough, hard, exciting experience. Its heavy burdens have been shared by Australians, New Zealanders, Englishmen, Scots, Indians, South Africans, French, Poles, Czechs, Slavs—and even in the closing stages by Americans, although America's part in this phase of the worldwide war has been largely confined to the production of war material, flying war planes to the front and learning through military observers how wars are fought by veterans who have learned in a tough school how war must be conducted.

The early stages of Rommel's retreat from El Alamein seem long ago and far away. There was the bitter five-day struggle for the stubborn enemy strong point called Thompson's Post, near the Hill of Jesus, where the tanks battled across the powdery, choking sand.

There was the jubilant entry into Matruh, where the enemy had left so swiftly he didn't have time to destroy his supplies and fuel. And the even pleasanter return to Tobruk, where black African soldiers who had been prisoners since June lined the road with their big teeth flashing in broad grins.

There were the days when the prisoners began pouring in—first in small groups of sullen, sweating men who were gathered into barbed wire enclosures and searched, while truckloads of those same grinning troops passed by going toward the front along a nearby road, waving and shouting the one expression which is all the English many of them knew—an expression characteristic now of Australian troops but generic with Anglo-Saxons and now part and parcel of every soldier's vocabulary as it was in the last war.

And the army passed over Halfaya and crossed the flat plateau of Salum and rolled on and on.

Bootleggers who used to drive truckloads of liquor in the dead of night without lights, knowing that hijackers were lurking somewhere to kill them, have some idea of what the journey to the appointment in Tripoli was like. Their experience compared to that of the Eighth Army's was like a Boy Scout troop marching out to a marshmallow roast.

Like most free people who have experience and appreciate the value of freedom, the British began this war with mines designed to delay, perhaps damage, possibly cripple the vehicles which happened to pass over and explode them. The Germans, accepting wars as a life's work, never have gone out for marshmallows. Their mines were built to wreck and kill.

Drive your car some night without lights over a road you never heard of before, knowing that if you make one mistake about anything you'll wind up dead. Do it as an adventure, and then, whether you like it or not, take it on as a steady life job, without vacations or Sundays off or movies, for your pay of two-bits a day and your most welcome reward a tin cup full of black tea before dawn tomorrow if you dare light a fire to boil it.

The Eighth Army pushed westward from the desert, where its soldiers had been cursing the heat for months and years, and into the hill country of Cirenaica. There they met the rain they'd been wishing for for months. They got it in their faces and in their kits and in their bedding and down their necks and backs, and they were so sick of rain they never wanted any more.

And the Eighth pushed on from the Cirenaica Gebel into the Tripolitanian desert again—into a bitter cold country compared with which the hub-deep sand of Libya seemed faintly to resemble a ballroom floor.

The Eighth Army entered Tripolitania. The Scots Highland division—so trained and disciplined that I, not understanding those things, when I first saw them clicking their heels in the Libyan wasteland, thought them fools—the Scots took the high road along the coast and the Seventh Armored "desert rats" took the low road inland through mountains and rocks and sand and rain, and the Highlanders got there just before we did. And up on the Seventh Division's left flank came the New Zealanders.

The Eighth Army pushed on toward Tripoli and beyond, seldom catching more than a sight of the enemy, sometimes leaving behind men and vehicles that hit cunningly buried mines.

And we made Tripoli on a morning three months to a day from that furious barrage which raised a sandstorm at El Alamein in October.

The Army is probably glad, in the disgruntled way of all armies, now that the march into Tunisia is under way. It's bully and biscuit again, but Churchill knew what he was talking about when he mentioned the "vengeance of the Eighth Army." When the Axis is actually pushed out of Africa, I hope and expect that the Eighth Army will do most of the pushing.

* * * * * * * * * * *

CHESTER MORRISON

Chester Morrison was a senior editor at *Look* magazine when he retired in 1966. A Philadelphia native, he went to Rutgers University and served in the Navy in World War I. He worked for the Associated Press, the Boston *Transcript*, and the Boston *Herald* before moving to the Chicago *Sun*. As a correspondent for the *Sun* and also the Columbia Broadcasting System, he covered the war in Africa during World War II. In addition to his talent for broadcasting, reporting, and free-lancing, he was praised for what he described as volumes of "innumerable magnificent but unprintable limericks."

Morrison died shortly after retiring.

"It's a Helluva Fighting Soldier You Are"

· · · · · · · · · · · ·

BY

GRAHAM HOVEY

INTERNATIONAL NEWS SERVICE STAFF CORRESPONDENT

WITH THE AMERICAN FORCES AT CASSINO (INS) Feb. 7, 1943—
"Lieutenant, it's a helluva fighting soldier you are—you haven't
heard a gun go off in three weeks," said Frank Clay to Alfred
Nelson.

"Lieutenant, that such a remark should come from the likes of
you is truly baffling—you haven't exactly been a Commando yourself," said Alfred Nelson to Frank Clay.

So they hiked off to Cassino together; checked up on how front-
line doughboys were making out in the embattled city, spotted four
German pillboxes and directed tank fire which knocked out all of
them, stalked German snipers and then trudged off home with a
Nazi Bazooka gun which they presented to the commander of their
armored task force.

I was at a command post when Clay, the 22-year-old West Pointer
son of Maj. Gen. Lucius Clay, of Washington, D.C., and the 25-
year-old Nelson of East Jordan, Mich., returned, grinning broadly,
their faces flushed as though they were schoolboys coming home
from a victorious sandlot football game.

I also listened in to the mock bawling-out their company commander, Capt. Frank Crittenden of Ridgewood, N.J., administered

to them for taking chances. Crittenden had trouble keeping a straight face.

"It was pretty enjoyable," Clay admitted to a group which included Lieuts. James Taylor of Big Stone Gap, Va.; Howard Simpson of Peoria, Ill., and Milton Weinberg of the Bronx, N.Y.

"We had crossed the Rapido and hiked past the ruins of Italian barracks north of Cassino when we found the Bazooka, intact, in a German dugout. They must have had a duel to the finish with one of our medium tanks.

"Anyway, the tank nearby was pierced by a Bazooka bullet-hole the size of a silver dollar at a 30-foot range. The projectile had gone through the turret near the telescopic sights and killed a gunner, but there were plenty of dead Jerries lying in the dugout around the Bazooka, too."

"From there," said Nelson, "we walked down the road to town. Jerry snipers gave us some attention. However, finally we were told we couldn't go any farther because of sniper's fire, so we took to the high route in the mountains west of the road and reached a position where we had a nice view of Cassino."

Clay picked up the story from here.

"We were lying there watching the town," he said, "when I saw a tracer coming from a big pile of rubble where the house had apparently been wrecked by shellfire.

"With our field glasses we picked up a machine-gun emplacement and watched until we had spotted two more.

"We had seen a Sheridan tank in the vicinity, so we found a tank commander and said: 'We've got some targets for you.'

"He said: 'I don't have permission to fire because we are in a defensive camouflaged position here.'

" 'Hell, call up and get permission,' " we said.

"And he did," declared Nelson.

"We crawled up the hill ahead of the tank and directed its fire. Before the first round I looked back and saw the tank's 75-mm. gun pointing right at us. I told Clay if the fire didn't clear the hill, we wouldn't have to worry about Jerry pillboxes. But it did clear. He pumped three rounds of direct fire into each pillbox and hit every one."

"By then," said Clay, "we had spotted a fourth pillbox, so the tank fired at that too. In a few minutes the infantry radioed that we had scored a direct hit again, knocking out a nest they had worked on with machine-guns for several hours. The infantry was grateful.

"There's not much more to tell. Snipers bothered us some and we started looking for them, but I guess it was a good thing we didn't find them because I only had a forty-five, and it's a funny thing, but I've found I can't hit much beyond five feet with it."

Nelson put in:

"We may go back tomorrow, though."

"Then again, lieutenant, there's a bare possibility you may not," said Capt. Crittenden, airily.

. . . .

GRAHAM HOVEY

After graduating from the University of Minnesota, Graham Hovey worked for two years as a combat correspondent for the International News Service, covering the war in Italy, France, and Africa. Shortly before the end of the war Hovey moved to Washington, D.C., and joined the Associated Press and later the *New Republic*, covering the State Department. In 1956, after teaching for several years at both the University of Minnesota and the University of Wisconsin, he went to the Minneapolis *Tribune*, where he worked as an editorial writer and a UN correspondent. Seven years later he went to *The New York Times* as a reporter and member of the editorial board. He retired in 1986 and returned to academics as a director of the Michigan Journalism Fellows Program. A professor emeritus, Hovey lives and teaches in Ann Arbor, Michigan.

Guadalcanal—First Jap Defeat in 1,000 Years

. . . .

BY

ROBERT C. MILLER

UNITED PRESS STAFF CORRESPONDENT

[Editor's Note: Robert C. Miller went ashore at Guadalcanal with the first wave of United States Marines last August 7, 1942. He was the only news correspondent to cover both the first and last battles at Guadalcanal. In this dispatch he describes the final action which crushed Japanese resistance on the island.]

GUADALCANAL, Feb. 11, 1943—The battle ended at sundown today in the first complete American victory of the war in the South Pacific, when two American columns working toward the northwestern tip of the island joined forces near Visalie, capturing or annihilating effective Japanese remnants.

The last remaining enemy troops were crushed six months and two days after American naval units prefaced the invasion with a deafening barrage and American marines splashed ashore in the first American offensive of the Pacific war. Old Glory flies unchallenged over the island.

Her navy smashed repeatedly at sea, her Zeros and Mitsubishis erased from the skies and her proudest regiments now masses of rotting corpses, Japan has tasted defeat for the first time in a thousand years.

To the only correspondent present at the beginning and conclusion of the campaign, it was a magnificent example of American bravery, tenacity and resourcefulness which the enemy was unable at any time to match.

The conclusion of the fighting was announced by Maj. Gen. Alexander Patch, commander of the American forces in the Solomons, who said the "17th Japanese army was smashed tonight and ground fighting has ended on Guadalcanal."

General Patch's announcement closed a campaign in which American sea, air and land forces met and crushed every counterattack of a desperate enemy who attempted through sheer weight of numbers to recapture this vitally strategic island and annihilate its valiant defenders.

Observers estimated that at least 20,000 Japanese soldiers and marines died in Guadalcanal jungles, many from disease, while another 30,000 died aboard flaming transports and warships blasted by American surface and air units.

The Abbey Becomes Another Famous Ruin

· · · · · · · · · · · ·

BY
GRAHAM HOVEY

INTERNATIONAL NEWS SERVICE STAFF CORRESPONDENT

ON A HILLTOP 5,000 YARDS FROM MONTE CASSINO, Feb. 15, 1943 (INS)—For the better part of an hour today, huge American Flying Fortresses unloaded thousands of pounds of block-busters on the ancient abbey of St. Benedict.

The giant aircraft, sent into action against a holy monument that the Germans had made into a fortress, blasted asunder one of Italy's greatest and oldest cultural landmarks because the Hun wanted it that way.

The steeple of robin's egg blue surmounting the bluish-white chapel of the Monte Cassino monastery was one of the first abbey landmarks to topple as the first wave of Fortresses hit the target at 9:20 A.M.

I had admired that steeple from a scouting plane in a flight over the abbey only two weeks ago. When the smoke cleared from the explosion of the first bombs, I looked for it through field glasses from this vantage point less than three miles away.

It was gone.

[Editor's Note: A British broadcast reported that 100 Flying Fortresses participated in the assault against the peak of Monte Cassino.]

From here it seems as though the first bomber to go over hit the abbey squarely. The first burst of swirling smoke seemed to come right from inside its white walls.

As I looked for the steeple through glasses, it appeared as though all the windows of the main building had been blown out and the southern section of the massed structures looked cream-colored rather than white—the way white stone buildings always look after a plastering by shells or bombs.

Since the time a second wave of Fortresses finished their bombing runs, smoke obscured the abbey proper.

White smoke, gray smoke and jet black smoke are rolling skyward.

There was nothing of surprise in this bombardment of a shrine of Christendom established by St. Benedict in the year 529. Leaflets had been dropped into the monastery yesterday pleading that all Italian refugees inside the buildings leave, inasmuch as the Germans had transformed it into an observation post and fortress, necessitating attack.

Perched high on Monte Cassino, overlooking the Via Casilini, which leads to Rome and the flat, easily negotiable Liri river valley separating the Eternal City from the present Cassino battle area, the monastery in German hands constituted a mighty garrison.

Enemy guns in its embrasures and battlements had raked the allied lines consistently, and field telescopes in its windows had spied upon the movements of American and British troops.

The leaflets pumped into the monastery's 1,300-year-old cloisters throughout yesterday left no doubt as to what the Nazis had made of them. Addressed solely to civilians who had taken refuge in the cool halls and stone cells where the followers of Benedict had for centuries devoted themselves to meditation and furtherance of culture and learning, these pamphlets said:

"Italian friends, beware! We have until now been especially careful to avoid shelling the Monte Cassino monastery. The Germans have known how to benefit from this.

"But now the fighting has swept closer and closer to its sacred precincts. The time has come when we must train our guns on the monastery itself. We give you warning so you may save yourselves.

Leave the monastery. Leave it at once. Respect this warning. It is to your benefit."

The leaflets were signed: "the 5th Army."

[Editor's Note: Correspondent Hovey later flew over the shattered abbey in an American scout plane and described what he saw in the dispatch which follows.]

ABOARD A CUB SCOUT PLANE OVER MONTE CASSINO ABBEY, Feb. 16, 1943 (INS)—The ancient abbey on the peak of Monte Cassino lay sprawled in smoking ruins today after the terrific bombardment loosed on the German-held monastery by American Fortress and Marauder bombers today.

"That's a pretty sight to see," said the pilot of the Cub scout plane in which this correspondent flew to observe the devastation wrought on the shrine.

"That had been a thorn in my side for more than a month," continued the pilot, Staff Sgt. Ernest McClelland, of Sebring, Fla.

McClelland shouted his words back over the motorboat-like sputter of the tiny Cub's engine as the plane hovered 800 feet over the deep craters on the hilltop. Sections of the monastery lay in piles of smoking rubble. Some walls stood torn and ghost-like.

But it was not a pretty sight to see, as "Mac" McClelland would freely admit if he had not been shot at by German machine-guns and small arms fire from the vicinity of the abbey of St. Benedict so many times recently.

"They're shelling hell out of it now," Mac yelled.

I looked and saw one geyser of black smoke with plumes and greenish rubble shoot up and felt relieved that we were banking sharply away.

Neither of us can spot any sign of life in the ruins below. That doesn't necessarily mean the Germans aren't dug in in that vicinity but the best guess seems to be that they at least may have departed from the main abbey precincts.

One indication of this conjecture is that our big guns are laying down plenty of high explosives directly behind Monte Cassino on highway six where it stretches northwestward through the valley of the Liri river.

There was apparently some movement along the highway, perhaps from enemy columns attempting to rescue equipment. It was encouraging to think that yesterday's onslaught not only wrecked the monastery as an observation post but blanketed the steep sides of Monte Cassino as well.

From here I can see huge craters practically ringing the mountainside below the abbey—the most logical spot for German gun emplacements.

The Germans may have fired small arms and machine-guns from the abbey itself, but unquestionably its chief value was for the observation it afforded for all of our troop movements from north of Cervaro all the way to the lower Rapido and Liri valleys.

If the enemy operated true to form, gun emplacements probably were blasted in the sides of Monte Cassino just below the crest where the abbey stood. That area now is extensively gutted and the whole hill is liberally pockmarked.

"I'll give you one more good look," yelled Mac, so we banked over the ruins again.

I looked vainly in the ruins for the light blue chapel steeple which had impressed me on a previous Cub ride some weeks ago. Nothing visible remained of it or the red tile roof which once covered the basilica.

Monte Cassino abbey now is just another San Pietro, San Vittore and Mignano—just another entry in a stiff price list Italy now is bucking for tolerating Fascism and a partnership in the axis.

I wondered again if it was necessary to do this job. Then I looked off to the southeast and saw two giant red crosses on the ground marking army hospitals where broken soldiers were fighting for life after suffering at enemy hands in the fight for Cassino.

Yes, I'm sure it was necessary to bomb the abbey.

86 Minutes Which Helped Fashion Victory

· · · · · · · · · · ·

BY

LEO S. DISHER

UNITED PRESS WAR CORRESPONDENT

[Editor's Note: The following dispatch tells for the first time of the planning of a top-level U.S. Eighth Air Force raid—Thursday's mammoth blow to disrupt German transport. No correspondent ever before had been admitted to the secret operations room of the Air Force and permitted to report a session.]

GEN. DOOLITTLE'S HEADQUARTERS, ENGLAND, Feb. 23, 1943. (UP) . . . Lt. Gen. James H. Doolittle's chief staff officers assembled in a secret, buried room. A fat-faced wall clock ticked off a total of 86 minutes before they finished two sessions.

But in that time they mapped the master tactics which sent 2,200 planes and 15,000 American airmen to strike their greatest blow of the war at German transport yesterday.

At 4 P.M. Wednesday some 30 officers had passed guards and were standing in the buried room, innermost part of the underground operations block of headquarters.

The room was only 30 feet long by 15 feet wide. Maps were on every wall. A long table was placed in the middle and at the upper end were four lounge chairs.

The hands of the fat-faced clock in a corner stood at 4:08 when heavy-shouldered, West Point Maj. Gen. Orvil Anderson, Deputy Commander of the Air Force, entered and took a lounge chair.

Without preliminaries, one of the most historic raid plannings in the history of the Air Force began.

Anderson sat so close to me I could touch him. Officers, some of them looking like college boys, sat around the general or stood behind him. The general leaned forward in his chair without speaking. Before him was a weather map.

"Probably fog on ground bases . . ." This came without prompting from Maj. Peter Pruett, 26, of Stevens, Ark., weather briefing officer. "For around three to five-tenths . . . low clouds around 5,000 to 6,000 feet. . . ."

When Pruett finished it was just 4:11.

Anderson sat with his chin in his hands. Abruptly he said:

"Let's have the maps."

This was the layout of targets for the day.

The talk moved rapidly from there on and was hard to catch. The general asked about targets, about flak pools and routes and checked with Pruett for more weather information.

At 4:15 P.M. the general was gazing absorbedly at a large wall map. At the right of him a chart showed details of an Eighth Air Force raid then in progress.

He sat down again after two minutes and for seven minutes there was silence. Finally, Anderson said:

"Let's get enough targets north and southwest of Berlin to absorb at least one full division."

The general said he wanted the route to miss heavy guns and he wanted to hit rail yards. If he could not hit freight yards, he wanted railroad bridges, viaducts and roadbeds. He was going to put in a raid at 7,000 to 12,000 feet.

Fighter, gun and navigation experts, young colonels and boy-faced captains, spoke to the general. He agreed with them or checked them and made decisions.

Thirty-six minutes after the conference began, he left the room. He returned at 10 P.M. for a final conference.

Meanwhile, Supreme Headquarters, which broadly had directed the plans, reported on all to the divisions of the Air Force.

In a final 50 minute conference, Anderson settled the final details of the raid.

It had long been apparent that what he was shaping up was the boldest attack ever made by the Eighth Air Force—two dozen targets to be hit with bomber groups scattered over the Reich at record low levels.

"We'll know a great deal more about the Luftwaffe at 4 o'clock tomorrow afternoon," one staff officer remarked.

"Hell, yes," answered another. "Never has man done anything more insulting to the Luftwaffe than this."

. . . .

LEO S. DISHER

Leo S. Disher was a reporter for the United Press during World War II. While traveling with the British Navy near Oran, Algeria, he was badly wounded during an attack by Vichy troops but managed to swim to shore. He was the first civilian to receive a Purple Heart during that conflict. *Springboard to Berlin*, written by Disher and three other correspondents, was based on the Oran battle experience.

After the war he headed United Press bureaus in Czechoslovakia, Bulgaria, and Romania. His marriage to Hanyi, the daughter of a key official in the exiled Czech Army, forced him to leave the Eastern bloc. He joined the United States Information Service in 1948 and was press attaché to several embassies worldwide before entering the field of international business in the private sector. He was fifty-seven when he died in 1969.

First Fortress Flight over Europe

. . . .

BY

WALTER CRONKITE

UNITED PRESS STAFF CORRESPONDENT

Editor's Note: One of the first six American correspondents to fly with the 8th U.S. Air Force on a raid in Europe.

U.S. FLYING FORTRESS BASE SOMEWHERE IN ENGLAND—Feb. 27, 1943—It was a hell 26,000 feet above the earth, a hell of burning tracer bullets and bursting flak, of crippled Flying Fortresses and flaming German fighter planes.

I rode a Flying Fortress into the midst of it with the 8th U.S. Air Force on their raid on the Wilhelmshaven Naval base in northwest Germany yesterday.

For two hours I sat through a vicious gun duel with twisting and turning Focke Wulf 190 fighters and held tight while we dodged savage anti-aircraft fire. My reward was to see American bombs falling toward German soil.

Luck was with us and our Fortress came through the torrent without damage. Other formations caught the brunt of the fighters' blows and we saw Fortresses and Liberators plucked from the flights around us. Altogether, seven planes are missing.

We knocked out our share of fighters, and as we swept back over the North Sea we saw great pillars of smoke pluming from the target area.

It was the first time correspondents had been permitted to accompany the Flying Fortresses or Liberators on any of their raids over Germany or occupied France. Eight reporters had qualified to go, but one was ill and another was aboard a ship which turned back because of technical difficulties.

We were skirting the Frisian Islands and still an hour from the target when our tail gunner, Staff Sgt. George W. Henderson, 22, of Columbus, Kan., sighted the first of the enemy fighters. Over the inter-communication system, he said:

"Locks like enemy fighters low at 6 o'clock—about six or seven of them."

"Six o'clock" in aerial parlance meant directly behind the plane.

It didn't take the fighters long to close in on us. Meanwhile, I was trying to scrape the frost from the windows in the plastic nose of the plane in order to see.

The fighters came toward us with guns spitting. We couldn't hear them because of the noise of our own engines.

Our tail gunner was the first to open up. We could feel the vibrations set up by his rattling gun. Then the waist gunners, Sgt. Edward Z. Harmon, 33, of Talue Lake, Calif., and Staff Sgt. Duvard L. Hinds, 23, of Los Angeles, Calif., took over.

Heck Balk, 22, of Temple, Tex., veteran of ten missions, was banging away from the ball turret on the belly of the plane.

A spurt of flames immediately overhead disclosed that Tech. Sgt. Charles E. Zipfel, 22, of Sigel, Pa., had joined in from the top turret.

Then the enemy planes swept by and the bombardier and navigator in the nose of the fortress began firing their guns. Clips of empty cartridges flew around the tiny compartment and the stench of burning powder filtered through our oxygen masks.

The bombardier, First Lieut. Albert W. Dieffenbach, 26, of Washington, D.C., turned around and lifted his thumb. That meant that our tracers had at least scared off the attacking enemy.

The anti-aircraft fire began as we started the bombing run into Wilhelmshaven and didn't end until we had passed the last tiny peninsula of the continent.

The first flak broke some distance below and to the left of us. There were tiny bursts of flame and small puffs of black smoke that gradually grew larger as the wind dispersed them. It surprised me not to be able to hear the burst.

Then bursts appeared in front of us; then to the right and not nearly so far away.

"It looks like they are laying out a carpet of that stuff for us," one gunner said.

I watched, fascinated, as the big Fortresses above and below took evasive turns and narrowly avoided flak, forgetting that some of the bursting shrapnel might pierce the nose of our own plane.

The crew told me that there was not much danger that flak would knock down a ship by itself, but once a ship has been damaged and is forced to drop out of formation, the enemy fighters gang up on it and hit it like kids on a merry-go-round plucking for the brass ring.

I saw one bomber several thousand feet below, under control but obviously damaged by anti-aircraft fire. Seven enemy fighters circled it, giving it burst after burst.

We had our share of enemy fighters. About twenty were almost constantly within attack range throughout the two-hour fight. With scarcely a pause, someone on the ship was calling out over the inter-communication phone the position of an approaching enemy.

"Six o'clock low!" . . . "Four o'clock high!" . . . "Two o'clock high!"

"The --- -- - ---- is coming in." . . . "Get on him!" . . . "Give him a burst." . . . "Keep him out there."

As our guns shook the plane, the voice of the skipper, Capt. Glenn E. Hagenbuch, 24, of Utica, Ill., rang out:

"That's scaring him off, boys. He won't be back for awhile. Nice work."

Your first impression of an oncoming enemy fighter is similar to your first impression of flak—nothing much to frighten you. You can't see his guns firing and you seldom see his bullets spurt by. You just know he's firing on you.

Once I saw a body plummet by. The parachute finally blossomed out below. Later, I saw a Nazi pilot bail out and his Focke-Wulf spiral down toward the sea.

FIRST FORTRESS FLIGHT OVER EUROPE

We saw Wilhelmshaven through broken clouds. It looked like a toy village from 26,000 feet.

The planes ahead were the first to drop their bombs. The "eggs" were plenty hideous-looking as they began what appeared a slow descent to earth.

Then Dieffenbach's left hand went out to the switch panel alongside him and almost imperceptibly he touched the button.

"Bomb away!" he said calmly over the inter-communication system.

That was it: Our mission had been accomplished.

It was a letdown. I couldn't see our own bombs falling and even our ball turret gunner was unable to see them hit the ground because of our extreme height.

I did see some bombs hurtling down, however, from almost immediately above us from another formation. They came so close to our wings that I could almost read the inscription on them. The crew members bluntly expressed their opinions over the inter-communication phone.

The trip back home was almost an anti-climax.

· · · · · · · · · ·

WALTER CRONKITE

Walter Cronkite began his long and admirable career as a radio and television news correspondent as a writer and editor at Scripps-Howard. At the United Press he worked as a respected correspondent and manager in several bureaus across the United States and Europe. In 1951 Cronkite went to CBS News as a correspondent and managing editor. He presided there for more than thirty years. As a news anchor he hosted dozens of groundbreaking special reports and won several Emmy awards. Other journalistic honors include the Peabody Award, the George Polk Memorial Award, the presidential Medal of Freedom, and many honorary degrees. He is the author of *Challenges of Change.*

Cronkite retired from CBS in 1981.

We're Going to Bomb Tokio!

· · · · · · · · · · · · ·

BY

RICHARD TREGASKIS

INTERNATIONAL NEWS SERVICE STAFF CORRESPONDENT

WITH THE U.S. PACIFIC FLEET AT SEA (SHANGRI-LA), Apr. 20, 1943 (delayed)—There was electrifying news aboard the ship this morning. As the carrier, which was part of our task force, moved closer, it was announced that we are going to bomb Tokio!

It is the action for which Americans have been wishing since the Japanese attack on Pearl Harbor.

"We're four months late, but we'll give it to 'em now," is the cry of a gunner at a midship battery as the word was passed around.

A quiver of anticipation seemed to run over the ship. This was certainly the greatest story of the war so far.

There was another wave of excitement as binoculars were trained on the giant aircraft carrier Hornet, which now moved closer to our ship.

A high, irregular mass on the deck marked the presence of much larger aircraft than [the] usual carrier planes. The ship drew nearer, we could make out the double tails, the wings, and tricycle landing gear of the Mitchell (B-25) medium bomber.

There are the weapons which will be used in the attack on Tokio—in a daring plan typically American in its ingenuity. Never before in wartime has such a maneuver as this been planned: to send land bombers twice as big as the deck of the carrier aircraft, from the deck of a ship.

Admiral William F. Halsey made clear some of the details of our planned assault.

Our force was told that they will approach to a point about 400 miles from Tokio. There the bombers will take to the air and we will hightail our way towards home.

Obviously, the bombers will not return to the carrier's deck, for the landing space is not large enough for them. But just where they will go is a mystery.

Admiral Spraunce suggested the possibility of landing in China.

The admiral was not over-optimistic about our chances of getting away unscathed from this expedition. He spoke of the long range of the Japanese patrol aircraft which might spot us; also of the hundreds of small patrol vessels known to operate along the Japanese coast. He spoke, too, of the need for lightning withdrawal after we made our thrust.

At supper, officers were as excited as boys. Humorous talk revolved around $1,000,000 in cash said to have been offered by various American interests as a prize for the first bomb dropped on Tokio.

How would the amount be divided among the squadron? the officers wondered. And if the bombing crews landed in China, would they be paid off in Chinese dollars?

Aviators speculated on the surprise angle.

"Those Japs'll be crazy to know how a flock of B-25's got there."

The Marine captain at the head of the table held up crossed fingers on both hands, and with his face screwed up in earnestness, shouted;

"Oh, oh, oh, God, may they get there."

This morning, talk was back on the subject of the bombing. One item in the news, which we had heard by radio, was stimulating to the conversation.

It was an announcement by Prime Minister Winston Churchill that a great Japanese fleet, including as least three battleships and five aircraft carriers, was operating in the Indian Ocean.

This fact lent a cheering note to the conversation—for five carriers and three battleships in the Indian Ocean are eight ships less for us to contend with in our assault on Japan.

Another cheering note is the weather. The sky is gray and stormy, and it is raining. The rolling and pitching of the ship is bothersome, but many a hand aboard is glad: Glad because the murky weather is a curtain to screen our large task force from enemy observation. We hope that this natural protection will continue until we have launched our bombing planes.

This afternoon there were moving pictures in the crews' quarters. The picture was "The Wizard of Oz," and everyone enjoyed it— but such colorful fantasy seemed to strike a bizarre note on this ship of war in the Pacific, amidst all these tense men bound on a mission of death.

There was news of a submarine alarm and some of our small craft went out to hunt for the enemy. But, according to the story, he was not discovered, and presumably the alarm was false.

In these days as we are nearing our objective, however, our patrols must keep a double check ahead and on all sides to guard against our being seen by the enemy.

One Japanese submarine, popping up somewhere along our course, could quickly flash word to the Japanese mainland and bring out a naval force that might thwart our plan.

Everyone seems to be growing more tense by the hour now, and time accordingly has slowed considerably. The men aboard are wearing out whatever literature is available. The magazines on the rack in the officers' wardroom, already well worn, have aged still more, and the ship's little library reports a heavy demand.

The sailor lads told me there are several popular games which fill in well if you don't happen to be in the mood for reading. Acey-Deucey, played on a checkerboard, is a long-standing Navy favorite. Cribbage is another standby.

Tonight at dinner the conversation still turned on the raid. Wistfully, every officer who speaks of the matter lays dreamy plans for engaging the Japanese home fleet, or blasting shore installations with our heavy guns.

There was conjecture as to the time of day for the launch of our planes. Some say late afternoon, as that would give us the cover of night in which to haul our ships away from the battle area at full speed; and also afford the bombers the advantage of darkness for their attack.

Others objected to a launch in the afternoon, because we would have to penetrate deep into Japanese coastal waters in broad daylight—while we were watching our launching point—and that, they suggested, would probably result in our being caught with our planes down, and the failure of our mission.

The wardroom radio was blaring a broadcast in Japanese. We are close enough to their coast now to pick up their programs on our standard wave-length band.

The skies continue overcast and the night is very black.

Today was the day before the great event and at mid morning we were still many hundred miles from Tokio, and our task force slowed in the choppy gray seas to have a parley. Under the overcast, lights blinked back and forth.

Talking done, we began to shove on speed. Our ship plunged ahead of the pack, tossing clouds of spume over her bow. She rode so fast that she jerked and shivered each time she rode a high one, and one of her propellers topped the waves.

It was perfect weather for the raid—for no Japanese "eyes" could be flying on such a day.

In the evening after supper, when the lights had gone out, a rather larger group than usual remained at the tables passing the time away—it was the night before—and not by a long shot was it the night before Christmas.

The ship's physician, Dr. James B. Maloney of Boston, Mass., sat with a young flier, Lt. Charles A. Shipman of Big Spring, Tex., doing anagrams. Ensign Ustick was reading a Thorne Smith novel at the same table. At another table Comdr. Shetky, the executive officer, played cribbage with three younger men. At a third table, Dennis S. Crowley, staff aviation officer, of Roanoke, Va., spoke earnestly on the subject of airplane armament. He had an audience of three, one of whom alternated listening with reading a novel.

Below decks other sailors and marines had turned into their tier bunks.

Out on deck, the only signs of human life were a few well bundled forms of sailormen passing in the dark. There was a stern rolling sea and a shrieking wind. Spray flew over the railing and smashed against the catapult towers. This was a fitting night before THE day.

Up at four o'clock this morning in the hope of seeing all the excitement of the day. There was a possibility that we had decided that the bombers might take off at dawn.

But they did not.

When the sun came up we were still 800 miles from Tokio.

At about seven o'clock, as we were sitting down to breakfast, one of our scout planes spotted an unidentified ship, but quickly avoided it.

Later in the morning came the electrifying news that the cruiser running just behind us had sighted a Japanese patrol ship. Contact was unavoidable this time, and putting on maximum speed, the cruiser dropped out of formation and darted off to our port side.

We could see her streaking towards the horizon, where the Japanese ship was only a faint smudge of gray on the horizon. At last we had met the enemy.

The cruiser was about four miles from us when she opened fire. But we could plainly see the brilliant flashes of her guns. She came alight with puffs of orange flame, like a gas stove touched off by a match, each time the guns fired.

Clouds of dirty smoke, a yellowish hue, were rising over the cruiser. And near the horizon we could see tall narrow geysers, like a line of white columns, springing into existence.

Then the small popping sound of the gunfire came to us from the distance. Sound is slow to travel in such vast spaces.

Almost immediately, the bright flashes of a second salvo burst along the cruiser's deck. And then the bright little sunbursts of color came in rotation, rolling up and down the length of the ship.

On the horizon a smother of spray columns had risen where the Jap ship had been seen. The cruiser's gunners had to hold their fire until the colonnade of splashes had settled and vision was clear again, so that they could see their target.

We were trying to exterminate the enemy before he radioed our position to his base. But it took a few minutes too long to sink him, and we feared that he had reported our position.

Now mechanics were warming up the motors of the big B-25's on the Hornet's deck—only a few minutes after the might of the cruiser had blasted the Jap to bits. We must get our bombers off post-haste, before enemy air or surface craft arrived on the spot.

A Grandstand Seat As Our Planes
Take Off for Tokio

· · · · · · · · · · · ·

EXCLUSIVE EYEWITNESS ACCOUNT BY
RICHARD TREGASKIS

INTERNATIONAL NEWS SERVICE STAFF CORRESPONDENT

WITH THE U.S PACIFIC FLEET AT SEA (Shangri-La) Apr. 20, 1943 (delayed)—It can now be revealed that a U.S. naval aircraft carrier launched the swift, two-motored bombers which raided Tokio, the capital of Japan, for the first time in history.

This amazing feat of Army-Navy collaboration was accomplished during a heavy storm within 800 miles of Tokio in an area infested by Japanese patrol craft.

I witnessed the dramatic sight as 16 great, landlubbery planes— the celebrated Mitchell (B-25) medium bomber—weighing 12 tons each took off from the pitching, rolling deck of the carrier while great waves crashed on the bow of the ship and washed over the flight deck. The daring, ingenious idea was carried out in broad daylight.

[An official War Department announcement in Washington identified the aircraft carrier from which the planes were launched as the U.S.S. Hornet, since lost in the battle of Santa Cruz in the South Pacific.]

These large Army planes with tricycle gear, never used in ordinary carrier operations, waddled along the deck, staggered into the air nearly stalling and struggled for altitude over mountainous seas.

They were heavily loaded with incendiaries, Molotov breadbaskets, and high explosives, besides extra gasoline for the long flight for Tokio and beyond to the secret landing point.

The cruiser on which I was quartered acted as a guard for the carrier. It afforded me a grandstand seat as we were only a few hundred yards away when the planes took off for their sensational raid on Tokio.

We were on tenterhooks lest the Japanese naval force should discover us before we could get all the planes, bound for Tokio, into the air.

We had been spotted already by one Jap patrol boat which a cruiser in our task force blasted to atoms. Almost immediately after the cruiser sank the enemy patrol boat, our carrier began to launch its planes.

However, we were afraid the Jap patrol boat had radioed our position to the Japanese mainland and we were anxious to get our planes in the air before a hot reception could be prepared for them.

We could see small figures of men, hurrying around the deck of the carrier in the gray stormy weather, starting the plane motors.

At 8:22 A.M., a quarter hour after the disintegration of the Japanese patrol boat, the first of our bombers waddled forward from the huddled herd of its sisters gathered on the carrier's deck.

I could hear the motors now as the bomber inched forward, gaining speed. Soon the craft was air borne, lifting gradually from the deck of the carrier as a great shout rang out on our deck from the sailors and Marines who were awaiting this sight for many days.

The bomber, now cleared the carrier, staggered into the wind and then levelled, moving steadily but low, over the waves and gaining speed.

As the bomber picked up speed, it swung in a slow circle to great cheers from our ship. It was the number one bomber off to Tokio in a heroic moment. Nobody spoke of the great dangers facing this intrepid crew.

A few minutes later a second plane moved forward on the carrier's deck, gained momentum and, hitting a blast of air, lifted as if on an elevator, cleared the carrier and slowly levelled to streak straight ahead.

The third plane took off in a like manner, but the fourth was nearly the first casualty as lads on our ship cried, "There she goes."

As this bomber climbed steeply off the deck it appeared to almost stall and it hung sluggishly over the sea, its nose pointed upward, but the plane fell toward the high waves.

A great groan ran along our deck as our boys, motioning upward, cried "Up, up." The plane sagged down a few feet more toward the white caps, then appeared to gain altitude, but bogged down again.

Our boys cried, "No, not yet." The plane was sinking, but finally gained speed, power and height, and streaked off into the stormy sky.

"That makes me feel good all over," said a Marine, watching it disappear into the skies toward Tokio.

The waves were increasing in size by now, breaking over the bow of the carrier.

Our lookouts were on the sharpest alert for Japanese air and surface craft. An ensign near me, with earphones on his head, snapped to a gun crew:

"Air craft 30,000 yards, bearing 300."

The gun crew moved close around the guns, ready to fire when the "identified as friendly" word was passed. The crews relaxed a little.

Now, the last bomber was moving along the wet deck of the carrier as a comber shot a fan of spray along each side, high on its bow. The last bomber ran along steadily, lifted, levelled and swung in a slow turn close over our ship and just clearing its masts.

Our sailors cheered loudly and waved farewell as the plane passed so close we could see the figure of one of its gunners busy in one of the great transparent turrets. We could also see the star and insignia letters, "U.S. army," under its wing.

Before the plane disappeared, our ship swung sharply in a U-turn toward home. The carrier followed now and our task force was hightailing, full speed for home, with all bombers launched with no casualties.

We were not in the clear yet because at 2:30 P.M. that day another Jap patrol boat was sighted. Again the same cruiser cut out of our formation and made steam toward the spot where the Jap boat was seen.

The masts of the enemy craft were noticed just over the horizon. It was of a type, about 100-foot long, which the Japs have in hundreds, prowling their home waters.

Now the masts disappeared on the horizon as the ship fled, but the cruiser gained inexorably. The cruiser was almost over the horizon when bright orange bursts of gunfire were seen along its length just before I saw white splashes on the distant horizon and I heard popping of distant gunfire.

A cloud of dirty yellow smoke floated over the area. Planes dropped bombs, giving birth to tall black water spouts. Then the cruiser pulled up and continued its dash toward home.

The same afternoon our planes sighted a Jap destroyer, but our force avoided the enemy who might have delayed us.

We steamed into the night, another good job well done, another big payment made on the debt marked "Pearl Harbor."

. . . .

RICHARD TREGASKIS

Richard Tregaskis began his career at the former Boston *American*, then became an overseas correspondent for the International News Service. His best-seller, *Guadalcanal Diary*, was written while he covered the U.S. Marines' invasion of the Solomon Islands. It was later made into a movie.

In 1943 he was seriously injured by a mortar shell while covering the fighting in Italy but miraculously survived and went on to cover the invasion of Normandy six months later. He also spent two years reporting in Communist China and traveled with American troops in Vietnam.

Aside from *Guadalcanal Diary*, Tregaskis wrote several books and screenplays, including *Invasion Diary*, *Stronger Than Fear* (his best, he believed), *Seven Leagues to Paradise*, *Last Plane to Shanghai*, *John*

F. Kennedy and PT-109, and *Vietnam Diary*. He also wrote for magazines and television.

Described as a "quiet and scholarly type of newspaperman" by his friend Ernie Pyle, Tregaskis was a native of Boston and held five scholarships from Harvard. He died in 1973.

Flight Report from Britain

· · · · · · · · · · · ·

BY

CHARLES E. GRATKE

FOREIGN EDITOR, THE *CHRISTIAN SCIENCE MONITOR*

July 12, 1943—We were 6,000 feet over the mid-Atlantic. It was a moment, coming home, to cast up impressions. The officer-not-in-uniform across the Clipper aisle inevitably asked:

"What's the biggest story you found in Europe?"

Usually, you can't answer that. But this time it was simple. The story is only a fragment. It has no denouement. It is the story of Chris.

Her name is really Crystal. She's one of the English girls loaned to the Americans to drive staff cars. She wears the legend "U.S. Driver" in a circle upon her shoulder. She drove our party of visiting correspondents around the still-smiling English countryside, looking at American military installations, for three days.

Rather a good driver, we thought, wondering where she learned. Then we came to Coventry.

The Major had to telephone ahead and it had been a long time since breakfast. Chris knew where there was a bakery, so we walked around the corner to see what we could buy without ration cards. And we remarked that she seemed to have been there before.

Chris had arrived in Coventry an hour and a half after the blitz. She was driving an ambulance. She drove it for sixteen solid days.

Her story is as simple as that. Except for bits that came out later, like the Junkers plane that crashed in the middle of things and how Chris helped get the Germans out . . . the rubble, destruction, and the heartbreak.

The English don't talk about the things that matter most. Especially when almost everyone is quietly being heroic. But you can't be in Britain these days without sensing the reason the island fortress still stands.

It was not only that the people did not know, in 1940, how near they were to the verge of defeat. It is rather that they possess a kind of inner conviction that the democratic and individual way of life— whether you express it on the cricket ground or by going to the church of your own choice on Sunday—is just something that will not perish.

There are, for instance, the two very British ladies who live in a flat somewhere overlooking the Thames. They produced tea—a bit nicer tea than they might be having were it not for a visitor—and talked about the war and how certain they were, all along, of the ultimate outcome. Of course they themselves, they said, had been very fortunate.

I overstayed my time. And in the end, they let me out the back way to dash cross-lots for the train. Only then did I discover that at least a quarter of the rear part of their building had been sheared away by a bomb.

They didn't speak of it. Like Chris, they are silent about some things that matter most.

It wasn't that they had forgotten the blitz. London hasn't forgotten it. The wide reaches of the City, the ruins in Limehouse and the block after block of uninhabitable houses in the West End are things one does not forget. But it's been cleaned up in a most amazing fashion—tidy even in its devastation. It's as if the British are saying that the fury of modern war may blast them out, but it cannot change their way of thinking . . . their tea, their cricket, and the right to attend whatever church they choose.

The churches, indeed, present an interesting aspect. So many have gone. Isolated spires and gaunt walls . . . but St. Paul's stands . . .

So, too, does most of St. Sepulchre's in Holborn. And at noon-times there is a recorded concert, attended mostly by workers and clerks who have eaten hastily to spend a half hour with a few great composers.

On the same day, a Bach concerto having been concluded, they were playing Beethoven's Appassionata. It was the recording of a great pianist, made some years ago before the time when he could have been accused of having turned Nazi. German music on the edge of the blitzed city of London. It takes a people who know something of lasting values to do a thing like that.

And then it rained—the one thing you can be sure ultimately will happen in London, even in June. So we took refuge under the arch of a doorway, unbothered in the deluge until someone accidentally leaned against a bell.

The clerk who answered had taken shelter in that same doorway the night the building across the way was bombed. His offices weren't touched, but some of the firm's records, in the building across the street, were destroyed. So were the records of hundreds of other firms in the financial district. And what did they do?

"We wrote to the customers we could remember and those we didn't remember wrote to us. People who had 'em sent us duplicates of our contracts and people who hadn't told us what they could remember of the terms. We patched it up all right."

Yes, they've patched it up. It hasn't left London the same, quite. If you want an ironing board you have to pay 39s.6d for it. It costs you two pounds to have an umbrella recovered with cotton. If you want a razor blade you likely can't buy it at all.

But if you want a joke you still can chat with a bus conductor. The men still may be the wittiest, but the women who are replacing them are learning the repartee of transit.

Change—that is silver—is a bit short in the early morning hours. But the conductress made the best of the one pound note. What would she have done if she hadn't been able to change it?

"I'd ha' taken yer watch," she said more than audibly. We wondered why the passengers were so obviously amused until we recalled that you can't even get a watch adjusted in London these days, let alone buy one. What you do is go to a newsstand and pay a shilling for a pamphlet telling you "How to Repair Your Own Watch or Clock."

Yet London manages to get down to it remarkably on time. And once there, there's a good bit of standing around in queues.

It's far from easy, this queuing business—two hours for a bit of fish and half an hour for some biscuits made of charcoal. Often it is time snatched from a war job and a bit of fire watching. But the reason the chore goes on without grumbling is that the rationing system has been worked out on a basis that is essentially fair, and to the British, that is the main thing.

You still can eat without ration cards in fashionable West End London, but only a three-course meal the content of which is rigidly prescribed. This is balanced by the fact that worker's canteens and meals for school children are on a far broader basis than ever before. There is a "black market," despite Lord Woolton's recent disclaimers. But it is limited to a few fashionable clubs and a few elite chiselers. In the main, the handling of the food situation presents an object lesson to some other nations.

There is sacrifice beyond what belligerents at a distance can comprehend. Big sacrifice, and a host of little ones. When you've put up with a blackout more than 1,200 times and taken on much factory work, and you talk of "part time housekeeping"—it begins to wear. And you understand the story of the Mayor of the little midland town who said that some of his people didn't know the war was on.

"Why, would you believe it," he said, "there's folks in this town who haven't had a bomb dropped within half a mile."

But one thing that keeps the British courage high is that it's their turn to drop the bombs.

The RAF and the United States Eighth Air Force are giving Germany a tenfold lesson in the meaning of the air war. As you see the might of Britain's bomber stations, it is incongruous to look at the remains of the preparations Britain once made to meet an invader.

Barbed wire in St. James's Park, blockhouses commanding the crossroads, barriers ready to be thrown across the High street of every village . . .

But England would have done it. You can't explain why you know. But you do know . . . even without encountering the woman who volunteered as an instructor when they talked of teaching women to shoot, sending in her application in utmost seriousness before her daughter reminded her that 97 was a bit beyond the acceptable age.

In those days, there was little to fight with except the resources of the spirit. It was this that stood behind the staunch words of the Prime Minister, who really meant to battle the invader "on the beaches . . . in the fields . . ." It is the memory of those days which gives the nostalgic touch to a current cartoon in Punch.

A sergeant is pictured preparing his men regarding intricacies of hand-to-hand combat, saying:

"Now you'll remember that back in '40 when you 'adn't weapons, you was taught 'ow to use 'em. Well, this course in unarmed combat will teach you 'ow to get along without 'em now you've got plenty of 'em."

Yes, England can smile. It has a reason to. It knows the war is past the half-way mark. Anyone on the London streets can show you why. Every taxi driver, every bus driver, knows.

For in May, the traffic lights were changed. Half of each red and blue disk is exposed now. You can see them in the daytime even though there isn't nearly as much traffic as there used to be. There's a gadget which the wardens can pull down to dim them a bit more if the air raids get really heavy and if a more stern blackout seems needed. But they look positively festive.

The difference is somehow important. You can't be in London without understanding that the lights are beginning to go on again.

· · · · · · · · · · ·

CHARLES E. GRATKE

Charles Gratke was born in Astoria, Oregon, on August 11, 1901, and got his first newspaper job at the Astoria *Evening Budget*. He then worked at the Oregon City *Enterprise*, the Portland *Oregonian*, and the Detroit *News*, before landing at the *Christian Science Monitor* in 1927. He was the paper's Berlin correspondent when Hitler took power in 1933, and in 1937 he became foreign editor, the post he held when he died in 1949.

The Show at Anzio

· · · · · · · · · · · ·

BY

JOHN LARDNER

NORTH AMERICAN NEWSPAPER ALLIANCE

WITH THE ALLIED FORCES ON THE ANZIO BEACHHEAD, Sept., 1943—The Anzio waterfront is a vaudeville show so rich and profuse that only the best acts, the real novelties, will hold an audience any more.

For instance, two German shells hit the water and sent up huge geysers of smoke and sea yesterday while Flight Sergeant Laurie Tambour, of New Zealand, was doing his number, and nobody on the beach noticed the shells at all because Tambour's act was so much better.

It consisted of a race between Tambour in a parachute and a rescue squad in a duck (amphibious assault vessel) on which the spectators bet freely. Tambour says the act will not be repeated, despite tempting offers from Anzio showmen who want to sell tickets. He says it was unrehearsed—his first parachute jump and his last one. Also, he wonders who that girl was in the boat.

I met Tambour today, but yesterday when I watched him jump he was to me, as to other beachcombers and loafers along the shoreline, just a stranger in a parachute. We were all very pleased with him, too, like the Main street bums in a Mark Twain story watching a fight between two very lively dogs.

Sgt. Tambour's Spitfire had engine trouble on the way home from the Rome area and burst into flame a couple of hundred yards off the Anzio beaches. There was nothing for the sergeant to do but jump, so he did. His plane hit the sea in a burst of foam and noise. Tambour came down more slowly. Everyone saw his white parachute open and flutter in the light Tyrrhenian breeze.

"There's a rescue boat putting out to pick him up," yelled a private.

"I'll bet he hits the water before they reach him," said another beachcomber.

"Two bits you're wrong," bawled a third.

As a matter of fact, it was a dead heat.

"I barely got my feet wet before they had me inside the boat," said Tambour. "I was swearing very freely, you know, because I thought it was a pretty poor show on my part when I suddenly noticed there was a woman in the boat. I'm sure she was a woman. A Wren or a Wac or a nurse or something. I was most frightfully embarrassed. I just shut up and let them take me in."

Sgt. Tambour comes from a little town called Waimauku, near Auckland. He said parachute-jumping was just like sitting in church—complete with prayers. He said he would not under any circumstances repeat the performance.

"But it was very interesting," urged your correspondent. "The boys on the beach didn't even notice the shells that were dropping around. Some of them think the boat will beat you the next time. They think with a couple more practice tries you can drop right into the boat. It's a good betting proposition."

"Very likely," said Flight Sgt. Tambour coldly. "I don't mind if they bet all day. But someone else will have to do the jumping."

As a postscript of this wholesome episode your correspondent is able to report that the girl in the boat was not a girl, but a sailor. I got this from the driver of the boat.

"I know who he means," said the driver. "That sailor wears his hair very long. It fools a lot of people. The pilot could have cussed all he wanted to. It's too bad."

· · ·

Once Knox College in Illinois was famous in fiction as "Old Si-wash." Then it got famous again for its football teams which lost 29 games in a row. Everyone knew about Knox in those days and your correspondent wrote at least one story yearly about this death-less chain of defeat, but I never met a Knox football player till this week.

It appears there is a formula which goes with meeting a Knox player.

"Where did you play football?" you say.

"Knox College in Galesburg, Illinois," says the subject.

"Oh," you say, "you mean the school where—"

"Yes, that's right," says the subject. "You've got it. Twenty-nine straight."

The subject in this case was Lieut. Col. James T. Stewart who commands a transport battalion supplying the Anzio beachhead. It's getting so you meet everybody in Italy. The place has become the successor of North Africa which, in turn, was the successor of Broadway and Forty-second street.

Col. Stewart's men have as tough and steadily tense a job as any in the army. They ride the ships between Anzio and a supply base almost as regularly as conductors ride a suburban railroad line. For obvious reasons, the Germans like to make this Anzio shuttle service red hot and they heckle it with every form of explosive trinket at their disposal.

Col. Stewart is wearing a small new wrinkle between his eyebrows in token of the responsibility of getting the job done and keeping the morale up.

"I won my first wrinkle in the retreat from Gafsa a year ago this month," he said.

He did not reveal himself as a Knox man until we had talked about the war for a half hour while I waited for an LST to take me back to the beachhead. Then the gruesome fact came out and he went through the Knox formula—"Yeah, that's right," said the colo-nel. "You've got it. Twenty-nine straight."

He added hastily that his playing days as fullback did not coincide absolutely with the great doormat era at Knox.

"Don't get me wrong," said the colonel. "I was a freshman when the great streak ended. What a day! We beat Beloit. Lloyd Burdett and then Ice-House Reynolds came along and got our football situation straightened out and during my varsity years we were doing pretty well. We won about 75 percent of our games, as I remember."

Not even the Fascist Italian army in its heyday could boast such a long and powerful losing streak as Knox and Col. Stewart, like other Knox men, takes a certain quiet pride in the fact.

"But I am glad we got it over with," he said. "There is such a thing as carrying a good thing too far."

The more you sift through Anzio beachhead history, which is now fifty-three days old and continuing to gain weight, the more unsung and half-sung heroes you find who contributed individually to the defeat of the great German counter-attack in the climax days of February 17 to 20.

After mining a dozen American and British field leaders from this mother lode of valor, your correspondent has now encountered an Australian who belongs right up near the head of the list.

Once you find Maj. Hyman Abramovich, of Sydney, it is a little hard to know what to make of him. Autobiographically, Abramovich is very sparse pickings. Aside from admitting he formerly practiced medicine and prefers active fighting in time of war, he will say nothing of himself. His men and his colleagues don't know how he made the jump from Sydney to the British Loyal Regiment, which is based fundamentally in Lancashire, England, but they agree wholeheartedly that he is one hell of a soldier and had as much to do as any other one man with putting the German voyage down the Rome–Anzio road into reverse.

One battalion of Loyals confronted the German regiment which spearheaded the attack and came up to the famous Flyver Bridge at Campo Di Carne, seven miles from Anzio Harbor, with the throttle still more or less wide open. One British company was overrun. Abramovich's company moved in to save the position, which it did by dawn of Feb. 18. It then, with Abramovich dealing out orders, counsel and assistance right and left, reinforced two companies on its flanks and helped to carpet the ground with German dead. The

THE SHOW AT ANZIO

enemy never got going again except in the direction from which he came.

Maj. Abramovich is not bashful in behalf of his men. At the drop of a notebook he will give you a catalogue of names of enlisted men or "other ranks," as the British call them, who played their positions brilliantly that day. The major carries a world of this sort of detail in his mind.

"Why NOT?" he says. "All I know about the war is the men who fight around me. That's all there is to my job."

To speak of the German dead in terms of carpets is not to exaggerate or "sloganeer." From the best of observation sources, we learned that the Germans were detected using bulldozers, big hauling and digging vehicles, to sweep loose earth over the remains of their own killed.

And I have since learned that in some places in the region back of Carroceto they used procedures even more hasty. The bulldozer burial was an elegant refinement in comparison. Between ditches and creek beds were piles of unburied dead in the first days of the German setback. And if you know how the Germans normally garland their dead, you know how tight the pinch was here.

Physically, Anzio has been the deepest single wound we have inflicted on them since we came to Italy.

A big fellow with a clipped brown mustache and named Lieut. Richard George Arthur Beal once fought a German in Hamburg and got a draw. He fought another bout in Berlin and won a decision, which he admits was quite remarkable, hometown judges being what they are and especially in Berlin where it has been practically illegal for ten years to whip a superman.

One day not long ago on the beachhead, Lieut. Beal got loose among the Germans again. This time he really raised hell with them. He had an armored car with a lot of firepower on it instead of boxing gloves, and the official confirmed score for him and his reconnaissance crew was two German self-propelled 88-millimeter guns, two infantry guns and two three-inch mortars and their crews.

An informal estimate at British reconnaissance headquarters says Lieut. Beal's car killed sixty German soldiers that day.

"That sounds about right," said Beal when I saw him. "Look, do you mind if I take my boots off? I've been out on another job and haven't had them off for nine days. My God, that feels good!"

Lieut. Beal comes from Sherwood in the Country of Nottingham. In school and college he was one of England's best amateur heavyweight boxers and in this capacity he made his brief raid on Germany in 1935, drawing once and winning once.

His raid up the beachhead roads toward the thorny German stronghold at Campoleone put him so far ahead that the Germans will probably never catch up without the assistance of Max Schmeling, who is said to be in a state of disrepair.

Probing at the head of his patrol, Lieut. Beal and car and crew found themselves among a Nazi outpost of paratroop division soldiers in strength of about two companies. The Germans were in various stages of shaving, washing and breakfasting, and Beal's car shot them up lavishly. In the first half hour, their "Beezer" guns, or mounted machine guns, fired off seventeen boxes of ammunition.

The picnic continued for five hours. At one point, Lieut. Beal came upon a German demolition unit of eighteen engineers about to blow up a railroad bridge and "removed" all eighteen.

At four o'clock in the afternoon, ordered by radio to withdraw, Lieut. Beal and crew fought their way out again—or almost out. The car got bogged in a swamp and a colleague and his driver had to dig them out, nonchalantly hooking on the tow chains, etc., while the Germans fired mortar shells at them.

"We were very fortunate," said Beal. "Speaking of heavyweight fighters, I don't believe Freddie Mills, of England, can ever beat Joe Louis. But I saw Tommy Farr fight Louis and Tommy almost beat him. Don't you think so?"

Your correspondent murmured something polite. This Beal is not the sort of character you like to disagree with.

The business of riding the shuttle between the Anzio beachhead and a supply base has its compensations. You get good food aboard ship, especially on the southbound run when the ships are less crowded. And you get real butter occasionally and always good coffee.

An LST is no luxury cruiser, but sometimes in the dining saloon, with its tables covered in green leather, its comfortable, upholstered chairs and sofa, with books and magazines lying around and a bright light shining—these are the strangest rarities to the front-line soldier—you have a fleeting, isolated sense of well-being. The radio is playing and, lying back in a chair, you listen to new songs and old ones sung by tenors and smooth-voiced women who all sound alike, and you find that by going long enough without it you have come to miss even this.

The radio is tuned to the British Broadcasting Corporation program from London. Pretty soon, a news broadcast comes on and the announcer begins: "On the Anzio beachhead today" and every soldier and sailor in the dining saloon comes to attention in his chair and listens quietly and completely to the latest word of this little wedge of seacoast which is now the mainspring of his life and work and the center of his small, wet world.

It's a curious experience, hearing about Anzio on a ship that has just come from there or is just going there. The voice that tells the news is remote, but it brings you back very quickly to the war you are bound up in. It reminds you where you are, which is on a sea route, compact and exposed and subject to every kind of attack the Germans can bring to bear.

The sailors are reminded more easily, for they ride this route more regularly, though some army troops from transport battalions have made the round trip a good many times. The sailors were doing this sort of work before the Anzio beachhead was born.

The LST on which I rode up to the beachhead this week was making its thirty-seventh voyage of the war. Here and there scarred walls and twisted plates recall the time the ship was shot up off a British Eighth Army base in southern Italy last September.

"That was a nasty jolt for the boys," said the chef, shoving a cup of coffee through a partition from the galley to the dining room.

"Do they like Anzio any better?" I asked.

"Quit kidding," said the chef with a smile, though kidding was not exactly the word he used. "Anzio is in a class by itself. You'll find milk and sugar there on the table."

. . . .

JOHN LARDNER

John Lardner, reporter, correspondent, and columnist, inherited his love of sports and his humor from his father, Ring Lardner. He began his career at the New York *Herald Tribune* in 1929 after graduating from Harvard. From 1933 to 1948 he was a sports columnist and war correspondent for the North American Newspaper Alliance. From 1939 Lardner worked simultaneously as a correspondent for *Newsweek* magazine. After his return to the states, he became a contributing editor and wrote a weekly sports column for *Newsweek* and a weekly radio and television column for *The New Yorker*. Additionally, he free-lanced for many publications and wrote many books, including *The Crowning of Technocracy, Southwest Passage: The Yanks in the Pacific, It Beats Working,* and an introduction to his father's book *You Know Me Al.*

Lardner died suddenly in 1960 while writing his *Newsweek* column, "Lardner's Week."

Mission Complete

· · · · · · · · · · · · ·

BY
BOB CONSIDINE
INS CORRESPONDENT

The following article appeared in the December 1943 issue of *Cosmopolitan* magazine.

LONDON (by wireless): I have an incredible story to tell. It has to do with the headless pilot of a Boeing Flying Fortress. It's a "Message to García" tale rewritten by Jules Verne. It concerns also a Fortress gunner who over his pitiable protests was flung down to the Germans from 25,500 feet in the sky, in the hope that the enemy would save his life.

No fiction editor would believe this sort of thing, yet it is all on file in the cold, adjectiveless prose of the United States Eighth Air Force Records. The moral of the story is obvious: Victory can be only the just deserts of the country which produces boys like these. Yet there is a more intimate moral, for this is principally the story of twenty-five-year old Flight Officer Johnny ("Red") Morgan, who proved one terrible morning over Germany that guts and a life of ease are not necessarily antonyms.

Things were always made easy for Red Morgan. His father and mother, who now live in a Sutton Place suite that's like a movie version of how rich New Yorkers live, saw to it that he grew up with every juvenile wish fulfilled. He was born in Vernon, Texas, and educated at the New Mexico Military Institute and the University of Texas. His father, a prominent attorney, wanted him to follow in his footsteps, but instead he went to the Fiji Islands, where he worked for a pineapple firm. Back in the United States in 1936, he built himself up physically by roughnecking for a Texas oil firm.

Red learned to fly when he was seventeen. He had a natural feeling for the air; he could charter a craft whenever he wanted, and he usually wanted. He was having one hell of a good time out of life. After his parents moved to New York, he visited there frequently and enjoyed most hanging out at the Stork Club. In short, Red lived as many others of his racy set lived—for the laughs. Into this pleasant existence war now intruded itself. It wasn't our war, we told ourselves, but Johnny wanted to be in it, so in August 1941, he dismayed his family by packing off to Canada and joining the R.C.A.F. Soon he was abroad fighting for England in a war that was going badly for her.

Last March Red transferred to our Air Force. The best our side would offer was a flight officer's rank, one step lower than a second lieutenancy, but Red accepted the tiny rank and went to work.

It was tough work, for Fortresses don't go out at night; they fly in broad daylight, exposed to everything Nazi ingenuity can send against them. They thunder along far beyond the protective cover of the Spitfires and Thunderbolts which escort them across the Channel, and they must defend themselves while they go into, over and away from pinpoint targets.

Red was (and is) the copilot of one of these Fortresses. His pal and secret hero was the pilot, First Lieutenant Bob Campbell, from rustic Liberty, Mississippi. Campbell's life had been the opposite of Morgan's but they were as close as good men can get. They shared a common love for their Fortress; they strove to do their jobs well.

They had tough times in the air. Last July Fourth, they brought their Fortress in though it was riddled from nose to tail, wing tip to wing tip, with two engines shot out and the controls ripped loose. They were given the Air Medal for that job.

Presently, they were up again in another Fortress. Their target was Hanover, deep in the industrial heart of the Reich. In "briefing" early that morning, their commanding officer had said that they must destroy this target because it supplied materials vital to the German war machine. They strolled together to the rare breakfast of real eggs given to men about to go on missions, and soon they were in the air. In strict formation the Fortresses flew out over the Channel, the umbrella of friendly fighters high above them, and on toward the teeth of the Nazi air defenses.

It happened not long after the fighter escort had turned back. A Focke-Wulf 109 tore in at Morgan's Fortress from the right, machine guns and cannons belching fire. A 20-mm. explosive shell shot through Morgan's window, missing him by no more than an inch, and struck poor Campbell in the side of the head. The shell exploded with such terrible force that it not only blew off the pilot's head, but blasted the arm off the top turret gunner behind him, Staff Sergeant Tyre C. Weaver, of Riverview, Alabama. Campbell's blood coated the windshields and controls, and his lifeless body slumped over the wheel. Weaver, terribly wounded, crumpled to the deck.

It was Morgan's ship, a great blind one-million-dollar bird with tons of bombs in its claws and its mission far from fulfilled. His buddy's lifeless lunge had sent the Fortress into a deep glide. Morgan is a strong boy, but it took all his might to pull the ship back to a level to keep and rejoin the formation. He had to make up his mind immediately whether to turn back and pick up the fighter escort or go on and complete the mission.

It was a hard decision for a boy who not long before had never been confronted with a decision much more acute than whether to have steak or chicken for dinner, but it didn't take him long. He reached over, pulled his dead buddy away from the heavy wheel, and with gloved hands wiped the blood off the windshield. Red Morgan was going in to the target.

The danger was extreme, not only outside the plane but inside. The formation was coming into walls of flak now and the very cream of Germany's fighter pilots. One of the ship's main oxygen lines, supplying the navigator, Second Lieutenant Keith T. Kosky, of Milwaukee, Wisconsin; the radio operator, Technical Sergeant John E. McClure, of Atlanta, Georgia; and the tail gunner Staff Sergeant

John E. Foley, of Boise, Idaho, had been shot out. These vitally needed men fell to the floor gasping for air, for by this time, the Fortress was 25,500 feet in the sky.

Focke-Wulf and Messerschmitt pilots love a cripple, and here certainly was one. They streaked at the battered, gory nose of the Fortress, hurling everything they had at it, then turning over and hurtling straight down at more than 600 miles an hour. The belly turret gunner, Sergeant Jim Ford of Chicago, gave the attackers all he had, but one of his two .50-caliber guns jammed. For a long time the other was the only gun the ship had.

When a German fighter attacks head on "from twelve o'clock," as the boys say, our pilots take evasive action. They continue to fly their Fortresses straight at the wildly approaching enemy, and when the German pilot opens fire our pilots put their bombers into a short dive in order to duck under the line of German fire. But each time Morgan did this, poor Campbell slumped over into the tandem controls, his weight pushing the nose of their Fortress down deeper and deeper, as his boots were snarled in the twin foot controls. Morgan had to pull him out of the controls, then pull the Fortress out of its dive, then duck more fighters, then evade the flak. And the target was still a long way off.

There was Weaver to worry about too. Lieutenant Kosky, revived by a portable oxygen tank, crawled back from the navigator's "Greenhouse" and tied a tourniquet around the small stump of Weaver's arm, but there was too little of the arm left and it continued to pour blood. Weaver was in unbearable pain, so Kosky got out his morphine kit and attempted to jab the drug into the wounded boy's covered body. The needle broke, fortunately, as we shall see.

Here was fresh travail for Morgan. He knew Weaver would bleed to death before the ship got back home, if it got back. Hours of flying hell remained. Morgan and Weaver were close friends; but there was only one thing to do and Morgan knew it. He ordered Weaver dropped out of the Fortress.

Weaver needed medical attention immediately. The Fortress was drumming over Germany now, but the only chance Weaver had of living was to be flung down to the mercy of the enemy. The kid struggled feebly against this. He might have thought of the reception he'd meet from the gunners on the ground. He knew, of course, that the kindest fortune that could befall him was immediate capture. If he were to drop into woods and not be found for hours, he would bleed to death.

But after a little time Weaver realized that he must go. Kosky unhooked the escape hatch beneath them and it flew into space. He took off Weaver's remaining glove, there in that sub-zero cold, and hooked one of Weaver's numbed fingers through the ripcord ring.

Kosky asked the wounded boy to try the cord, to be certain it wasn't stuck. Weaver did, but he pulled it too much and a rush of wind from the open pit below caused yards of silk chute to burst from the bag. The little compartment was filled with surging silk as unmanageable as a frenzied horse and the footing was precarious because of the open hatch. Poor Campbell had fallen back on the controls and Morgan was fighting for the control of a ship that was like a fifty-ton truck skidding down an icy hill as German fighters attacked savagely and flak came up in torrents.

But somehow Morgan kept the bloody nose of that Fortress aimed directly at the distant target.

Kosky finally overwhelmed the ruptured chute, stuffed it back into the bag and at last Weaver dropped down through that bottomless well of thin air. Ford saw the chute open. If the morphine had entered Weaver's veins he would not have had enough strength to pull the ripcord; he would not have had the pitiable little chance of survival actually given him.

And so that Fortress went on carrying its message of TNT to the war machine that had threatened to rule the world. Morgan sent it directly over the target with a dead man lying on the tandem controls, flak coming up in sheets and fighters attacking suicidally. The ship's bombardier, Second Lieutenant Asa J. Irwin, of Portland, Oregon, dropped his bombs squarely on the target. It was wonderful teamwork with Morgan, for the ship's communication lines had been shot to bits.

It was a long trip home and full of aerial savagery. Between them, Morgan and Kosky managed to get Campbell out of his seat. It took forty-five minutes and all that time Morgan also had to fly the ship and keep it in formation despite everything the Germans could do to separate it from the others. During one brief respite, with the automatic pilot operating, Morgan helped Kosky to lower his dead buddy into the compartment behind the cockpit. The deck was covered with their blood and Campbell's and they slipped and nearly fell through the escape hatch, but it was a danger that had to be accepted, for even if the ship did get back to its field, it could never be landed with Campbell in the controls.

Morgan brought that Fortress home with no radio to guide him, no communication with the crew and little or no brakes left. Landing a Fortress is a two-man brake job at best, and Red did it alone.

This, the first war in the air, is filled with high heroism. Incredible feats of valor are a dime a dozen. But when the boys sit around their lounges at night and when they talk shop they often speak of Red Morgan. What the former playboy did that awful day was miracle flying, an unparalleled saga of fortitude, determination and muscular strength. His hands and arms were thick with welts and both knees were sprained when he hobbled away from the ship to make his routine report. But he had manhandled that huge bomber into subjection. He accomplished his mission—as Bob Campbell would have wanted him to.

. . . .

BOB CONSIDINE

Bob Considine was born in Washington, D.C. He worked his way through George Washington University as a clerk for the State Department, where he claimed his disorganized filing system may have been a direct cause of World War II. His first job was as a sportswriter for the Washington *Post* (for thirty-five dollars a week). Shortly thereafter the Washington *Herald* gave him the position of sports editor, from which he was promptly fired for lack of "executive savvy."

From there he went to the Hearst International News Service as a war correspondent and columnist. His column, "On the Line with Considine," was syndicated to hundreds of publications. He was known for his fast and prodigious writing, and colleagues enviously observed Considine "bat out a swell column on the base-running of the Cardinals in exactly nine minutes, with his typewriter on a baggage wagon and the conductor yelling 'All Aboard.'" His war story *Thirty Seconds over Tokyo* became a best-seller and hit movie. Other books include: *MacArthur the Magnificent, The General Wainwright Story, The Rape of Poland,* and *The Brink's Robbery.* His Christmas classic, "No Room at the Inn," was written for *Collier's* magazine, for which he wrote often.

Considine died in 1975 following a stroke.

Up Front with a Roosevelt

· · · · · · · · · · · ·

BY

JOHN LARDNER

NORTH AMERICAN NEWSPAPER ALLIANCE

WITH THE AMERICAN FIFTH ARMY, ITALY—When the news of Brigadier General Theodore Roosevelt's presence in this theatre was released, the British army field newspaper, "Union Jack," took a hasty look at his genealogical chart and did not have time before deadline to dope the whole thing out. Hoping for the best, it printed a brief report on the matter under the headline:

"PRESIDENT'S SON HERE IN ITALY."

Now this statement is, of course, correct on all counts, so the editorial staff of "Union Jack" did not pretend under pressure that it had the right president in mind.

"We take the line," a reporter told your correspondent in confidence, "that when you speak of Roosevelt, you are pleased in calling him 'president's son.' After the war, our form sheet will doubtlessly be brought up to date, and all bloodlines double-checked."

The subject of the aforementioned headline takes the business genially as he takes everything else in this war. His family and his aides do not object to the genial phase of his attitude. They object to his disposition to look for trouble and to go up hills where nobody has been before. Much of the real estate traversed by General Roosevelt in the last thirteen or fourteen months has become copiously embroidered with mines, bombs and shellfire. He seems attracted by this sort of terrain.

Early in the Mediterranean campaign, he had a letter from his daughter, Grace, a lady of the greatest sense and perspicacity, which said, in part, "Don't go around being brave; stick to business."

The general's steadfast aide and jeep driver, First Lieut. W. H. "Stevie" Stevenson, of San Antonio, a large, bald fellow with a large mustache and a soft heart, shares this view, though duty as well as a personal fondness for adventure keeps him from enunciating it as often as he might.

"When the general takes us into a hot spot," says Lieut. Stevenson, "I figure the best thing is to go along and see what he has in mind because generally it adds up. He is very good at this war racket."

Thus, in the battle of Gela in Sicily, when the First Division's foothold on the beach was threatened by counter-attacks, it was General Roosevelt, agent on the ground for Major General Terry Allen, who first spotted the German threat and stopped an American retreat which might have been disastrous.

Both Roosevelt and Stevenson, now a long-standing team, have been decorated by the French army, to which they are attached at present. In Tunisia, last winter and spring, they made a daily tour of the frontlines which won them a reputation as trouble shooters which in turn was admitted by all hands to be very good for the morale of the division.

Your correspondent made a battlefield tour last April with these same two characters which was noteworthy for the nonchalance of the regular members of the cast.

Our jeep, after touching all the warmer points in the line, was headed home. The general, one of the world's most fluent reciters of verse, was in the middle of the second stanza of Grantland Rice's tribute to the First Division in the last war. Messerschmitts came over the road with their machine guns popping. The jeep stopped and General Roosevelt disappeared in one direction and Lieut. Stevenson and your correspondent in another.

Five minutes later we were back in the jeep, on our way again, and the general, after two seconds' thought, picked up the poem of the Poet Rice where he had left off and recited it to the end and with great relish.

He is still shuttling around battle lines and still in a rhythmic state of mind. The other day at a restaurant, between battles, your correspondent observed the general haranguing an acquaintance over the hot clam broth. Approaching closer, I found the strategical topic to be the greatness of the poetry of Edwin Arlington Robinson, with samples. And so it goes with the war effort in Italy growing stronger by the minute.

The Death of Captain Waskow

· · · · · · · · · · · ·

BY

ERNIE PYLE

SCRIPPS-HOWARD NEWSPAPER ALLIANCE & UNITED FEATURE SYNDICATE

WAR CORRESPONDENT

AT THE FRONT LINES IN ITALY, Jan. 10, 1944—In this war I have known a lot of officers who were loved and respected by the soldiers under them. But never have I crossed the trail of any man as beloved as Capt. Henry T. Waskow of Belton, Texas.

Capt. Waskow was a company commander of the 36th Division. He had been in this company since long before he left the States. He was very young, only in his middle 20's, but he carried in him a sincerity and gentleness that made people want to be guided by him.

"After my own father, he comes next," a sergeant told me.

"He always looked after us," a soldier said. "He'd go to bat for us every time."

"I've never known him to do anything unkind," another said.

I was at the foot of the mule trail the night they brought Capt. Waskow down. The moon was nearly full, and you could see far up the trail, and even part way across the valley. Soldiers made shadows as they walked.

Dead men had been coming down the mountain all evening, lashed onto the backs of mules.

The Italian mule skinners were afraid to walk beside the dead men, so Americans had to lead the mules down that night. Even the Americans were reluctant to unleash and lift off the bodies, when they got to the bottom, so an officer had to do it himself and ask others to help.

The first one came early in the morning. They slid him down from the mule and stood him on his feet for a moment. In the half light he might have been merely a sick man standing there leaning on the other. Then they laid him on the ground in the shadow of the stone wall alongside the road.

I don't know who the first one was. You feel small in the presence of dead men and you don't ask silly questions.

We left him there beside the road, that first one, and we all went back into the cowshed and sat on watercans or lay on the straw, waiting for the next batch of mules.

Then a soldier came into the cowshed and said there were some more bodies outside. We went out into the road. Four mules stood there in the moonlight in the road where the trail came down off the mountain. The soldiers who led them stood there waiting.

"This one is Capt. Waskow," one of them said quickly.

Two men unleashed his body from the mule and lifted it off and laid it in the shadow beside the stone wall. Other men took the other bodies off. Finally, there were five bodies lying end to end in a long row. You don't cover up dead men in combat zones. They just lie there in the shadows until somebody else comes after them.

The uncertain mules moved off to their olive groves. The men in the road seemed reluctant to leave. They stood around, and gradually I could sense them moving, one by one, close to Capt. Waskow's body. Not so much to look, I think, as to say something in finality to him and themselves. I stood by and I could hear.

One soldier came and looked down and said out loud:

"God damn it!"

That's all he said and walked away.

Another one came, and he said, "God damn it to hell anyway!" He looked down for a few last moments and then turned and left.

Another man came. I think he was an officer. It was hard to tell officers from men in the dim light, for everybody was grimy and dirty. The man looked down into the dead captain's face and then spoke directly to him, as though he were alive:

"I'm sorry, old man."

Then a soldier came and stood beside the officer and bent over, and he too spoke to his dead captain, not in a whisper, but awfully tenderly, and he said:

"I sure am sorry, sir."

Then one man squatted down and he reached down and took the captain's hand, and he sat there for a full five minutes holding the dead hand in his own and looking intently in the dead face. And he never uttered a sound all the time he sat there.

Finally, he put the hand down. He reached up and gently straightened the points of the captain's shirt collar, and then he sort of rearranged the tattered edges of his uniform around the wound, and then he got up and walked away down the road in the moonlight, all alone.

· · · · · · · · · ·

ERNIE PYLE

Ernest Taylor Pyle was a native of Indiana and was educated at the University of Illinois for several years, though he quit before graduating to become a newspaperman. He worked on a small Indiana paper until he was hired by the Washington *Daily News*, then a subsidiary of Scripps-Howard, where he worked for fewer than three years. After an extensive vacation traveling around the country with "that girl" (a consistent reference to his wife, Geraldine), Pyle ended up working briefly in New York at the *Evening World* and the *Evening Post* until he was brought back to the *Daily News* as telegraph editor. Meanwhile, he had developed a passion for aviation, which got him a job as aviation editor for Scripps-Howard and a column as well, and he was soon promoted to managing editor of the *Daily News* and eventually to roving reporter for all Scripps-Howard papers.

Then Pyle became a war correspondent, and his travels with American GIs through England, Germany, Africa, Italy, and the South Pacific gave him the material for his columns, which ran in more than three hundred newspapers at the time. After going to Normandy to cover the invasion, Pyle returned to the states for a brief rest in Albuquerque and Hollywood, where a film based on his experiences, called *G.I. Joe*, was being made.

In 1944 he won the 1944 Pulitzer Prize for correspondence, Sigma Delta Chi's Raymond Clapper Memorial Award for war correspondence, and a host of other citations.

In 1945 Pyle traveled to Okinawa, where he was killed by a Japanese sniper on the island of Ie Jima. A memorial stands on the spot where he died. Pyle is buried in the Pacific Memorial Cemetery in Hawaii.

Tregaskis Speaks for the Wounded

· · · · · · · · · · · ·

BY

RICHARD TREGASKIS

INTERNATIONAL NEWS SERVICE STAFF CORRESPONDENT

Jan. 25, 1944—The first shell of the barrage hit me—and then when consciousness came back, and I knew I had been badly wounded, I came to realize something I had long suspected: that there was absolutely no sensation of pain in such a situation. It was like a movie without sound.

Often I had seen badly wounded men—in Italy and in the Pacific—and it had struck me that their eyes had been filmed over by some barrier to the contortions of pain.

That barrier was shock, the fortunate mercy of the wounded soldier.

Now I knew that shock had dimmed my perceptions, just as I had seen other men cut off from pain by shock.

But though all my senses were dulled, I knew that I must catch up with Col. Yarborough (Lt. Col. William P. Yarborough of Staunton, Va.) if I wanted to get off that mountain that night.

Col. Yarborough and Capt. Frank Tomasik, of New Bedford, Mass., had gone a little ahead of me, on our way back from the top of the mountain. I had stopped off for a few minutes to round up a successful day's notes. Then I got hit.

Getting a wounded man off the hard rocky slope of Mt. Corno, west of Venafro, I knew would take a crew of eight to carry me down the virtually impassable slope to the nearest jeep trail, nearly a mile away.

Since I was all alone, it did not seem likely that I would be able to find eight people to help me. The thought of self-preservation came strongly through my shock.

Blood ran warmly down my face but I half sat up and tried to shout at two soldiers who were running at a crouch a few feet away. My own voice rattled faintly like a broken gramophone and I realized that the words didn't make sense.

Surprised, I tried again and another time to make words. I had lost my power of speech.

A shell was coming; I automatically grabbed the ground and listened. But this time too I heard the familiar sound muffled as if it were rattled nearly off the sound track, as if my whole head were joggling.

The usually frightening sound of an approaching shell and the explosion were ghosts of themselves, almost comic.

A frightened soldier had skinned his way into the rocks next to me during the arrival of the shell and I tried to talk, fumbling over the words, trying to say, "Can you help me?" coming out finally with the words "can help."

Another shell burst further down the slope and then the soldier's fear-hallowed face was looking back as he was running away and saying: "I can't help you, I'm too scared."

Then I realized that my chances of getting off that night depended on my getting up and walking. Blood still ran down my face and I knew I was badly hit. I saw my helmet lying on the ground, a hole like an open mouth in the front of it and another in the side. My glasses had been blown off but miraculously not broken. I put on my helmet and glasses unsteadily with my left arm because my right arm had been knocked out of action. It felt like a board against my side.

I stood up and began to stagger down the rocky trail. I dropped my helmet and stopped to pick it up and thought that it would be a good souvenir if I survived—probably that was the only extraneous thought I remember except that I felt my pockets to make sure that I had my notes.

Then a shell was coming and I heard the same ragged, distant whistling of the movement and the rattling, loose explosion. I was on the ground for a little time and then I found a medical soldier wrapping my head in a bandage and saw that he had stuck my right arm with a morphine surette, but I was not aware of the thrust of the needle. I picked up my right arm in my left hand and it felt like a foreign body and when I dropped it, it fell inert.

Then the medic was gone and I became again consciously alone and helpless.

I got to my feet again, and stumbling, dropping my helmet time after time, picking it up with my left hand and dangling my right arm, talking my ape-jargon and with blood running down my glasses, I must have been a grotesque sight.

But in this peculiar way I was still trying to catch up with Col. Yarborough. That was the focus of my stunned mind and the arrival of each rustling and rattling shell halted me only temporarily while I hit the rocks. Once a shell burst so close that I felt I could have touched it—it towered over me like a geyser, but I was not frightened, only startled, at its proximity.

Then there were more shells following me and I found a small cave which a German had evidently dug a few days ago against this sort of danger when the Germans held the area. I began to wonder whether I would be able to catch up with Col. Yarborough after all, or whether I would stay the night on the mountain, but the mechanism of shock made the thought seem unimportant, in which case I would probably die. Meanwhile, bursts in a rattling succession hit close below my little cave. I felt something like relief about being wounded even though I might die tonight. It seemed somehow that after so many close ones my luck should at last catch up with me.

My being hit had been totally unexpected and would have surprised me, if I had been capable of being surprised in my present shocked condition.

After having watched an all-day hand grenade battle between the Germans and the Rangers on the ridge of Mount Corno, I had thought that my job of reporting was over for the day.

I had started down from the peak along the rocky trail and had estimated it would take me about two and a half hours to negotiate the two mile trail down the mountain.

On the long, sweaty climb up the mountain to the box-seat for the hand to hand battle, I had been struck by the continuous trail of blood sprinkled brightly on the calcite rocks. It was the first literal trail of blood I had ever seen over such a long distance.

Nearly every day there had been casualties on this trail, particularly at one point where the Germans were able to bring a heavy concentration of artillery to bear. Yesterday, from the foot of the mountain I had watched the dirty grey puffs of shellfire sprouting from the mountainside and had seen the wrecks of injured men. I hadn't thought that I would be contributing some of my own blood to this crimson trail.

However, here I was in the cave, badly wounded through the head and, as I thought, also in the arm.

Thinking back over the time, I remember, however, that I was singularly unconcerned about my plight. I seemed vastly good-natured and nothing seemed to disturb me—but the automatic force of self-preservation seemed to be telling me what to do.

When the shells slacked off, I climbed to my feet again, dropping and retrieving my souvenir helmet several times. Then I staggered down the rocky trail, still impelled by the force which pushed me in the direction of Col. Yarborough.

Like a robot, unsteady on his feet but under directional control, I stumbled over the rocks and fell automatically each time I heard the fuzzy sound of the approach of a shell, got back to my feet and went ahead.

Time did not seem to be moving fast or slowly; time seemed to be in neutral gear, but I knew that the distance I walked was long.

Around a bend in the trail I saw Col. Yarborough, bending over a bleeding enlisted man who sat on the ground. With Col. Yarborough was Capt. Tomasik, and I felt a surge of pleasure at seeing them again, like a dog wagging his tail at the sight of some familiar person. Then I knew that somehow I would be able to get down the mountain that night, because I had found Yarborough. Fortunately for me, Yarborough and Tomasik had stayed behind to care for one of their men whose arm had been blown off a few minutes ago.

From then on, down the long trail, Yarborough helped to support me, and the long haul might have seemed like a nightmare, if I had not been shielded by the impervious barrier of shock. As it was, this was not a particularly unhappy dream.

It must have been a half an hour later that we reached a peasant's house, where the bare mountain mass of Mt. Corno stretches down on the dirt floor, and waited for transportation.

Still I tried to talk, and uttered inane unconnected syllables, and lifted my paralyzed right arm in my left hand and tried to indicate that I thought it had been hit. They stripped the sleeve from my arm and it was untouched. Still the blood ran down my face and coated my glasses.

Across the room I saw a line of soldiers standing with that fascinated, awed look written on their faces, as they stared at me, the badly wounded man—and to know that those fascinated spectators felt more imagined pain than I did actually. Such is the power of shock and the will to preservation.

More than a month later, when I was recovering my power of speech and the use of my right arm, and a great hole in the side of my skull was healing, I asked a doctor who was a patient in a bed next to mine, the question which had occurred to me many times since I had come through the experience of being badly wounded.

The doctor said that he believed that almost all of the men badly hit feel no pain at the time.

That, I think, is the only worth-while bit of information gathered in that otherwise unproductive day of news-gathering, November 22, 1943.

Prelude to Battle
and How Victory Came

· · · · · · · · · · · ·

BY
HOWARD HANDLEMAN
INTERNATIONAL NEWS SERVICE STAFF CORRESPONDENT

ABOARD A TRANSPORT IN THE "MARSHALLS," Jan. 30, 1944 (delayed) (INS)—The officers who will lead the infantry attack on Enubuj Island on Kwajalein Atoll tomorrow morning gathered in the dim mess hall aboard this transport tonight for the last word from their commander.

The imminence of war and wholesale death was evident on every hand. All day this convoy has been in the Marshall Island area, skirting Jap bases by thin margins. All day there has been the uneasy fear that the Jap planes would come, that torpedo bombers would drop death on the crowded troop transports that are scattered over the ocean as far as the eye can see.

The red lights, dim red lights, in the mess hall were evidence of war. Until tonight the mess hall had bright white lights, under which men could read and play cards. The hall was dimmed out tonight to protect against a vagrant flash of light over the ocean when a hatch is opened.

The officers gathered as soon as the orderlies had cleared the tables of dinner dishes. Second Lt. Gerald Helder, 23, the good-looking intelligence officer who was a commercial artist and sales promotion man for a Holland, Mich., furnace company, gave the final word on the pass words and maps, and told company officers to report to the CP after the meeting to see aerial photographs taken this morning and rushed to troopships.

Then Lt. Col. Edward P. Smith took over. Smith, commanding the same battalion he led on Attu last May, is a 27-year-old West Pointer whose father is a fire captain in Boston.

He minced no words.

"The platoon leader fights the war," he said. "He does the dirty work. He has to make the decisions on which I base my decisions. I have every confidence that the platoon leaders will make the right decisions, but I don't give a damn whether they make the right or wrong decisions so long as they make some decision and carry it out. If it's the wrong one, we'll pull you out of it somehow.

"Some of you have been in combat before. As I've said before, you're going to be scared. So is everybody else. Anybody who says he isn't is a liar.

"Your first impulse when you're shot at is going to be to hit the ground. It's the man who can get up and move forward fast who is the good leader.

"Your respect for the American soldier is going to go way up. You'll see him do things you thought impossible and that you thought man couldn't do. You'll have to prove yourselves worthy of leading these men. Don't put them in an impossible situation. Lead them so they'll have a chance to use their superiority over the Japs man to man.

"Your job is to go in and kill. That's a cruel word, but it's your blood or his. When you have to take a position and it's tough, just remember that if you don't take it now you'll have to take it three hours from now. Go on in and get it over with.

"Good luck and good hunting."

The men rose in the darkness as one and saluted the short, well-built youngster who is their leader.

KWAJALEIN ISLAND, Feb. 3, 1944 (delayed) (INS)—Last night and most of tonight I scrunched on my belly under bullets fired by Japs who hid in holes and fired at Americans while waiting for death they knew was inevitable.

A sniper who was doomed and knew it awakened us at dawn with bullets whining over Col. Curtis D. O'Sullivan's command post in Sandy Gully.

The belly crunching began then while soldiers spread out to find the sniper and silence him. This done, everyone was freed to get on with the business of war.

Keith Wheeler, Chicago Times War Correspondent, and I attached ourselves to Lieut. Roy Skipworth, 22, of Fort Sumner, N. Mex., lanky leader of an intelligence and reconnaissance platoon, who started for the front early.

Skipworth's 13-man patrol, bolstered or weighted by two correspondents and an Army photographer, Sgt. Bob Carson, Wheeling, Va., bumped into the shooting long before shooting was to have been heard. Bullets blazed several hundred yards behind the front lines as listed on G-2 maps. But the Japs didn't read the G-2 maps and holed out while front line troops went by, trying to disorganize the rear when mop-up soldiers came along.

Skipworth and his men and guests walked right into battle. With bullets pinging away, "Skippy" ran and dodged, leading his party to a sandbanked building which apparently had been demolished. A grotesque dead Jap lay half covered with sand in a shallow trench we sat in.

The soldier closest to the Jap hollered for a shovel, couldn't get one so he used a palm branch to finish covering the Jap. Presence of a dead Jap indicated the war had passed the place at least.

Skippy sat atop the sand pile looking ahead. Somebody started shooting over our heads from behind. A soldier on our left flank shouted, "Cut out that damned shooting!" And another soldier ducked and dodged to the rear to tell the shooting soldier personally.

Gunfire from the rear brought a general trying on one of the checkered identification panels American soldiers wear on their backs, and a happy-go-lucky private shouted, "Hey, Skip, better get down, some trigger-happy so-and-so is shooting."

Then the shooting from both sides of us died down and Skip ran ahead of the party again, first to a shell hole a block-buster bomb must have scooped out, then to the ruins of a Jap shrine where everyone huddled with three stone steps for protection.

That protection was needed. Bullets traveled overhead both ways. The din was terrific. Tanks, including one labeled pistol packin' Mama with a gun named Mama's pistol, rocked pillboxes and the earth with great blasts.

The engineers made worse explosions with satchel charges of TNT. Machine guns stuttered constantly. Rifles and grenades at close range, and artillery and Navy gun fire at long range, added to the noisy confusion.

And the siren from a boat in the lagoon sent an eerie note cutting through the heavier sound.

Lieut. James Bean, 24, of Saginaw, Mich., came up with a frightening report. He told us three Japs were killed in the sandbanked building just after we left.

The war was all over hell on the island.

Soldiers for several hundred yards in any direction, including back, lay behind tree stumps or in shell holes, keeping under cover until they were called on for active duty pillbox busting.

Skippy, who wished he had a rifle platoon instead of an ostensibly non-combat intelligence platoon, moved ahead again, a strange looking figure in camouflaged helmet and with eyebrows and upper lip green, all that remained of paint he put on three days ago for camouflage.

His next hop was well into a destroyed Jap village. Some of the squad continued up the road toward the skeleton of a house which still had a shady porch.

Staff Sgt. James Richmond, 22 today, of Larkspur, Cal., moved along toward the house while two others covered him with rifle fire.

No more than 10 yards from the house Richmond saw a Jap leap to the porch uttering a soprano scream, "AI!" Richmond fired twice and ducked back and the whole squad scrambled to fighting posts.

Wheeler, Carson, and I leaped to the back side of a concrete wall after seeing several Japs run to the porch shade. We were really non-combatants. Skip's squad engaged in a quick battle. One man was killed with a bullet through the head. Another, firing from a tree no more than four inches wide, got a Jap but got winged in the shoulder himself.

Richmond came out congratulating himself, "If that guy had kept quiet I'd have gone right up to where we could have shaken hands and he'd have plugged me sure."

The incident at the house seemed to set off a whole series of Jap counterattacks and sniper bullets made a deadly cacophony overhead. Soldiers unable to see who was shooting at them scrambled a few yards to the rear to a Jap bomb shelter.

The doctors couldn't take to the shelter though because there was a wounded man ahead. They sneaked forward, got him, and by the time they carried him by on a stretcher his right shoulder was bandaged.

Little groups of men moved back in spurts all along the flanks. Skip was mad, but finally he had to tell the squad to move back. The men leaped through the battlefield rubble.

The first shell hole resting place had one dead American and two dead Japs. The second had a bloody pool of water. The third resting place was back at the shrine.

That was a bad place to be at 1 P.M., for a Jap sniper had a bead over our heads, and not far over our heads either. Everybody hit the dirt, crouching behind the shrine steps, the stone foundation, the sacred stone pedestals before the steps and behind fallen logs.

It was another stubborn Jap, firing from a hole he knew would be his death place.

Sweating, tired, hungry soldiers lay with faces in the dirt for 40 minutes waiting for someone to stop the sniper's bullets. The wait got on the men's nerves. One soldier shouted, "Why in hell don't we get out of this place?"

His words were hardly uttered before a new burst of bullets screamed overhead. Another soldier answered, "That's why."

The sniper finally let up, and the most miserable 40 minutes of the day ended with the rapid retreat of 16 men—a retreat through skeleton jungle left by big American guns.

Skip led his men back to the command post where he gobbled a K ration and returned to the front again with a fresh squad.

Wheeler reached into his pocket, found his cigarette lighter missing and started back with Carson and me to look for it.

We never found it, but we got chased to the ground three more times by Japs, those stubborn, damned Japs.

• • •

ABOARD EXPEDITIONARY FLAGSHIP, ENIWETOK ATOLL, Feb. 22, 1944 (delayed)—The blackest month in Japan's military history was drawing to a close today, with the American flag floating over Eniwetok Island and American troops ready to storm the shell torn beach of Parry Island where the Japs await death like men in some prison's condemned row.

For three days the Japs on Parry, under day and night bombardment themselves, could look across two miles of water to Eniwetok Island and almost see American soldiers and Marines slaughter hundreds of their compatriots.

The conquest of Eniwetok Island was a noisy prelude to death for the Parry Japs. Saturday (Feb. 19) Army and Marine troops went ashore at Eniwetok in landing boats, and the Japs on Parry could see the waves of the small American boats easily.

Ever since then, they have been able to hear American rifle and machine gun fire, grenade explosions and the roar of demolition charges, as the Americans went about their grim and determined task of wiping out every Jap they saw.

By watching smoke from grenade and tank gun bursts, the Parry Japs have been able to chart the Americans' swift progress.

Daily the explosions and smoke bursts have been moving closer to them, and they are now powerless to lift a finger to escape inevitable death.

Parry has been a South Sea death house for days, and the Japs garrisoned there know it. All they could do was wait their turn, wait until the Americans got around to them.

That personal attention will be given them when the Marines go ashore to annihilate the last of the live Japs on the Atoll.

The Parry Japs underwent the most harrowing experience of all the Nipponese this month, the day-to-day wait for death, but every Jap in the Pacific suffered more during February than ever before, in the opinion of Rear Admiral Harry W. Hill, of Oakland, Cal., and Washington, D.C., commander of amphibious forces.

"Japan has never had a blacker month," he said. "In three weeks we moved 800 miles closer to Tokyo, and that is a tremendous advance in any man's war when you are moving on the enemy's capital."

In one sense the Tokyo Japs felt the advance in the same way the Parry Japs are feeling presently.

They saw their cozy hold in the central Pacific lost in three weeks—three weeks in which America won island masses from which land planes will be able to pummel hitherto unreachable Jap strongholds.

Our losses at Eniwetok Atoll, as of February 21, stood at 150 dead and 350 wounded. In fact, American losses in the whole great campaign have been amazingly light, as Japs on most islands were beaten into submission from the sea before our troops ever went ashore.

And every Jap island garrison had to fend for itself, as the Seventh Army Air Force and Navy planes kept other Jap air bases unserviceable during the attacks.

The twelve-plane raid by the Japs on Roi Island February 12 has been the only air attack on American Forces so far and that came a week after the Kwajalein Atoll was secured, too late to affect the American foothold in the Marshalls.

Officially, Eniwetok Island was declared secure at 4:45 P.M. yesterday (Feb. 21), after a three-day fight in which 22nd Division Marines and the 106th Army Infantry dug Japs out of their palm covered fox holes.

Admiral Hill and Brig. General Thomas E. Watson, of Oscaloosa, La., commanding the joint Army and Marine invasion troops went ashore for the flag raising ceremony.

Actually, the fight on Eniwetok is not over yet, and won't be for sometime, because island warfare against the Japs never ends with the securing of a battle ground.

Scared little Japs hide out alone for days and our soldiers have to flush them from their holes.

Yesterday afternoon, for example, with only a few hundred yards to go through tangled, jungle-like underbrush, Lieut. Col. Harold I. Mizony, of Spokane, Wash., led tired soldiers through this stuff until they reached the island's tip. Every soldier fired ahead to preclude opposition and to pour out such a blanket of lead as to probe every Jap hideaway.

Even though the Americans control every square foot above ground, a few disorganized and dazed Japs maintain their sovereignty over dust-choked rat holes still to be found by Americans.

Meanwhile, the Parry invasion was being prepared by a terrific bombardment from surface craft which leveled whole sections of the island, whose fortification was begun only recently by the harried Japs.

John R. Henry, International News Service correspondent, saw the bombardment from the deck of a battleship and declared:

"We were so close to the beaches we were able to see the Japs on shore. One was killed by machine gun fire from our ship which also poured on salvo after salvo of murderous bombardment from its heavy guns."

Simultaneously, other ships stood far out at sea, lobbing shells high enough to plunge them into underground defenses.

For three days now, the Parry Japs have been kept awake with the constant bombardment, under the plan to leave the survivors dazed and exhausted when the Marines begin their invasion.

· · · · · · · · · · ·

HOWARD HANDLEMAN

Howard Handleman was a California native who began reporting for the *Orange Belt Daily News* in San Bernardino after graduating from the University of Redlands. In 1935 he became a reporter for the International News Service, working in a number of cities before covering the war in the Pacific as a correspondent. After the war he was the INS director for the Far East, was the San Francisco bureau chief, spent two years as chief INS diplomatic correspondent, and was appointed its chief European correspondent.

Handleman quit the INS in 1958, whereupon he worked for the Office of Civil Defense and Mobilization in Washington, D.C., until he returned to journalism by taking a position as diplomatic editor and correspondent at *U.S. News & World Report*. He retired in 1978.

Howard Handleman died of heart failure in August 1994. He was eighty years old.

Retreat from the Ukraine

· · · · · · · · · · · ·

BY

DAVID M. NICHOL

CHICAGO *DAILY NEWS* FOREIGN SERVICE

ON THE UKRAINIAN FRONT, March 21, 1944—The Nazis' road to Rumania is littered alike with the hopes and wreckage of the German army.

It is a road that leads away from the richest area in the Ukraine, the section on which Hitler and his leaders had based their entire colonial program. It is a path that has jarred German morale to its very foundations and it has been one of the costliest retreats in the history of this war.

I am not altogether a stranger to the confusion that is left in the wake of any major engagement, but I have never seen anything like this. Mile after muddy mile of Ukrainian highways are lined with every kind of conveyance in various stages of destruction. Sometimes these lines are double. Sometimes they are faced in two directions as the Germans in their flight tried to find escape only to become entangled in their own columns.

There are trucks and half-tracks of every variety, staff cars and smaller automobiles, field kitchens, mobile radio stations, heavy guns mired to the hubs of their oversize wheels, and immense Mark V and Mark VI tanks, their guns at crazy angles and their treads deep in mud.

Not all this equipment was moving when the slashing Red Army attack compelled the Germans to set it afire and abandon it completely. Some of it is almost new. At the tiny railroad station at Potazh, for example, there were tanks enough to equip an entire division.

Only a few ever actually participated in the fighting. Some of the guns had never been fired. Red Army engineers tallied 240 tanks there, most of which had only just arrived as replacements and reinforcements for four tank divisions which were concentrated in that area.

So impassable are the roads that it is impossible from the ground to get an adequate picture of this destruction. We tried once in a jeep to go from Uman about fifteen miles north to Potazh, but the mud stopped us and we changed to inspection by air.

For this there is the admirable Russian airplane called U-DVA, or U-R, a tiny two-seater biplane with an open cockpit that is universal throughout the Red Army and might well be described as the jeep of the aviation world.

Originally designed in 1927, it has trained whole generations of Soviet fliers. At the front it is used to carry bombs, rush wounded to hospitals and ferry officers about from point to point. It lands or takes off at about 30 miles an hour from fields or highways and flies comfortably at about the speed of a modern passenger car on a good road. The Russians have a dozen affectionate names for it. The Germans, when they can speak printably about it at all, call it the "coffee mill" or "sewing machine."

Skimming along at tank-turret level, it was possible to reconstruct the disaster that overtook the Nazi army.

The village of Mankovka, about fifteen miles north of Uman, was the place where the Germans first broke. One officer described it as the "crisis" of the entire Uman operation in the sense that while action continued several days longer, it was here that the final outcome was determined.

Three days earlier, Marshal Ivan S. Konev's troops, in the wake of an intense concentration of artillery fire, pierced the German defense lines which had been located some fifteen miles farther north. It was not an easy job. Some Soviet assault units suffered as much as 25 percent casualties in the first stages of the fighting. The Germans retired doggedly in good order, prepared to hold Mankovka.

Early on the morning of March 8, Red Army infantry advanced along both sides of the highway that leads to Mankovka from the north. Here, as elsewhere in this offensive, the secret of their movement was no secret at all. It was simply slogging on foot through mud with a minimum of motorized transport. The ordinary Soviet soldier is openly contemptuous of German dependence on trucks and automobiles.

The Soviet T-34 tank likewise proved its adaptability. Its high clearance, broad treads and powerful axle take it through conditions which bog down German tanks, officers say. The Red Army has a wholesome respect particularly for the Mark V or "Panther," but low clearance and an axle that sometimes breaks in mud handicap its movements. This and the potent morale factor of a victorious army seem to be the answers to the Soviet success.

As the infantry advanced from the north, two columns of Soviet tanks swung wide around Mankovka, cutting the roads to west and east and appearing suddenly south of the village, where the Germans least expected them. While this was going on the Stormoviks, which the Germans call "Black Death," attacking in waves of nine and eighteen, had been pouring a merciless fire into the concentrations in the village.

Mankovka shows the effects of this pounding. Much German equipment was crippled there.

With the equipment they could still use the Germans hastily tried to defend the southern edge of the village. It was here, officers said, that the element of bewilderment appeared among the German forces. Their only road to the south was under fire from both sides by Soviet tanks. They fought a brief engagement, then fled, leaving Mankovka's streets lined with abandoned transport.

South they rushed, towards the important east-west railroad, but the narrow crossing there was a bottleneck. Like a dammed stream, the German columns spread to either side and sunk into the fields.

What was not fired by Soviet airplanes the Germans themselves put to the torch, then moved farther on.

The Soviet tank column to the west of the road continued to parallel retreat, harrying the Germans at every step. But the column to the east of the road was after bigger game. Red Army scouts had learned of a tank concentration at the station at Potazh. They headed for it, swinging south and then east, cutting the station off from the lines of retreat.

What they found there puzzled them. Twenty-eight Tigers were grouped to the front of the station. Apparently the German reconnaissance was thoroughly confused. Only a small number of machines were guarding the southern approaches. They fought a brief, savage engagement, then lit out across country.

Not only was trainload after trainload of almost new tanks captured, but the booty included an immense fuel dump and stores of ammunition wired to be exploded but which the Germans never touched off. Many tanks in good condition had already been moved. The captured ammunition will suffice for some of them. In others, Red Army mobile repair crews are installing Soviet guns. There is a story that tells of one commander who placed twelve Tigers around his command post rather than stop to build fortifications.

Meanwhile, alarm and uneasiness, approaching panic at the immediate front had been spreading back through the German lines much more rapidly than the line advance itself. In Uman, the supply columns began to move. At the little town of Voitovka, about five miles to the north, the Germans installed a battery of field guns, but the pursuit continued.

The people of Uman told us of almost solid streams of Nazi transports, virtually nose to tailgate, that moved spasmodically along the roads to the south throughout March 8 and 9, and of columns of cursing, sweating Germans trying to free themselves from the clinging mud and sloughing off equipment as they went in an effort to lighten their load. One German tank division commander, his Prussian military dignity completely gone, escaped through the town on a Soviet tractor.

By nightfall of March 9, the Uman roads were hopelessly clogged.

German demolition squads had blown up and burned the few principal buildings when, at 10 o'clock, rocket signals flared along the whole line. Precious gasoline streamed out over the roads. The German retreat became a serpentine path of fire.

What had been confusion now approached panic. Soldiers threw down their packs. Helmets and gas masks littered the streets. Valuable staff records were thrown to the winds. It is difficult even now to walk along the two principal thoroughfares leading south through the city, so closely packed is the wreckage. In three short blocks alone, I counted more than 88 heavy vehicles, motorized infantry transports that had rolled so insolently into Russia three years ago, searchlights, mortar-batteries and field kitchens.

These streets bear mute testimony of Nazi looting—smashed sewing machines, torn feather quilts, pots and pans and even household furniture. Some of the burned trucks contained potatoes baked in the flames.

Some supply dumps were left virtually untouched. In the yard of what formerly was Uman's principal machine tractor station stands a solid line of entirely new tank motors. The yard itself is crowded with tanks in various stages of repair.

At the airport on the outskirts of Uman the Germans left 12,000 barrels of aviation fuel and immense piles of parachute cannisters that had been intended to relieve the forces which had been trapped earlier at Korsun-Shevchenko. These are now being dropped to advancing Russian troops by the Soviet transport.

Near the fringe of the field is the burned skeleton of an immense transport plane.

Soviet air officers hesitate to identify it positively. They suggest it may be a Messerschmitt 323. It has six motors, four heavy caliber machine guns and two cannons, mounted oddly in power-driven turrets in the wings. It may have been designed as a new German challenge to this front. It lies hopelessly wrecked in the mud.

. . . .

DAVID M. NICHOL

David M. Nichol was born in Ontario, Canada. He went to the University of Michigan and began working on the *Iron River Reporter* shortly after graduating. The Chicago *Daily News* hired him three years later as a suburban and special assignment reporter, then as a correspondent. He covered World War II developments in Germany and Russia.

This Is It! D-Day
and What Followed

· · · · · · · · · · · ·

BY

JOSEPH DRISCOLL

WAR CORRESPONDENT OF THE NEW YORK *HERALD TRIBUNE*

ABOARD ASSAULT HEADQUARTERS WARSHIP, June 6, 1944—This is it! This time there is no fooling. This is the real thing. At last the Allied invasion of western Europe is begun. The long-heralded second front has been opened in a big way. Our warship has the honor and responsibility of leading troop transports and tank-landing crafts through the enemy minefields.

The objectives are quite simple. First, to gain a foothold or two on the continent; second, to march on to Paris, and Berlin.

It's as simple as all that, and yet the greatest amphibious forces in the world's history, including tremendous naval, ground and air forces, are employed.

Several thousand warships are involved in the massive operations, and this total does not include the smaller landing craft and coasters. With them the number might be doubled. As far as the eye can see is a gray forest of masts and superstructures of all sizes, shapes and purposes. Relatively speaking, the water is as jampacked with men of war as a Long Island commuters' train on racing days.

This is a race too, and for classic stakes. Our job is to blast a hole into Hitler's vaulted Atlantic Wall, and land sufficient troops and equipment before Marshal Erwin Rommel can counter-attack and try to drive us back into the sea. It is a race the like of which no warrior has ever seen, not even Napoleon, or Julius Caesar, and countless lives are being staked on our chances of smashing to victory.

The fact that the eagerly awaited, long delayed invasion was getting under way at last became known to correspondents when they were summoned to the Admiralty at short notice.

For a month, as Prime Minister Churchill had predicted, Allied headquarters had engaged in a series of feints and a war of nerves to deceive the Germans, keep them constantly alerted and break down their morale. No doubt it had a tendency to do this, but it must be confessed that the public over here was also getting a trifle anxious and impatient.

As part of the studied program of feints and for the misinformation of enemy agents in London and the countryside, correspondents themselves engaged in a series of false starts and dry runs. To them the eve of invasion was better known as "the eve of evasion." The deceptions were so clever that even some of their own people were fooled. As recently as last Sunday, an American officer solemnly assured me in Hyde Park that the invasion talk was a hoax and that western Europe was too tough to tackle.

But when we taxied to the Admiralty before breakfast we were ushered upstairs into a guarded conference chamber and quickly informed:

"This is not to be a dry run. This, gentlemen, is the business."

Our informant was a young American liaison officer who addressed the correspondents gathered around a green baize table. At one end of the room was an open fireplace, at the other a tight-lipped portrait of an Admiralty Lord Advocate, Lord Stowell in his robes of office.

Further briefing of correspondents was done by two pipe-smoking British officers who outlined "censorship stops"—that is, certain matters which it is forbidden to publish, such as secret weapons and tactics, and serious casualties to men or ships, and speculation on future operations.

Having been made privy to all the secrets of D-Day, correspondents were then told that they were "sealed" from then on and would be kept together and away from outside contacts. With the lives of thousands of men depending upon the secrets being kept secret, the correspondents were warned with grim humor that they would be "sealed at both ends if necessary."

From the Admiralty we were escorted to a bus and sped on to our port of embarkation. In London, queues of customers were already forming outside the butcher shops, the newsstands and the pubs. In London, the skies were weeping gloomily, but as we bounced over the rolling countryside, the skies brightened and the rare beauty of the English countryside unfolded itself. England never appeared more peaceful, except for a few portents.

Two motorcycle policemen preceded us to assure the right of way. In every English village through which we passed, American military policemen were on traffic duty at the intersections and the householders peered from their windows at passing convoys which had been rumbling through the streets night and day. Once we were delayed by a convoy of cows and bulls that refused to yield possession of the highway. Of them, a wit remarked: "There's the O.W.I. unit."

Easing any jitters in our group was a talented writer with a German harmonica on which he softly played "Waltzing Matilda" and "Red River Valley," and "Yankee Doodle Dandy," the latter revived as our invasion theme song.

And so, after a tedious, jolting ride, we came to a coastal zone where American jeeps were everywhere to be seen. The English approve of the Americans being there but do not tell them so because there are posted signs which enjoin "civilians must not loiter, or talk with soldiers."

Still "sealed" away from the public, we were taken out to our warships to be briefed further. Without ado, the officer went to a safe the size of a kitchen icebox and showed us pounds and pounds of his secret orders. He did not get to read the orders, but he did produce a detailed chart, and he said:

"Here's where we're going in and what the plan is."

The officer added that he had instructions to tell us everything and he made good. For an hour he explained the chart and told us in the freest details what forces were available and how they had prepared to kill all the exposed German personnel and to knock out the batteries of enemy as a preliminary to seizing the beachheads for the drive to Paris and Berlin.

He spoke of the difficulties of supply and of novel plans to overcome this and of secret weapons to be used for the first time, and of the exact number of units, to be landed within so many days after D-Day.

The officer even spoke about the weather, which, it is to be hoped, will favor the Allies, who are on the side of the angels and would prefer sunshine to fog or darkness.

Anyway, here we are crossing the water and the Germans, who once upon a time sang that they were sailing against England, are now cowering behind the Atlantic Wall, which our guns are pounding with a sound and a fury like the worst storm multiplied a million.

One of the most heroic stories of the war is coming out piecemeal. When all the pieces are put together, it should be difficult to find an epic involving more human courage and resourcefulness under fire.

The story concerns a little group of Rangers assigned to be the first of our ground forces to establish contact with the enemy. Their specific mission was to storm and capture enemy gun positions at the top of a cliff which juts out into the bay not far from the center of our Normandy invasion front. The Germans had cunningly concealed themselves in chalk caves at the very summit of the 200-foot cliff.

So long as the batteries remained in action it was impracticable for Rear Admiral John L. Hall, jr. to land his assault forces. Careful surveys indicated that the arc of fire from the German batteries would sweep the whole transport anchorage area and endanger not only the transports but Admiral Hall's flagship and bombardment warships.

Therefore, it was imperative to knock out the German batteries before the invasion forces could be landed. On the other hand, the Germans in their caves at the summit of the cliff enjoyed natural protection plus concrete and steel improvements.

Not knowing it was impossible, the Americans attempted the impossible and succeeded. All the Rangers were picked men and volunteers. For about a year they have been training where there are plenty of cliffs to climb. The Rangers knew long in advance what their mission was to be and they were eager for it.

Under cover of darkness, the Rangers approached the cliff in LCTs which were transporting ducks especially fitted with serial extension ladders like [the ones] firemen used to ascend skyscrapers in big cities. The LCTs cut off their engines and slipped to within a mile of the beach to let down the ramps. Down the ramps rolled the ducks into the water. But when the amphibious vehicles tried to swim up on the sands they were blocked by huge bowlders. It was simply impossible for the ducks to get in close enough to place the extension ladders up against the cliff where they could do any good.

So the ducks and ladders had to be abandoned and the dismounted Rangers waded into a beach of not more than twenty-five feet in width of sand and boulders before they came to the towering cliff.

From a mortar, the undaunted Rangers shot a grappling hook into the air and it caught on the top of the cliff. One man shinnied up the line leading to the hook. Around his body he carried four rope ladders which he draped over the side of the cliff.

Up the ladders ascended the Rangers carrying what equipment they could. As they went up, the aroused German gunners were waiting for them with hand grenades. They probably would have swept aside and killed all the Rangers except for four factors:

One, the Rangers were busy throwing grenades with baseball accuracy.

Two, the cliff was undercut, the top of it jutting out farthest so that the climbing Rangers found some protection under the overhanging ledge.

Three, down on the narrow beach a few Rangers had been left behind to fire 60 mm mortars which had a tendency to keep the Germans from sticking their noses out over the topside.

Four, a few more Rangers had been left farther along the beach where they created a diversion and distracted the Germans by firing their guns and yelling like Indians, the methodical Germans not being accustomed to such outlandish tactics.

Gaining the summit, the Rangers rushed four of the enemy gun positions and knocked them out by flinging TNT charges despite opposition on machine-gun fire. They found a fifth gun had already been knocked out by a direct aerial hit and a sixth gun had been moved two hundred yards inland.

After daylight, as they rushed this sixth gun, the Germans came out with a white flag. As the Rangers advanced to accept surrender, machine-guns opened up on them. The Rangers not only knocked out the gun, but thereafter they took few prisoners.

The battle was far from being ended. The Rangers had knocked out the batteries and accomplished their objectives. But now they had to fight for their lives all over again. The Germans brought up reserves from the neighborhood and counter-attacked repeatedly.

The Rangers were pinned down to an area one hundred yards wide and three hundred yards long. They had a choice of holding that area or jumping over the cliff. They held it at fearful cost, exhausting most of their ammunition and food. Their wounded they lowered on lines to the beach where litter cases remained unattended throughout Tuesday and Wednesday.

The Rangers suffered casualties. Some were captured by the Germans. One patrol was sent out and lost. Toward the end, only a few Rangers were left to hold the point. Their leader was wounded the first day, but refused to leave his command.

Finally, the destroyer Harding was sent inshore to bombard the Germans and drive them back. Under this protection, the wounded Rangers and twenty-eight German prisoners were brought off and reinforcements sent in. Tonight, the good word is that other Rangers and Army units on their left have at last made contact with the surviving Rangers. The siege has been lifted and the epic struggle is closed.

Rear Admiral Hall said today that "things are going pretty well now." Coming from the admiral, a conservative Virginian, this statement almost approaches optimism regarding a somewhat confused situation.

The admiral cited a case where sixty Germans surrendered after shooting their commanding officer who had refused to surrender, and said it was a good sign of a break in German morale.

Hall, returning from an inspection of the assault armada, told correspondents here he would not delay reinforcements because things were "tougher than it had been thought they would be," but added he had never had any idea that the area assigned to him would not be a tough job.

Francis is a first-class welder from Brooklyn who wonders today how and why he ever landed on a beach in this part of the world.

"If I never see another beach, it'll be too soon," says Francis, a small man with a little black mustache and big brown eyes that fill with tears as he relates his D-Day experiences.

"I never saw so many men die before in my life," says Francis, "and they were not grown men either—just kids."

Francis went into the Army in November, 1940, and was honorably discharged a few weeks later. "I would rather have stayed in the Army, but my legs gave out and I couldn't keep up with the marches," says Francis. So, bowlegged Francis went to work as a welder in the Kearny shipyards until November, 1943, when he was inducted into the Navy, which he thinks was a mistake.

"These boats make me very seasick," he confesses. "I was sick eleven days coming over. I'm sick every day now on the small boats. I just don't tell anybody any more."

Francis went into battle with a sick stomach and a heavy heart. He had tried to get into the Seabees, where he could have followed his trade of welding, but the Seabees were full up, so Francis was shunted into the amphibious corps and he is hardly the amphibious type. But what really weighed him down at dawn yesterday was the fact that he had quarreled with his wife, with whom he is much in love—the wife who has borne him one child and has another on the way.

"It seems the older I get the stupider I get," says Francis, who will be 38 next November, if he lives that long. "I didn't get my mail from home for six weeks and I wrote a pretty nasty letter to my wife. Then I got twenty letters all in a bunch."

It was as a turret gunner on the stern of an LCVP that Francis chugged yesterday into an objective which some one with a quaint sense of humor had designated on the charts as "an easy beach."

"We were supposed to hit the beach at 6:30," Francis remembers, "but we had trouble with our pumps and we were taking in water, so we laid up for ten minutes to empty the boat.

"When we went in, the Germans still had everything. None of the beach obstacles had been knocked out and they had rifle, machine gun and shell fire. The only thing they didn't have was planes. Thank God for that.

"Well, we lowered our ramp and let the troops out okay. When we tried to back out a strong tide worked against us and piled us up on one of those wooden underwater obstacles that the Germans had built on the beaches.

"Then they started shooting at us from the cliffs above the beach. One shell hit the bow. It was either a direct hit or a near miss; I didn't wait to find out. I jumped overboard and stayed around a sand bar for ten minutes. Then I took a chance and swam 200 yards to the shore; on the way I picked up a machine-gunner who had lost his life jacket and couldn't swim. He was hit on the way in.

"Finally, our side overcame the machine-gun positions above us on the hill. Twelve LCI's moved in to unload troops. One was hit on the main deck by an 11. She moved in anyhow. And one exploded below her water line. She teetered, but came in and disembarked with one or two casualties. I started out on her, but she was stranded on a bar, so we all had to swim back in. The skipper gave us blankets and sandwiches.

"There was a lot of trouble on our right flank. A couple of batches of 11's were knocking out a few of our landing craft. I saw an LST blown up, probably by a 7.7. The 11's were knocking out smaller craft—LCI's and LCVP's and LCT's. Their main battery was three or four miles away, behind a clump of trees. If it had been any closer, it could have hit our destroyers.

"I helped the corpsmen to give blood transfusions, that blood plasma stuff. I thought one fellow was dead, but we gave him two bottles and he came to. I saw a couple of boys bleed to death because there were not enough corpsmen to go around.

"Anyway, my wife should be happy to know that her blood was

helping out too. She gave it to the blood bank back home."

This was the first time under fire for Francis and most of his comrades.

"I was trying to save my hide," Francis recalls, "but you can't be yellow, with kids out there walking up and down the beach. I saw so many killed. Maybe you don't mind so much on dry land, but I saw them killed right in the water before they had a chance to fight."

Francis assisted in the capture of three German air force prisoners.

"Two were very young and one was old," says Francis. "The old man's clothing was decrepit and the others wore hand-me-downs. The German prisoners were glad to get caught. They sat down under a tree and made no effort to get away.

"A funny thing," mused Francis, "I guess we Americans aren't revengeful. We could have shot those Germans then just as easy as this."

Francis marveled at the courage of his fellow Americans. "I saw boys wounded and lying around for hours without even a moan out of them."

Having seen enough for one day, Francis hopped a ride on an LCT at 4 P.M. The craft was swamped and he had to swim back to the beach again. Finally, he swam out to another LCT and was pulled in, exhausted. He had a bad cold, he had swallowed some oil and his dungarees were shredded.

Francis lives in Brooklyn. He swears his three-year-old son is "the biggest, brightest, cleanest, strongest and blondest guy you ever saw," and he adds, "my son probably thinks I'm winning the war single-handed."

. . . .

JOSEPH DRISCOLL

Joseph Driscoll was born and raised in St. Louis, Missouri. He began his career in journalism at the St. Louis *Times* and the St. Louis *Post-Dispatch*. He became a reporter, then a correspondent, for the New York *Herald Tribune*, for which he covered every newsworthy event from the Lindbergh kidnapping to the British royal family to war developments in the Pacific and Europe.

He was the author of three books: *Dock Walloper, War Discovers Alaska*, and *Pacific Victory*.

In 1947 Driscoll returned as a national correspondent to the St. Louis *Post-Dispatch*, where he worked until his death in 1952.

Shot-by-Shot Story of D-Day

. . . .

BY

RICHARD L. STROUT

STAFF CORRESPONDENT OF THE *CHRISTIAN SCIENCE MONITOR*

ON BOARD THE HEAVY CRUISER U.S.S. QUINCY OFF FRANCE, June 7, 1944—This is a round-by-round story of the invasion of France and the opening of the Second Front.

It covers the secret passage of the invasion fleet under fire and the most glorious sight of the arrival by glider of 10,000 air-borne troops.

The battle continues as this is written.

The ship jolts with the explosion of shells.

But one thing is certain. Our beachhead is established.

The degree of organization disclosed is so amazing as to augur Hitler's overthrow.

The story begins on the open bridge of a United States heavy cruiser (the U.S.S. Quincy), Capt. Elliott M. Senn, United States Navy, commanding.

It is 2 P.M. Monday, June 5. I am standing under the sky. I am dictating this story as it happens.

We have just left our anchorage. We are headed almost due east in a single line of capital ships flanked by outriders. History hangs on the weather.

On our left are the cliffs of England. We are in an Anglo-

American task force. The ships' names mingle like a chant. Those of the British have come down through history. The American names sing of the New World.

Our vessel, with its home port at Boston, is one of the fleet's newest and finest. There is another task force. The combined flotilla with landing craft will be vast. There are French, Dutch and Norwegian ships.

Already, another convoy is visible carrying its own barrage balloons.

The sky is overcast. The sea is lead-colored but quiet. There is hardly any wind. Even a squall no worse than last night's would hamper landing craft, result in thousands of casualties, maybe upset the whole show. Well, we have done what we can—the weather is nature's business.

This high, open bridge covers three sides. Forward and below are three decks and gunturrets. The biggest turrets carry triple sticks of long range, dangerous-looking guns.

The prow comes to a razor edge. Like most of man's weapons, this appears beautiful. It is slim as a race horse, rhythmic as a poem.

It is so new that 1,000 of its crew are green. They speak every American accent. This spot is a magnificent grandstand seat for history's greatest show.

5 P.M. We have overtaken and are passing the landing craft fleet formerly seen on the horizon. They make slow headway; their barrage balloons tied front and stern of larger craft tug ahead as though pulling.

These craft are chock-full of assault troops and supplies. They will catch up to us as we anchor in the night.

6 P.M. We have hoisted a fresh, clean battle flag. It will fly there till the engagement is over. Blue-coated figures in steel helmets are sweeping the sky and sea around me, chanting observations like football quarterbacks.

The air is tense and the men are consciously trying to break the suspense by horseplay. This has gone on for weeks. Our ship has known its mission and has been sealed. Now it is coming the gun crew is skipping rope.

We are leaving England. The great adventure begins. The coastline fades as we steam slowly. Right under the haze close to the distant shore is another line of vessels, alternating big and little ones, moving our way stealthily under the shore line.

We look and wonder. Something marvelous is going on. All the world's ships seem to be going our way.

Rumors fly about. Yesterday, at the peak of uncertainty, came the radio news that a New York press association had falsely reported the invasion already under way. I have been asked dozens of times if this kills the whole thing.

7 P.M. A voice breaks the silence over the loudspeaker system. A battle message has been received for this task force.

"I will read it," says the voice. It is terse, pungent, without false heroics.

"Let's put the Navy ball over for a touchdown," it concludes. The sailors chuckle.

And now the chaplain offers the final prayer before the battle. All over the ship, out here in the breeze and down in the engine room beneath the surface of the sea, the men pause with bared heads.

The voice goes over the ship and into the evening air: "Our help is in the Lord."

"Ask and it shall be given, seek and ye shall find," the solemn voice concludes.

8:30 P.M. Zero hour tomorrow is 6:30. There will be general quarters tonight (which means battle stations) from 10:30.

That is the loudspeaker announcement. A hush falls on the crew, only two hours before night and day watches set in, with compartments sealed watertight.

Hurried last minute preparations are made. I walk through the compact crew compartments. Some men sit by themselves, others write letters home, some are on bunks in the canvas tiers. The voices are cheerful.

I turn in for a final nap.

10:30 P.M. The boatswain just piped, followed by the electrifying cry, "All hands man your battle stations!" Now the bugle blows "general quarters."

The sky is overcast. Somewhere up there the moon is one night from being full. Behind us are a few red streaks of sunset. Will this thick cloud conceal us? Is it possible German planes haven't spotted these great ship lines? All afternoon the number has been swelling. But the enemy has given no sign.

Midnight. It is June 6, D-day.

The breeze has freshened. France is off ahead. There is a spurt of distant tracer bullets and a falling meteor that is really a falling airplane.

There is a gray light and we can see one another. We keep peering out, wondering when the enemy will go into action, but nothing happens.

Here is a wonderful thing: Out here in the open Channel we are following mine-swept safety lanes clearly marked so even a landsman can read them, for there are little pinpricks of buoys. Nothing that has happened has so given me the sense of extraordinary preparation.

We steam slowly. Our ship is flanked by shadowy destroyers. Only occasionally does a muffled signal flash and even on ship in the corridors, there are only his red battle lights. Now and then there is a hint of moon in the cloud blanket.

1 A.M. For an hour, airplanes have gone over us. Occasional star shells fall off there in France. Once, the moon glowed out and cast us in full relief and a silvery patch. As I dictate this, suddenly a batch of lights twinkles like July 4 sparklers. Anti-aircraft stuff! Now it is gone.

I keep thinking of home. It's 7 P.M. there now. The family is just finishing supper. It's the same in millions of American homes, children doing home work, mothers at dishes, fathers reading papers. And here we are on the dark sea moving at half speed toward history.

2 A.M. France is just over there twelve miles off. There must be hundreds of ships around us. It is impossible to see. I couldn't have believed we would get so far undetected. The Germans must know we are here. But nothing happens. Just bombers.

A few minutes ago a great flock came back from France flying low and scudding past like bats showing the prearranged signal of friends.

Behind tiny wedges come stragglers, some with limping motors.

Again and again the lights blaze on the French coast. The moon dodges in and out.

Something extraordinary in bombing must be going on. When I was a child, I could see the distant glow of fireworks at Coney Island. This is like that. Just as I dictate, a fountain of sparklers sprays upward—dotted lines of tracer bullets shoot out. This must seem pretty bad on shore, but they don't know what's to come.

3 A.M. We have arrived. And the slower landing craft meet us here. Then we go in with them to six miles offshore.

There will be simultaneous attacks by the Americans and British. Our beachhead is the one farthest north, the one nearest Cherbourg.

Here on the open bridge I hear the order, "Be ready to fire."

It just doesn't seem possible they don't see us. If they do, why don't they fire?

This must be the greatest concentration of bombing in the war. Everything is going off. We strain to read its meaning.

The only thing we know is that we are in Act 2.

Our performance is to reverse Dunkerque.

4 A.M. Well, this is the most spectacular bombing display of all. This must be the commotion kicked up by our parachute landings.

As I write, the roar of planes is like an express train going over a viaduct. I dictate this to Chief Yeoman Charles Kidder. As I speak now, flares blaze out in fifteen to twenty clusters. I can read my watch. Flames still drop. They coil out long wriggling trails of white smoke. The water seems jet. I am so wrought up I can hardly hold still. The tension on the ship is reaching a peak.

We are going inshore. The bombs on land are so near and so big I feel the concussions. Our big guns are trained ahead.

Everybody is tense for the shore battery which does not come.

The moon is gone and it is darker than it has been. We are getting an acrid smell of torn-up soil. The eerie flares have gone out.

Well, here we go!

4:50 A.M. We are a few miles offshore. And no comment from the enemy. More fireworks stuff. I never imagined anything like it. The most horrible thing was two falling planes—ours, I suppose— that crashed down with great bubbling bursts of oily flames when they hit.

All nine big guns are pointed at the beach. It's getting lighter. There are yellow streaks in the cloud blanket.

5:30 A.M. It's come!

This is the bombardment. My ears pound. Our big guns are just under me and every time they go off—as just then—I jump and the ship jolts.

We all have cotton in our ears, but it is noisy just the same and we feel the hot blast on our faces.

We crouched behind the rail for the first one and are bolder now. We will pound the beach for an hour, picking up where the bombers quit.

Enemy shore batteries are ineffectual so far. They produce only geysers of water.

I hear the crunch of our neighbors' big guns. We all are pounding away for miles off the coast.

Here is the picture:

Dawn is breaking. There's more light every second. The sea is calm as a lake. The sky is mostly overcast.

By moving around the semi-circular bridge, I can see two-thirds of the horizon. We are in a sort of bay. We have moved in and the landing craft are coming in.

Dawn found us on Germany's doormat like the milk bottle.

The big ship to our left is firing tracers and they go in like pitched baseballs.

The whole bowl of sky echoes with our din. While we are concerned mostly with our own beach, we see tracers from other ships zipping ashore, see the flame from guns and a few seconds later, get the report.

I can see the flag waving at our mast and the long streaks of sun-touched cloud are like its stripes.

6 A.M. We bang away regularly like a thunderbolt worked by clockwork. The individual drama goes on all around. Somehow I never imagined it would be like this.

I thought it would be all a motion picture close-up. Actually, the immensity of sky and land dwarfs everything and you have to strain at the binoculars to see what is going on. I guess that is true of all battles.

If you are right in them, you can't figure what is happening.

But here are details:

An airplane laying a smoke screen for the landing just crashed. It looked as though it was hit in midair.

We are smashing in salvos at specific objectives and every time the guns go off the whole ship jumps and so do I.

A sound like milk cans is the shells being ejected from the five-inch batteries.

Our third salvo seems to have silenced one shore battery and we have moved to the next.

Now at 6:30 the landing craft should be hitting the beaches.

It is H-hour.

7 A.M. An American destroyer has been hit. It is heartbreaking to watch. The enemy fire splashes again and again. We shift our guns to knock off a battery.

A whaleboat leaves the destroyer.

Distress signals blink. A cloud of steam or smoke appears. A sister ship moves in right under the fire to pick up survivors.

Forty-five minutes later, the same din, the same animated scene.

A line of ships goes ashore. And empties are coming back.

A little French village with a spire nestles at the cliffs that look so like England across the Channel.

The drama has shifted from ship to harbor.

Things probably are moving fast, but it seems amazingly slow.

8 A.M. The sun shines gloriously. This probably is the best weather ever picked for an invasion—cloudy at night, bright by day now.

Our destroyers are practically walking on the beach, blazing into the cliffs as they move. We get radio word that one emplacement in concrete and the destroyer can't rack it. Our turrets sweep around.

Bang they go! Now a second time!

It is almost impossible to stand still, so great is the will to urge that long new line of invasion barges forward. Any one of the runny little amphibious beetles makes a story in itself.

It is like picking a particular ant.

Here in my binoculars I see an ugly squarish little craft making for shore with a lace of foam in front. It reaches the beach, the white disappears, it waddles up. I can't see, but its guns are probably going.

On the sands are hulks of other boats—motionless. They have hit mines.

9 A.M. No sleep—and a plate of beans for breakfast. It seems as though it must be afternoon.

Our radio has just picked up a German radiocast denying any troops are ashore. They seem thoroughly befuddled.

They say we made an attempt at Dunkerque and Le Havre. It seems a complete surprise.

Noon. Everything depends on speed. We have a landing, but we had that at Dieppe. Can we stick and can we go in fast enough to pinch off Cherbourg?

The whole drama is that line of ships. What it looks like is an ant line.

One line moves an army with crumbs and another returns to the crust. Here they are moving like that—little black ships, but all sizes.

A big one with a whole rear end that unfolds on the beach or a little one with a truck or two. They are all pretty squat and ugly— and the most beautiful sight I ever saw.

Yet it looks so quiet and peaceful. The splashes of water look like top splashes. Except when the splashes come in our direction.

There is one persistent battery that keeps trying to get us. It quiets after we fire and then comes on again after we shift to something else.

One earlier target we got in the first salvo.

2 P.M. I have just had on the head phones in the communications room. Shore groups with walkie-talkies are telling the parent control what they find.

It is all in a jargon of communications nomenclature. The parent voice calls out loudly and commandingly through the static.

More and more crackling static. Suddenly a quiet voice identifies itself.

"I am pinned down," says the quiet voice. "I am between machine-gun and pill-box cross fire." So that's it.

And now our radio leaves him.

A station reports that "firing from the bluff is continuing." It reports that the water obstacles are being taken care of. The incoming tide is helping.

That's what a battle sounds like under the scream of shells. We can't really tell what's happening. We are in it, but we might be losing for all we know.

4 P.M. Well, things are going well. We know because we have just heard a BBC broadcast! BBC seems delighted. It says reports are splendid. O.K. by us.

That far bluff is still spitting fire, though, and the elusive shore battery has splashed us with water. What does BBC advise?

But we are so weary now we are going to sleep on our feet anyway.

6 P.M. Six of the clumsy LCM's go by—the most angular craft ever built. Their front end, that ought to be high, is low, and vice versa. Not even its mother could love it. They are like wallowing watering troughs.

They carry a five-man crew and will lug a tank ashore. They come in abreast closer than anything so far. Those six, somehow, epitomize the whole affair. I can pick out figures—almost faces—with my glasses. To the men on shore they must look like ministering angels.

I can see the burly captain and even at this distance notice his arms akimbo. He is contemptuously looking at our towering warship and staring it out of counterance.

Then he sweeps the battle with uncomplimentary eye—the very image of a Hudson River tugboat captain. If I talked to him, I bet he would have a tough Jersey accent and would take backtalk from nobody, see—not from the Germans, nor from a warship.

We let go an eight-inch gun salvo over his right ear that must at least establish a feeling of joint respect.

All the time I have been typing, the ship has been blasting ahead. The typewriter jumps with the jolt.

Midnight. We are, I think, winning the battle. And here is the place to stop because I have just seen the most glorious sight of all. The paratroopers have come in. It was a scene of almost unbelievable romance and it probably revolutionizes warfare.

Right out of the east came suddenly a bigger and bigger roar of sound, as if all the planes in England were droning, and then here appeared line on line of big bombers, each towing a glider.

They curved over us in a mighty crescent and sped over the shore into the sunset.

Then, as the first batch passed and the second appeared, the bombers of the first were coming back again singly, this time having released their gliders filled with crack troops to reinforce the weary invasion companies that have battled all day.

Just at 11 o'clock, a new batch, even bigger than before, skimmed over in the late dusk of double summer time. They were so close you could see the rope that bound plane and glider taut as a fiddle string—all in perfect formation.

In each of the three earlier flights, there were many planes and as many gliders. Just now there are even more.

It was a fantasy out of the future.

Last week, when correspondents on the battle fleet were briefed, we were told something about airborne troops. It seemed fantastic— the number was so large. But I am beginning to believe it.

What a sight that overhead reinforcement must have been to the muddy, blackened men below. It had the dash and elan of a cavalry charge.

After seeing the things I have in the past 24 hours, I know one thing—the road may be tough, but we can't lose.

. . . .

RICHARD L. STROUT

Richard L. Strout, called the dean of the Washington press corps, grew up in Brooklyn, New York. After graduating from Harvard University with a degree in economics, he served in the Army during World War I. His first job in journalism was with a small newspaper in Sheffield, England. After returning to the states, he worked for less than a week at the Boston *Post* before joining the *Christian*

Science Monitor. Three years later he went to Washington, D.C., where he stayed until his death in 1990.

In addition to his authoritative reporting for the *Monitor*, Strout took over the *New Republic's* then-anonymous TRB column in 1943. From his first column came the famous quote "When a man dies, he wants to die for something important," about U.S. soldiers at war. He was widely celebrated for his physical descriptions (he particularly focused on the hair of various political figures).

A collection of his columns was compiled into a book entitled *TRB: Views and Perspectives on the Presidency.* His other book, *Farewell to the Model T,* was cowritten with his friend E. B. White and published in 1936.

Strout continued to write for the *Monitor* for more than sixty years, and for the *New Republic* for more than forty years, earning him a 1978 Pulitzer Prize for lifetime achievement. He retired at the age of eighty-three.

Glider on a Rooftop Captures
First French Town

· · · · · · · · · · · ·

BY
RICHARD L. TOBIN

WAR CORRESPONDENT OF THE NEW YORK *HERALD TRIBUNE*

SUPREME HEADQUARTERS, ALLIED EXPEDITIONARY FORCE, June 9, 1944—This is the story not only of the greatest air-borne operation in history, but also of unexampled Allied planning and unqualified success. It also is the story of an American colonel who made his first parachute jump on the night before D-Day, how he hung in a French tree, heard the cows moo in the silence of a northern French meadow and couldn't tell a German soldier from an American because of those new-fangled Yankee helmets.

The story was told to a spellbound assembly of war correspondents at supreme headquarters today.

During his story he told how the town of Ste. Mère-Église, on the Cherbourg peninsula, was captured by 7 A.M. on D-Day because an American glider landed on top of a French farmhouse and the Germans inside were too astonished and frightened to fight.

In the beginning the colonel, a small, baldish man with ribbons in three rows across his left breast, dropped with his men because someone had to be in charge, and anyway the colonel wanted to see what was going on. Actually, he was A.W.O.L., but his commanding officers more than forgave him later.

The colonel and his men took off at 11 o'clock Monday night.

He was one of many hundreds of specialists carried in towed gliders. His glider train got a bit off its course in the dark, but on the whole the liaison was excellent. The specific point of attack for this airborne squadron was the Cherbourg peninsula, well behind the beaches.

The colonel was making his first parachute jump. The jerk of his 'chute gave him a terrible jolt, but then he floated so gently that he did not realize he had come near French earth until he found his 'chute tangled above him in a tree.

"A parachutist is unsatisfied," said the colonel, "unless his parachute is tight enough so that you grunt three times. So I had the devil's own time getting out of the parachute in the tree. We knew we were in enemy territory and that we were the first folks there. So when I saw a man crawling along the ground I didn't shout at him and start wiggling, because I couldn't tell an American helmet from a German in the semi-dark.

"Finally, I cut myself away, threw away my own helmet, because I had a hard time hearing with it on, and followed the trail of discarded parachutes to the rendezvous. The cows were mooing and chewing their cud, just as if there wasn't any invasion going on."

The colonel had seen five hundred parachutes in the air at once from his own landing force. As many of these men and anti-tank guns and jeeps and arms of many calibers as had been landed in the area and could be brought together assembled their massive power, these many miles behind the beachhead that was still untouched by Allied feet.

The moon was bright at 3 A.M., but by 3:30 when other rendezvous were to be made with glider troops, the weather had deteriorated. It was so dark that the new-coming gliders could not see the signals placed below by the pathfinders.

In spite of this handicap, the gliders hit landings promptly on schedule, making remarkable noises when they piled up.

But the astonishing thing was how little damage was done to the men and the war machinery inside. Five gliders in a row were smashed in landing within the colonel's sight, yet no man was hurt nor a piece of equipment put cut of action. The parachutists were disappointed that the Nazis in the neighborhood gave in so easily and were so few in number.

Hundreds of big troop-carrying gliders set out from their bases in Great Britain in the hours before D-Day officially began, and they have reinforced and landed behind the enemy ever since. They were pulled by airplane tugs, pulled high over the choppy sea and the coast of the Cherbourg peninsula, where they were to drop their men to turn the earth for sea-borne planting at dawn.

It was one of these troop gliders that, failing to find a landing that had been selected by advance parachutists, plopped directly on top of a French thatch-roofed house at Ste. Mère-Église, and led to the capture of this middle-peninsula village. Troops and jeeps and artillery spilled out of the broken glider as it quivered between the chimney and the side of a hill. The noises were so incredible and the amount of equipment and man power so immense that the Germans billeted inside came out with their hands up.

Thus it was that Ste. Mère-Église became the first French town to fall into Allied hands at 7 o'clock on D-Day morning, even before the beaches had been stormed or the shore batteries reduced by Allied battleships, cruisers and bombers.

There were 2,500 men in one field, ready to botch up German coastal defense from the rear and to move toward the sea shore to meet and guide the incoming landing parties. Of these 2,500 air-borne soldiers, only four to five percent had been injured or killed getting there.

The colonel and his boys moved from place to place, gumming up German liaison and making a nuisance of themselves. In one French farmhouse they asked for something to drink and the happy Frenchman brought out his best white wine. He also brought milk, fresh from his cows, but the Americans protested that the milk was warm. They like their drinks iced.

As the sky broke into morning, the glider soldiers moved to meet their comrades wading ashore to direct them to places already seized by air-borne arms. It had been the greatest air-borne operation in history. It had insured the invasion of Europe.

. . . .

RICHARD L. TOBIN

Richard Tobin, a native of Chicago, became managing editor of the *Michigan Daily* before his senior year at the University of Michigan. He was a sportswriter for the South Bend (Ind.) NEWS TIMES before moving to the New York *Herald Tribune*. In 1944 he went as a correspondent to England where he wrote the book *Invasion Journal*. He also wrote *Reporters Tell the World*.

Ernie Pyle Thought He Would Die on D-Day

. . . .

BY

GORDON GAMMACK

DES MOINES *TRIBUNE* STAFF WRITER

LONDON, ENGLAND, June, 1944—Ernie Pyle had a deep fear that he would be killed in the invasion of Europe.

"I have an awful feeling that I won't live through this one," he said to me one day. "It's a terrible feeling. I can't sleep, and it is like a constant weight, night and day."

Unlike a few correspondents who have a reckless love for the thrill of combat, Ernie usually dreads it—but goes ahead because it is his job. However, he said not until this time did he have a feeling that he would not survive.

I knew Ernie's assignment, and the part that frightened him. It was the first two days he worried about, and now they are past.

Several days before the invasion, I had dinner with Ernie, Don Whitehead of the Associated Press and Duke Shoop of the Kansas City Star. We created a mild sensation with the restaurant manager, his wife and staff, with the ruse that Pyle was Dr. Pyle, a famous American professor of psychology, and that we three were his prize pupils and we were having a reunion.

The manager beamed and gave us the best of everything and Pyle gave an impromptu lecture on psychology.

Next day, Ernie planned to take us to see the famous Peter Pan statue in London Park which he likes the best of anything in London. But the next morning he left hurriedly. He was off to cover the big show.

. . . .

GORDON GAMMACK

Gordon Gammack began his career as a reporter, correspondent, and columnist at the Des Moines *Register and Tribune* after working briefly for the Hartford *Courant*. As a correspondent he traveled to battlefronts in North Africa, Italy, France, and Germany and later to fronts in the Korean and Vietnam wars. Although he was born, raised, and educated in New England, his reverent tributes to the Iowan soldier fighting in World War II and the everyday Iowan at home earned Gammack many journalistic honors. His column, which started shortly after World War II, was first called "Gammack Says," then "See Here!" In addition, he was a broadcaster for the Des Moines station KRNT Radio and TV.

Gammack died at age sixty-five in 1974.

Nightmare over Yawata

· · · · · · · · · · · ·

BY

CLAY GOWRAN

CHICAGO *TRIBUNE* PRESS SERVICE

ABOARD A B-29 SUPER FORTRESS OVER THE YELLOW SEA, June 16, 1944—The Super Fortress "Nightmare" has just carried me away from the flak spangled, searchlight-swept skies over Yawata, Japan.

Behind us is a blazing cauldron of fire which was Japan's largest iron and steel works producing one-fifth of her high-grade steel. In the longest raid in the history of the war, United States super bombers have just struck for the second time at the sacred mainland of Japan.

The "Nightmare" is one of the Super Fortresses belonging to the secret 20th bomber command, which for more than a year has been grooming planes and crews for what happened last night and early today.

It was worth waiting for—those four minutes we spent in our bombing run, pinioned by a half dozen searchlights and tossed and rolled by countless bursts of heavy anti-aircraft guns. So was the sight of the great plant belching great surges of flame hundreds of feet into the air.

This probably will be a very unpolished story, but who could remember all the details of a trip to hell and back at 200 miles an hour? I am writing on the corner of the navigator's table, seated on a pineapple juice crate, with a hooded black-out light for my only illumination.

Ahead of us stretch more than a thousand miles of danger and hazards before we reach our home base. We've stirred up a hornet's nest, now we have to go home through it.

To watch the crew of this plane you would think that bombing Japan was just an ordinary day's business. The plane's commander is 28 year old Lieut. Col. Robert B. Sullivan of Los Angeles, who looks much older because of the nine hundred combat hours he flew in a B-17 during seven months of service in the South Pacific.

The co-pilot is Lieut. Robert H. Marshall, 24, of Champaign, Ill., who is calm despite the fact that this is his first raid, although he has been flying for the Army for three years.

We have just finished fighting the Japs and now we face another bitter battle—the fight to get home, to make our gas cover the hundreds of miles of Yellow Sea and occupied China which lie between us and safety. The pilots nurse every extra foot out of every gallon of gas.

Behind them Flight Officer Calvin Hagins, 26, of Johnstown, Pa., our flight engineer, glues his eyes to his instrument panel watching engine temperatures, air speed, and his other precious indicators. Beside me sits Capt. Reimar Peterson, 25, of Gunnison, Utah, checking and double checking his navigator's charts.

Others of the "Nightmare's" crew are Lieut. Walter Dinnison, 27, of Pierce, Idaho, bombardier; Lieut. Eddie Williams, 22, York, S.C., and Lieut. Maurice Blum, 27, New York, whose occupations are secret; Sergeants David Miewski, Mount Vernon, N.Y.; Melvin Breshears, Wirt, Okla.; Chapman, Bloomville, N.Y., and Dan Yahnke, Culver City, Cal., gunners, and Tech. Sgt. Salvatore Tambascio, Newton, Mass., radioman.

Correspondents and the crews of the Super Fortresses had been waiting for weeks for the action. Finally, yesterday noon it came. We were called to a rough briefing hut surrounded by sentries. Col. Richard Carmichael, 31, of Austin, Tex., and Olean, N.Y., commander of the group to which I was assigned, gave it to us simply.

"Gentlemen, you have been waiting for a long time for someone to say, 'Tonight we attack Japan,' " he said. "That time has come.

Tonight your target is the Imperial iron and steel works at Yawata on the north tip of Kyushu. There you will find tremendous coke ovens, huge rolling mills and great open hearth furnaces. It is the largest works of its kind in Japan. Destroy it."

From maps, we learned more about Yawata. It lay on the sickle-shaped Maeda anchorage of important Wakamatsu harbor. Around it were railroad tracks for supplying it, and the anchorage itself provided facilities for ships bringing in raw materials and embarking with finished war products. We would make our approach from the northwest, striking inland across the anchorage and the tracks and drop our loads on the works itself. It was a target we could not miss, open hearth furnaces to the left, converters to the right and great coking ovens in the dead center of our target run. We hit it!

Late yesterday, in dreary, rainy weather, we climbed aboard the "Nightmare" at its China base. Probably the biggest thrill, next to the actual bombing, was getting the "Nightmare's" far more than 100,000 pounds off the soggy runway built for her and the others of her brood by 95,000 Chinese laborers.

As Sullivan gunned her west, we sat taut in our positions. She gained speed slowly. Marshall's voice came over the interphone, "Eighty miles an hour, ninety, one hundred, one hundred ten." A warning cry came from Hagins, "Cylinder head temperature, No. 2 engine, approaching danger point." With only a few hundred feet of runway left, "Nightmare" lifted, bounced, lifted again, and staggered off the end of the air strip.

A word about the "Nightmare" herself. The crew gave her the name because they say she is destined to keep the enemy awake. On her streamlined nose is the body of a beautiful, unclad girl. But in place of a girl's head is the ghastliest horse's head imaginable, with foaming mouth and ugly red eyes.

The flight to Japan was uneventful. Gaining altitude, we swung almost due east and settled down to the long grind as night swept down over China's terraced hillsides. Tambascio nudged me, pointed to a house fly crawling across his desk, and said: "He doesn't know where he's going. Sure picked a hell of a wagon for a ride." I watched the fly. I could sympathize with him. I began to ponder what I was doing here.

During almost eight dreary hours to the target we listened to music obligingly transmitted by Radios Tokyo and Saigon. Shortly after reaching the China coast we picked up Radio Shanghai. Apparently the Japs never knew we were coming because Tokyo stayed on the air during the entire raid.

About 10 P.M. western China time we reached the Yellow sea and saw lighthouse beacons flashing off the right wing. Then hours later came a sharp bank to the right. We had reached tiny Okino Island, off the coast of large Kyushu, our destination.

We caught our first glimpse of what lay in store. A red ball of fire ten miles inland showed that other bombers already had visited the steel works. Searchlights and bursting anti-aircraft shells combed the skies.

Dinnison's voice came on the interphone: "Navigator, how long to the target?" Peterson answered: "Eleven minutes."

We closed our prominent lights and the fire ceased, then the searchlights came on again, reaching for us with long tentacles of silver. The fire at the plant was plainly visible. It seemed to have spread over a vast acreage. Occasionally, a blast would send flames leaping hundreds of feet toward us.

"Steady on target run," called Dinnison, crouched over the bombsight.

Standing between the two pilots, I watched the searchlights. Two seemed sure to get us, but at the last moment we passed through untouched.

Suddenly, our plexiglass nose glowed as a light caught us. Immediately, five others pinned us, then the guns opened up. Unable to deviate from the bombing run, we had to sit there and take it. Ahead, I saw at least a dozen heavy guns flashing. Red tracers flicked by. The sharp crack of shells bursting around us smacked our eardrums and the ship quivered and tossed in the turmoil of the barrage. With a shower of sparks and flame something hit us.

For ages we held our course, the pilots crouched in the cockpit to keep from being blinded by those damned lights which never lost us. Finally Sullivan's voice came: "Are bombs away, Dinnison?" No answer. Again "Are bombs away?"

Then came Dinnison's voice: "Yes, sir. Sorry, my interphone came undone." "O.K., let's get the hell out of here," said Sullivan.

With the lights still on us, we pulled up sharply, then dropped in a steep bank. Reluctantly, the lights left us and the guns quieted.

Nose down, we poured on coal and roared away from Yawata and its fires. Occasional new bursts of flame showed other super-bombers at work behind us, hammering Japan where it hurts most.

Breshears at the tail guns reported lurid explosions and towering flames from the steel works still were visible one hundred miles from the target. Every few moments great blossoms of fire would bloom skyward.

But we had worries. Worriedly chewing his lip, Peterson moved his pencil along the line of our homing course. In the dim light I watched the five cent wooden pencil cross the Yellow sea and the coast of China, wend its way slowly through occupied China and finally mark an "X" far, far away across the map. That marked our base.

In turns, the rest of us sipped pineapple juice and munched on the inevitable Spam sandwiches.

As we ate there, in the depths of the Super Fortress, we talked about the raid. The biggest question was: "Why were there no Jap fighter planes around?" We concluded the big American bombers had caught Japan napping and were gone before protection could be sent up.

As we sat, and talked, and dozed, "Nightmare" droned on and on westward into the night.

(The following was written shortly after our return to the base.)

The remaining night hours provided slight relaxation for "Nightmare's" exhausted crew. The plane was wrapped in stormy weather and, barring collision with another Super Fortress or a wandering Jap interceptor, we were fairly safe. But dawn brought new worries.

Daybreak caught us still deep in Jap held China and we waited gloomily for the swarms of Jap fighters we thought surely would come. A few minutes later Dinnison gave a strangled cry over the interphone and pointed down. There, only about 6,000 feet below, was a Jap airfield.

But apparently the Japs still were unaware of us or ignoring the fact we had blown their biggest steel works off the map. Not once during the gruelling trip home did we sight an enemy ship.

Finally, worn out by the weight of the heavy combat gear we wore, we began shedding. There was a lot to shed—flak helmets, calk vests, life vests, parachutes, first aid kits, canteens, jungle kits, flight helmets. We had gone in on Japan prepared to walk or row back if necessary.

About 6 A.M. Marshall crawled back into the navigator's compartment for a moment. At the controls since the previous afternoon without a minute off, he looked like a sleepwalker. Hanging at his dials and switches seemed to have aged him years.

Shortly before 8 A.M., hoping for the best, we started to let down through heavy clouds. Again the "Nightmare's" luck held. Just as we broke out of the overcast and picked up the grayish, rainswept hills of China, Tambascio suddenly jumped to life at his radio. A few minutes later he crawled forward to Sullivan with a big smile across his tired Italian face. He had contacted the base and been given homing directions.

We knew where we were. An air field, hot coffee, ham and eggs were waiting for us a few miles farther on.

The "Nightmare" had taken her thirteen men to Japan and brought us home again.

. . . .

CLAY GOWRAN

Clay Gowran was an award-winning member of the Chicago *Tribune* staff for more than thirty-four years. After earning a degree in journalism from Northwestern University, he worked at the Evanston (Ill.) *Review* and the city news bureau of Chicago before joining the *Tribune* as a general assignment reporter. In 1942 Gowran went abroad as a war correspondent, covering activities in South America, the South Pacific (for which he won the *Tribune* Edward Scott Beck Award for excellence for his account of the attack in the Solomon

Islands), Japan, Italy, and Greece. After the war he was a foreign correspondent in the Middle East.

After serving several years as a radio and television editor, Gowran was appointed associate editor of the Chicago *Tribune* magazine in 1969. He died at age fifty-eight in 1972.

A Shell Through
the General's Window

· · · · · · · · · · · ·

BY

IRA WOLFERT

NORTH AMERICAN NEWSPAPER ALLIANCE

WITH THE U.S. INFANTRY, WEST OF ST. LO, July 1944—Everybody took his tone from the general, and this was a very quiet tone. A colonel strolled in from the front like somebody off Fifth Avenue with a handsome, leather-handled cane. I made exact note of their conversation after greetings were exchanged, and this is how it ran:

"Are they moving?" asked the general.

"Yes, sir. We captured three of them at this crossroad," said the colonel, putting his finger on a point of the map.

"Good; good," the general said. "That means we're moving all right."

He kept looking at the map a long time although he could see every coordinate on it in his mind with his eyes closed.

"Well," he said at last, "keep them moving. That is the thing. Keep them moving."

When anybody came into the farmhouse headquarters, the general asked the same question. First he'd ask: Are they moving? Then he'd ask: How do you know they are moving? He wanted to be sure you weren't just trying to make him feel good by yessing him.

Across the little entryway from the general's room there was a room full of staff officers working at one of those long, French, wooden kitchen tables. Radios, tuned in on the front, were outside the back windows and you could hear the young high, excited American voices talking their strange jargon. Artillery spotters were talking to their guns; airplanes were talking to one another and to ground bases; and the infantry was talking, too, calling for mortars, saying where the enemy is and where his mortars are.

Then the infantry ran into three German tanks bunkered down and were waiting to mine them up and you could hear the fellows talking from cover, asking for something more than rifles to deal with the tanks.

Sometimes the German infantry waves a white flag when they see tanks nowadays, but our fellows lay low and hope for the best. Soon some of our tanks started coming down the country lanes. There were other tanks to the left of them and the commander there was saying to his tanks:

"There are friends coming down the lane; big friends with doughs; big friends with doughs; coming down the lane to our right; to our right; don't shoot at them; don't shoot at them; now make sure of that—not to shoot, you guys, not to shoot."

Then the tank commander, moving on three German tanks, said:

"Off the air, please. I can't spare the air. Get off the damn air. Get off; get off, please!"

The general heard this and grinned. "I like a man who knows what he wants and goes for it," he said.

The tank commander spent a long time moving his tanks through the trees to get into position against the Germans. The general went into his room to telephone back to Lieut. Col. Richard Marr, of Oak Park, Ill. I stood alongside him. "Well," the general was saying, "there's still lots of the fog of war around here."

Then I heard a funny sound. I don't remember what it was—just something that attracted my attention—and I looked across the little entryway to the doorless room where the staff officers were working and saw a hot white and orange fire flicker by the window sill and leap up into the room.

Why, that's a high explosive, I thought; just like that, and I stood stunned. Then I heard a big whamming bang and saw a cloud of dust, and the dust flew up my nose with the force of gravel. The dust flew way high up into my head.

I didn't know what to do, so I just stood, and I wasn't even sure what had happened. Then I heard the general say over the telephone in his soft, quiet voice:

"Just a minute, Dick, a shell just came in the window and it's noisy here."

There were chairs crashing in the next room and there was the spattering sound of plaster falling and the sound of people scrambling. Then there was quiet for a moment and there was only dust to see—a whole acrid pall of it—and only the general's voice could be heard saying quietly over the telephone something about which battalions had moved where and what kind of fire they were up against.

After that the screaming began—a fellow saying, "Oh, oh!" bringing the sound up from way down deep in the bottom of his guts; and another saying, "Oh, my Holy God!" over and over; and a third was just screaming unintelligibly.

"I am sorry, Dick," the general said. "I will have to hang up now and call you back later."

Nobody knew which way to turn. We were sure more shells would be coming and you could see men standing all over, moving their arms aimlessly and turning aimlessly, but held quiet by the iron quiet of the general who moved with deliberate slowness into the next room. There were two officers lying on the floor there and a third sitting on the floor holding the stump of one leg up. The shell had taken his leg off clean about halfway down from the knee and he was looking at it and groaning from the pit of his stomach.

The shell was from one of those three German tanks whose end we had been listening to shape up over the radio. It had come right in the window of the room and had gone right through the sill.

It had been an armor-piercing shell, and the sparks it had struck going through some fancy iron work on the window and through the sill made me think it was a high explosive shell. Then the shell, careening downward, had sheered through the leg of the staff table, had hit the floor and had skipped, and as it rose it took off the captain's leg as he sat at the table. Then it went through the back wall and into a little closet-like room there.

Lieut. William Cool, of West Pittston, Pa., had been resting on a mattress in that room and his back had been to the wall when the shell came in just above him and dropped just beyond him on the mattress, covering him with a large chunk of wall but leaving him unhurt.

The two other officers lying on the floor of the room in which the captain's leg was shattered—a major and a captain—had been hit by rocks or splinters of wood. The only one badly off, however, was the captain who had lost his leg, and he kept looking at the stump of it. His mind was still clear, and the shock of the amputation had been so sudden that it had not yet reached his mind.

"If you just stop looking at it," I told him, "and lie down."

He didn't seem to hear me and I touched him on the shoulder and said it again. But he didn't pay any attention. He just groaned, "oh, oh!" bringing each "oh!" up from the bottom of his guts and he just looked at the stump. His face was wild and the white flesh of it strained wildly as if it were trying to run away from what its eyes were seeing. It was plain now that the captain understood exactly what had happened to him, and he was groaning, "oh!" over a new, terrible future that opened so unexpectedly before him.

The general sent for doctors and told everybody to get away from the windows and then he picked up the telephone and went back to the war.

"Yes, Dick," I heard him say. "Three were hit, but only one badly. Poor fellow."

He talked above the groans from the next room, but his voice remained quiet and courtly as he told Col. Marr how things were going.

When I went back again to the radios out in the back, after the wounded had been taken away, the tank fight was ended. The three German tanks had been destroyed and our tanks were moving on to something else.

A handful of men were grouped about the radios, listening solemnly, and one radio was saying: "This is six. This is six. All negats; all negats and all doughs, I see a white flag. Do not fire. They are coming out to surrender. Do not fire on them! They are waving a white some damn thing, flag or drawers, or something. I see it. Do not fire over."

"Well, well," said the general, bustling among us, "this is like listening to a football game over the radio, isn't it?"

He looked right at me, and I thought the hell it is. Then the general looked away from me and at the men around the radio. He was smiling brightly, and suddenly all the solemn faces began to loosen and shorten and then began to smile. You could see the echo of the captain's groans going out of their minds and you could see their spirits warming again to the fight.

Chasing the Buzz-Bombs

. . . .

BY

WILLIAM RANDOLPH HEARST, JR.

CORRESPONDENT, NEW YORK *JOURNAL-AMERICAN*

AN AIRFIELD, SOMEWHERE IN ENGLAND, July 3, 1944—Last week, while thinking unprintable thoughts about the "buzz-bombs" the Germans have been sending over Southern England recently, my eye caught a paragraph in a newspaper to the effect that an RAF pilot had nicknamed them "doodlebugs."

Typical of the English, I thought, to make light of such a serious business. Typical of them, too, to give new gadgets a nickname.

They always refer to the Germans, whom they have reason to hate with passion, as "Jerries," which is more like an undesirable relative than an enemy.

The English call their terrifically fast light bomber a "Mosquito."

Suddenly I got an idea.

Along with everyone else who has ever been annoyed by these things, I longed to get back at them in some way.

Supposedly, only very fast fighters can catch them. But if I could get a fast enough ship and cruise around the Channel area through which they most frequently pass—

I grabbed a phone and called Maj. Tex McCrary. He is famous for cutting red tape and handling tough jobs.

"Have the Americans got anything that will fill the bill?" I asked him, telling him briefly what I had in mind.

"Elliott Roosevelt is your man," he said. "His outfit has just the type of plane you need."

I called Elliott, and in a little while went out to see him at his headquarters in the country.

"That clinches it," he said. "Be at —— airdrome at 8 o'clock tomorrow morning. I will have our courier plane meet you and fly you up to my field, and you can start from there. In the meantime, I will work out the details."

I thanked him profusely, meaning every word of it.

We took off next morning in a drizzling rain, but when I arrived they told me it would be impossible to do it that day.

My pilot was to be Lt. Richard N. Geary, Santa Clara, Cal. In addition to our Air Force wings, he wore those of the RAF over his right breast pocket.

He had gone to Canada early in 1941 and joined the RCAF. In 1942 he switched to the American Air Force, but he remained attached to the RAF night fighter group. He had only recently transferred to Elliott's group.

Although only 24, his experience with the RAF made him perfectly suited to the work we were going to do.

Next afternoon we took off for an RAF fighter field on the edge of the Channel.

The weather was better down there, and we expected to get in a little hunting that afternoon, but in landing we blew a tire.

There being no other planes of that type operating near by, we phoned back to our base and the commanding officer said he would send down a new ship by dawn the next morning.

We left a call for 5 o'clock and when we got out on the field the next morning our new ship was waiting for us.

It was fairly light now so we took off.

Our plan of operations was to cruise around several thousand feet above the level at which pilotless "buzz-bombs" generally come in, listening in by radio to the flying control officer as he directed the fighters, then joining the chase.

Fighters passed us in both directions. Suddenly, behind Dick's shoulder, I saw aircraft diving.

We banked steeply, and there below us I saw the little thing, its tail aglow, going like a bat out of hell.

As we dove on it, a couple of more fighters did likewise.

Our air speed indicator showed 360 miles per hour.

As I watched, I saw the fighter closest to it hit the "buzz-bomb" a glancing blow. It made a little flash. They call it a strike.

On we went. Suddenly came a spurt of orange flame. It had been hit.

A couple of seconds later, the bomb proper struck the ground with a terrific flash, and a huge cloud of smoke slowly rose from the field where it had fallen.

We could hear the boys talking over the radio.

"Good show—wizard," I picked up on my earphones.

We now turned and resumed our patrol and only then realized how far we had come.

The chase itself had only lasted a few minutes, but at that speed you cover a lot of ground.

The fighters returned to their bases, but our ship had sufficient gas for several hours, so we went back and waited for the next "buzz-bomb."

A few minutes went by, and again we heard the voice control officer directing us to a location further down the coast.

We were both peering outside trying to get a glimpse of it, but instead we saw flak coming up and bursting all around us.

Apparently the little thing had slipped beneath us, and guns were firing away at it.

It was a funny feeling having your own guns shooting at us, so we banked around and got away in a hurry.

This time we were doing close to 400 miles per hour. The little thing was about a quarter of a mile ahead. We could see it quite distinctly.

Two fighters were on its tail, another just off our wing.

Dick had the throttle wide open, and the plane's motors were literally screaming.

We kept off a little to the side, the better to see the show.

Someone must have scored a hit, for it slowed up, enabling us to pull alongside it.

The pilotless "doodlebug" was now only about 100 yards off our right wing on my side.

As I looked out of my window, I could see flashes from the fighters' guns pecking away at it.

It was probably one of the most exciting moments of my life.

I could see it quite distinctly. There it was, the bomb itself, with its wings attached, and above it a little cigarette holder—shaped jet propulsion mechanism.

Even as I watched it, one of the fighters hit it.

The thing suddenly banked sharply toward us!

There was no time or need for consultation on strategy.

Dick pulled the plane up and then banked it vertically over to the left.

The bomb passed underneath us on its downward last journey.

We kept banking around steeply to keep it in view.

Down it went, and we saw the great flash it made as it exploded.

Boy, what a kick it was, far more exciting than any other kind of hunting in the world.

Added to the thrill of the chase, and the spectacle of the thing being destroyed, is the good feeling you get in the knowledge that, by knocking it down out here in the open country, you probably have saved the lives of innocent people and their homes from destruction.

On top of it all, I could not help feeling pleased with myself at having been the first war correspondent to have actually participated in this newest British sport, "doodlebug hunting."

In the language of the RAF, it was a "wizard show," I thought, as we banked around and headed for home.

· · · · · · · · · · ·

WILLIAM RANDOLPH HEARST, JR.

William Randolph Hearst, Jr., son of the newspaper magnate of the same name, began working at New York–based, Hearst-owned newspapers at a very young age. His journalistic career began at the New York *American* as a police reporter, then as publisher in 1936. From 1943 to 1945 he was a war correspondent for the *Journal-American*, where he became acquainted with colleagues Kingsbury Smith and Frank Conniff. In 1955 the three of them wrote a groundbreaking series based on several exclusive interviews with the leaders of the Soviet government that won the Pulitzer Prize for international reporting.

The same year Hearst was elected editor in chief of the chain of Hearst newspapers. He wrote his weekly column, "Editor's Note," for nearly forty years. He was eighty-five when he died in New York in 1993.

The Carpet Slippered "Frenchy"

. . . .

BY

JOHN M. CARLISLE

STAFF CORRESPONDENT OF THE DETROIT *NEWS*

WITH THE AMERICAN FORCES, LE MANS, FRANCE, Aug. 13, 1944 (delayed)—The boys in I Company call him "Frenchy," and they like him. They are, in fact, very proud of him. He goes everywhere with them now, since that first dark night in Le Mans.

He goes everywhere with them when he is not "out chasing snipers." He goes everywhere in his battered French helmet, his Garand rifle, his faded blue trousers, his very dirty khaki shirt—and in his carpet slippers. The last we heard the boys from I Company were out "scrounging around" through the battalion trying to find "our Frog some salvaged GI shoes."

The lieutenant speaks excellent French. He is the only one in I Company who can really talk to "Frenchy." So "Frenchy" follows him everywhere. They jabber away in French incessantly. The lieutenant once spent a few years in Paris, the old Paris of peace times. There was a pretty French gal, a very pretty gal. So the lieutenant got so he could parley-vous very well.

"Frenchy" and the lieutenant are now pals, though the lieutenant was very gruff with him the second day in Le Mans.

"What the hell," the lieutenant said, "are you still here?"

The Frenchman said he wanted to join the company.

"You can't join the company," the lieutenant said. "You are a very brave guy. You are swell, but you can't join the company. I can't put you on the rolls."

The next day "Frenchy" was still around. The lieutenant said, "You got to beat it out of here, 'Frenchy.'"

"Frenchy" looked very pained. Part of the company gathered around. They looked very pained. They liked this Frenchman. They had given him K rations. He got them water. They gave him a towel and soap and a razor. He saved them from being ambushed by snipers as they set up their camp.

The lieutenant looked very pained. He is a very smart young man, a college graduate. He finally settled it all, speaking very slowly in French.

"Now, lookit, Frenchy," he said, "I can't put you on the rolls, but if you hang around, I can't do anything about that either. Franco-American relations, n'est-ce pas?"

"Frenchy" caught on quickly.

"Where you go, mon capitaine," he said, "I go. To Paris, to Berlin. Maybe, back to America, maybe."

So I Company got a new recruit. The last time we saw a strapping master sergeant from Texas, he had a gang of GI Joes around him.

"Now, look, you guys," the sergeant was saying. "This Frog doesn't get any pay and he's one of us. How about putting into a kitty every month and giving him a GI's pay?"

The boys liked that. "Frenchy" will get paid.

"Frenchy" just sidled into the company that dark Tuesday night as it came slowly into town. It was very dark. The company came in slowly, sort of feeling its way in. There were other Yanks from the column coming in all over town. Some had come in earlier.

Some Detroit boys slept on the sidewalks in full gear that night. Soldiers like Pfc. Edward Krainick, 28 years old; Pvt. Bernard Lasko, 24; Pfc. Otto J. Gremel, 23; and Sgt. Bernard Driscoll, age 30.

"I aged 100 years going into Le Mans," Private Lasko said. "Everything was so quiet. We had been fighting the Jerries for days, after taking Mayenne. The suspense got me."

"Coming in," Pvt. Krainick said, "I crawled up to a Jerry truck.

"It was empty. I turned off the lights."

Pvt. Krainick had a grenade attached to his rifle, like so many advancing Yanks in the dark, on the alert for light Jerry tanks.

"I slept on the sidewalk next to a building," said Pvt. Lasko. "It was a bed of stone. But I never noticed it. Hadn't had much sleep out there on the road."

Other Michigan soldiers slept on the sidewalk that night, after fighting with the Yank column that won the town. Others like Pfc. George W. Scott, Jr., 20 years old, Detroit; Pfc. Melvin E. Olson, 32, of Pontiac; Pvt. J. D. Wade, 19, of Birmingham, a Bazooka man.

Still others like Pfc. Bruno G. Wisniewski, 21; and Pfc. Eugene Marszalek, 20, both of Detroit.

On the way into the city, a Nazi officer jumped up with an automatic pistol. Pfc. Scott killed him with his Browning automatic. Pfc. Marszalek had wiped out a pocket of Jerries earlier with a few well thrown grenades.

And still earlier in the day, Pvt. Wade was drinking some fresh milk a French farmer had brought out on the road, sitting there in a jeep drinking it, when a shell hit the jeep in front of him. But Wade was uninjured—though he dropped the milk.

The boys in I Company had crept slowly into town in the dark, too. As they advanced into a main street, this Frenchman joined them in his carpet slippers. He had a pitcher of cool water. They drank it quickly. He got them another, and still another, and more.

There was a crack of a sniper's bullet. Down went a Yank and up came a medic. This fellow "Frenchy" grabbed the fallen Yank's rifle, and ran down the street and up into a house.

There was the sharp crack of a Garand. "Frenchy" threw a Jerry body out the second story window. Another sniper was dead. He came back to the company. He offered the Garand to a non-com.

"You keep it, 'Frenchy,'" the non-com said. "You're damned handy with it."

A corporal dug up a used bandolier of bullets for "Frenchy." Then he disappeared. Some of the boys were disgusted. "All he wanted was a gun," one of them said. "He's gone."

But "Frenchy" was not gone. He came back 10 minutes later with his helmet on.

At dawn, our boys got a good look at him. He had been shooting at snipers at night.

We found out that "Frenchy" was 23 and had been a sergeant in the French army and fought until France fell. He had been aching to get back into action ever since.

The Price Valya Paid

· · · · · · · · · · · · ·

BY

DAVID M. NICHOL

CHICAGO *DAILY NEWS* FOREIGN SERVICE

UMAN, RUSSIA, Aug. 1944—Valya Markarovna was a lighthearted girl of 18 when the Germans arrived here on August 2, 1941.

One whole lifetime has passed since then. She is trying now to find something new, something that will make her again a useful citizen. Laughter has not entirely left her brown eyes, but it comes more rarely. Her voice still has in it the soft musical tones of the Ukraine, but she is no longer at ease, except among her closest friends.

Valya's family was a simple, ordinary one. She lived with her father, mother, 13-year-old brother and 3-year-old sister in a two-room cottage near the city's outskirts. Her father was a baker, then a laborer in Uman's power station.

When she finished the standard seventh class in school, Valya began to study to be a telegrapher, working meanwhile as a railway guard. After the Germans arrived she did nothing—that is, until Feb. 12, 1942.

About 2 that morning a raiding party of Nazi police came and routed the family from its sleep. Valya was ordered to dress. They took her under escort to School Building No. 4 in the center of Uman, a building that was to become notorious as an interim detention home. Three hours later she was on her way to Germany as one of Hitler's "volunteer" workers.

She still shudders when talking about that trip. There were seventy persons in each box car, without benches, without food, without a suggestion of sanitary arrangements.

But on the train she met and became the close friend of another young woman whose experience was strangely to parallel her own. She was Galina Ivanovna Medvedchuk. Now 31, she had been with the first Kolkhoz Theater in Kiev for ten years. Her husband had been stage manager there. He had joined the Red Army when war broke out and she had gone to live with his parents in Uman. She has heard nothing from him since.

Valya speaks slowly, but Galina is a verbal machine gun. What follows is a composite of their stories as told to us as we consumed a dinner of rich Ukrainian food and for hours afterward.

Their road led through Lwow, then to Peremyshl, where Nazi guards checked their limited baggage and took away some warm clothing, saying, "You'll get all you need in Germany."

By this time there were about 1,000 persons on their train, they estimated, of whom only a handful were men. The rest were single women, up to 30, and wives without children.

Somewhere along the line they spent almost two weeks in a forest camp, with little food and subjected, Galina said, to constant maltreatment. She estimated that sixty girls died during that period from hunger and illness. They again were loaded on trains and moved to the west. At Vienna they received a cup of soup. Ultimately they arrived at a large base camp in southern Germany.

Here, in addition to Russian men and women, were British and French prisoners. To them the girls will be forever grateful. They threw biscuits and bits of chocolate over the barbed wire fences that divided the camp sections, when the Russians failed to receive anything but boiled turnips.

For the first two days the British prisoners created so much fuss that the girls were given additional rations of barley and margarine. They also received blue cloth badges marked "Ost" (meaning "East," that is, from eastern front areas) in large white letters, which they were compelled to wear at all times.

Then the paths of these two friends divided. Valya was sent to a Munich suburb, with fifty other women from Uman, to work in a flax factory. They lived, she said, in wooden barracks within the factory grounds and were not permitted to leave except on "free days," which they spent loading railroad cars or working in the fields.

Working in the same place were Belgian, French and Italian men who also lived in barracks, but were permitted, Valya said, a certain amount of freedom outside. She spoke no German and the only contact she had with the Germans was the daily 200-yard walk to the shop to which she was assigned.

The routine was a deadly one. They were up at 5 and worked without food until 2 in the afternoon, when they received 100 grams (3 1/2 ounces) of bread and some boiled turnips and returned to the barracks, while the second shift took over. They had nothing to do, she said, except wait for the evening meal—three or four small potatoes and a cup of sweetened ersatz coffee. For this work they received a net of 70 pfennigs weekly—not enough to buy newspapers, had they been permitted to do so.

The factory was dusty and dark. They received no clothes or uniforms. They began to suffer visibly from malnutrition. With the native wisdom of the Ukraine, the girls found wild garlic growing in the factory yard and rubbed their teeth and gums with it to protect them. It merely served additionally to infuriate their foreman, who ordered that there should be no more of it and kicked Valya when she failed to understand his heated German words.

She sank deeper and deeper into despair. Several times, she said, she thought of suicide while watching the freight cars rumble past the factory, but what remained of her youthful buoyancy prevented this. She even considered the possibilities of pregnancy, but the only opportunity would have been to accept work as a housemaid for a man of "50 or 60." She thought of her family and home and decided against it.

Then, "one Friday in July"—time seems to have been a vague thing to these modern galley slaves—Valya solved the problem. She closed her eyes, put her left hand under the cutting knife of her machine, and sheared off four fingers at the base.

For a month she was in a Munich hospital. Three months more

she spent in barracks, unable to work and going regularly to Munich for dressings. The factory director urged her to stay and offered to teach her German and give her a job supervising a kitchen. She declined. It was not as generous offer as might appear. He was required to pay her fare in the event she was sent home.

A German woman who once had given her the few pfennigs she required for carfare to Munich advised her to visit the local arbeitsamt. She did, was given clearance and shortly afterward was loaded again into a freight car to begin the journey home. At Brest-Litovsk she met Galina, a vastly different girl than when they had parted a few months before.

Galina was chosen to work in a hat factory in Ulm. She lived in barracks that housed 380 women from the Ukraine and the region of Kursk and 200 men from Cherkasy. French, Belgians, Italians, Czechs and Poles were all working for this concern, but they lived outside the factory grounds.

Among these unfortunate people grew a guarded friendship, fostered through smuggled notes and hasty conversations. The French and Czechs posted illegal letters for them and often gave them extra bits of food from their larger rations.

It was an Austrian who ultimately showed Galina how to escape. He provided her with a handful of cigarettes, told her to make a brew of six of them and poison herself with nicotine. She retched violently the first time she drank the potion, but she was successful the second time and went to a hospital with an ailment that puzzled the German doctors during her entire stay. She had a few additional cigarettes, which she soaked in water and drank. She was under treatment for more than two months and finally sent home as a heart case.

At Brest-Litovsk she rejoined the mutilated Valya, who has not yet overcome her self-consciousness about her hand. Days later they reached Kazatin, about ninety miles northeast of Uman, where they traded their last bits of clothing for food. On foot and in wagons they finally got to Uman.

Rest, food and the skill of a dentist, who replaced four teeth that had been loosened when she was struck for interfering in another girl's beating, have removed the physical traces of Galina's stay in

Hitler's reich. She is made of tougher fiber than Valya, who will carry her torn hand as a lifelong memorial of her hatred of slavery and her yearning for home.

We asked Galina about other members of her family.

Three months ago, in the village of Zhashkov, she said, her sister-in-law was shot, she thinks, by her second brother, Feodor, who was working with the Nazi police.

"I'd shoot him with my own hands," she told us fiercely. "He's simply corrupt."

Now that liberation has made it possible for these girls to begin a new life, that is one of the first things Galina plans to do. She is going to Zhashkov in an effort to learn more about her sister-in-law's death and try to locate her mother. The village was heavily bombed during the fighting and she doesn't know what she will find.

Valya hasn't any plans.

McCall's 45-Minute
Paratroop Course

. . . .

BY

ROBERT VERMILLION

UNITED PRESS WAR CORRESPONDENT

WITH THE PARATROOPERS IN FRANCE, Aug. 15, 1944—I went into southern France with the paratroopers. It was my first jump.

My total training consisted of "McCall's 45-minute paratroop training course."

Capt. George McCall, of Salt Lake City, had taken me to a parachute shed and said: "This is a parachute." Then he took me to a plane and showed me how to jump, adding, "But you won't do it that way. The guy behind you will kick you out."

That completed my training.

We took off. In the blacked-out plane the men sat bowed under the weight of their equipment. Our plane was the ninth to leave the ground. I sat directly opposite the open door and across from the battalion commander.

As the commander shouted, "Fifteen minutes to go," the men already were jamming down to the plane's door.

I quivered with excitement and fear, which I wouldn't admit even to myself, as I stood behind the commander in the open door. Below us sped past what appeared to be clouds. I watched the spot where a flashing green light would signal us to jump.

It was then I realized I was still wearing my spectacles.

I jerked them off and fumbled for my pocket snaps lest I be forced to jump with them in my hand. Broken spectacles would have left me with poor vision in this type of warfare where recognition of friend or foe must be instantaneous.

I was shaking so that I had trouble putting my spectacles in my pocket. The tension was so great I wanted to yell. Then the green light flashed. The commander jerked through the door. I leaped out after him, forgetting all I had been told of how to do it. The propellor blast seized me and swept me beneath the plane's tail. Then came an agonizing shock as the chute opened. I felt as if I were being torn to pieces. Green, red and yellow lights flashed like a high score on a pinball machine. A moment later, all motion had ceased. I seemed to be hanging in midair.

The next thing I knew, I crashed through the slim branches of stubby pine tree and hit a slope with an impact that again sent lights flashing and bells ringing.

I knelt, shaking my head to clear it. The buzzing in my head stopped. There was no sound except the chirping of crickets. Darkness was complete. I began fumbling with my parachute straps when I heard the crackling of dry twigs. I froze. Then slowly reached into my pocket for my handkerchief, careful not to make the slightest sound which would reveal my presence.

I got out my glasses and put them on. I heard sounds further down the hill and I began stepping softly that way.

I slipped and rolled six or eight feet, crashing into a bush with a noise that seemed to echo in the hills. I lay there not moving until I heard a brief low whistle. I whistled in reply, and then decided to make contact with somebody. So I took a chance that the whistler might not be a German. I softly called the password which identified Allied troops. There was no answer immediately. I waited. Then a soft voice called, "Down here."

I stopped being cautious then, and skidded down the slope. I met a dark figure huddled against a rock.

It was Capt. Bill Howland, of Heflin, Ala., who had followed me out of the plane.

"You didn't have to push me, did you?" I asked.

"Hell, no," he said. "You went right out."

I felt pretty good then.

We didn't know where we were, but Howland called the password and it was answered. We stumbled over rocks and through bushes to this third person. It was a lieutenant-colonel from Staunton, Va. Soon, we picked up two more paratroopers including one boy who was so incoherent from tension and the impact of the fall that he could not identify himself properly. The colonel went to a hilltop and flashed a brief flare. Slowly we gathered a force on the hill.

We were puzzled by the lack of enemy activity. Top Sergeant Bill Sullivan, of Galesburg, Ill., warily turned his head to one side as we walked:

"Boy, we sure pulled a sneak on them," he said.

At daylight, there still were no Germans.

We saw our first Frenchman about 7 A.M. He was walking across a field carrying rabbit traps. He was not at all surprised to see us, since two Americans had dropped in his front yard. He invited us in for wine, but the colonel said:

"Hell, no, we're looking for krauts."

There was no action during the day, but at 6 P.M. we saw one of the great spectacles of the war. For one hour and 40 minutes we stood in awe watching a great fleet of transport planes and gliders dropping troops in a sunlit valley.

The colonel said in a low voice: "Oh, my God, let that be all; it's all my heart can stand."

Sgt. Sullivan said: "It makes me want to sing the Star Spangled Banner."

. . . .

ROBERT VERMILLION

Robert Vermillion served as a combat correspondent for the United Press. During World War II he covered the fighting in Italy and Africa, then headed the UP bureau in Miami until the onset of the Korean War.

In 1954 Vermillion and his wife founded a newspaper in Japan called the *Okinawa Morning Sun.* They sold it three years later. He returned to the United States and as general editor, joined *Newsweek,* where he worked for twenty years until his retirement in 1977. Vermillion died on May 2, 1987, from complications of diabetes.

Death Overtakes a Last Dispatch

· · · · · · · · · · · ·

BY

TOM TREANOR

LOS ANGELES *TIMES*

LOS ANGELES, SEPT. 9, 1944—On the very eve of his death, Tom Treanor dreamed he was in liberated Paris. In his dream he felt the thrills he had eagerly looked forward to as he sped along with Gen. Patton's army toward the environs of that city. He wanted to relate his dream on an N.B.C. Radio broadcast to America, but because of transmission difficulties he was unable to do so. Yesterday the *Times* received the broadcast as he had prepared it on his portable typewriter. It was dated Aug. 16, two days before his tragic death.

"I am going in search of a good story," he radioed London just before he set out to keep his tryst with destiny. Following is the text of his last message:

ON THE WAY TO PARIS, Aug. 16, 1944—"All I can report tonight is that I had a dream. I can't say whether it was a waking dream or a sleeping dream. It was kind of in between.

"I dreamed I was in Paris walking down the middle of the Champs Élysées. Flowers were under my feet and a thousand hands were holding out champagne. It was a kind of futuristic dream in which French girls were blowing kisses and shrieking: 'Vivent les Alliés.'

"I felt confused, and I said, 'What day is this?' And there was such a jumble of voices I couldn't catch a clear answer.

" 'Soon, soon,' some cried. And some cried, 'Thursday,' and some screamed 'Friday,' and there were some screamed all the other days of the week. I felt as though I had been drinking too much of the champagne that was held out to me, and I tried to clear my head to learn what day of the week it was, but it was all mixed up, and I only heard 'Thursday,' 'Friday,' and all the other days of the week mentioned.

"There was one voice which even kept saying, 'Man, you aren't dreaming. Wake up. You aren't in Paris at all. You're in a town called Le Mans, which is 120 miles from Paris. You're not only dreaming, you're snoring.'

"And then I saw the Eiffel Tower in my dream, and it was all lighted up like it used to be with a single word. Only the word wasn't Citroën then, as it was when I last saw Paris.

"There was a new word on the Eiffel Tower which winked on and off. The lights flicked another word into my dream:

" 'Liberation. Liberation. Liberation.'

"And then I dreamed I saw the Madeleine and it was all aglow with candles. A thousand people prayed there in thanksgiving.

"Next I saw the great dressmakers, snapping their fingers before the mannequins, who walked into a blaze of lights, wearing the latest chic—costumes in red, white and blue, with low-cut 'V' for victory at the bosom.

"And then I dreamed I was Gen. Patton, twirling two pearl-handled revolvers and backing a Nazi general into a corner, and the Nazi general said, 'Kamerad, kamerad. You can't blitz us. We invented the blitz.'

"And I twirled my revolvers and said, 'This is the super blitz. My name is Patton. I come from California where we grow everything bigger than anywhere else, including blitzes.' "

. . . .

TOM TREANOR

Tom Treanor was a correspondent for the Central Broadcasting Service and the Los Angeles *Times* in France. On August 19, 1944, Treanor was killed after a tank ran over his jeep. He was en route to the front near Paris. He was thirty-five.

Trolley Ride into Grenoble

· · · · · · · · · · · ·

BY

EDD JOHNSON

CHICAGO *SUN* FOREIGN SERVICE

GRENOBLE, FRANCE, Aug. 23, 1944—I rode into Grenoble today on a streetcar.

Just one week since we landed on Green Beach on the French Riviera our troops are in contact with the enemy on three sides of this important provincial metropolis.

But I didn't see a single German in the course of a trip through the city proper taken in a streetcar, on a bicycle, atop the cab of a partisan troop truck and for a considerable distance on the shoulders of the cheering, weeping, shrieking populace.

Nobody ever deserved less and received more adulation than has come my way due to the accident which permitted me to leave the spearhead of our forces a few miles outside of Grenoble this morning and jump aboard an interurban streetcar which carried me into the heart of the city.

Now I know how a swoon-crooner must feel when the tides of worshipful femininity rise up and engulf him. Nobody will believe this, but after the first five minutes it is simply a terrifying experience.

Officially, Grenoble may or may not be captured. From a room in the Grand Hotel of the Three Dauphins, where this is written, it is impossible to know what the communiqué issuers and Army staff officers call it.

But the people of Grenoble have gone mad and are declaring with tears and laughter that they are at last liberated.

Last night, as soon as we were going down beyond those breath-taking peaks of the French Alps, I left a command post with the colonel commanding my favorite regiment. The colonel had armored columns and infantry disposed beyond.

Since we have moved faster here than the best blitzkrieg the Wehrmacht ever thought of, the colonel wanted to make some personal reconnaissance.

The colonel was disposing his tank destroyers and artillery when the trolley car marked "Grenoble" passed.

The interurban train consisted of an engine and baggage car and two passenger cars. The motorman crawled through the back window of the baggage car, leaving the train to run itself, when he heard the screams of joy from the passengers.

With difficulty we persuaded him to return to his controls. But at the next stop he snatched a French flag from a little group of persons that had knotted up to cheer a passing truck of French Forces of the Interior who were patrolling a highway paralleling the train track.

The motorman climbed to the top of the train and fixed the Tricolor to the trolley arm. Then he was ready to proceed.

During the hubbub of my being kissed, pinched, hugged and patted atop my battle helmet by the passengers, I tried to frame sentences in French that would be adequate to the situation. And more passengers were piling aboard at every stop, and by the time the streetcar reached the city line I was wedged on the front platform, and the whole train was festooned with French men and women screaming to pedestrians, pointing to the Tricolor and announcing that the Americans had arrived.

I had heard there were several hundred prominent Frenchmen from the resistance movement in a prison opposite the Gestapo headquarters, and I made a pact with the conductress—poor thing, she hadn't collected a single sou since she recognized my uniform—

to escape from the trolley when we reached the street where the prison stood.

When the trolley stopped at the correct street, she smiled and nodded and I eased myself over the railing and ran down the street. But the shouts of the passengers attracted people in the street, and soon I was engulfed again.

On reflection, it seems I remember kisses of bewhiskered old men more vividly than those of scores of pretty girls. After all, almost everyone has been kissed by a pretty girl sometime before.

There were probably two hundred citizens in a milling mob around me when a truck carrying F.F.I. men drew up at the curb to see what had happened. I got one arm loose and waved frantically for help.

They stopped and three young fellows broke through the mob and dragged me to safety.

They hoisted me atop the cab of their truck and drove off down the tree-lined business street.

From everywhere people came streaming into the street to cheer - and throw their kisses and blessings. I shouted to a youngster riding astride the hood of the truck that I wanted to visit the prison where the political prisoners were held. He stood up and shouted in my ear that there was none left.

He said our airmen had scored a direct hit on the Gestapo headquarters a few days earlier, and that last night the people had broken into the prison across the street and released seven hundred prisoners. He shouted, with curses, that the Gestapo had shot two hundred twenty-five before Grenoble's "Bastille" night.

As the truck toured the city, all of us accepted all manner of effusive applause. Then it stopped in front of F.F.I. headquarters and a youth in a maroon sport shirt, named Jean, broke in to say that the only way to travel the streets of Grenoble was by bicycle, because automobiles attracted too much attention. He proved to be right.

With a plump blond girl on a bicycle at my left and Jean at my right, I hunched over the handlebars of a bicycle and pedaled furiously.

Jean shouted, "Attention! Attention!" in a loud voice to clear the streets, but when we had passed, he looked back over his shoulder and said, "Américains!"

The result was, we left a wake of startled, if somewhat frustrated, French citizens behind us.

A short distance ahead was the public square, jampacked with Frenchmen out to cheer the F.F.I., and there Jean's shouts availed us nothing. We came to a crashing stop against the legs of the populace, and a half minute later my uniform was recognized and I was hoisted on the shoulders of the crowd and carried about the square.

I finally persuaded those holding me by the legs to head toward a building and they deposited me in front of a startled, frock-coated manager. Then I was borne off to another office outside and around the building.

There I faced a swoon-crooner's nightmare. When I was sufficiently smeared with lipstick, one French girl snatched my handkerchief, which had been tied around a bloody knee, wiped off part of the lipstick and then kept the handkerchief as a souvenir.

Jean eventually clawed his way through this mattress of feminine charm and asked where I wanted to go. A thought of the privacy of my own bathroom at home suddenly flashed through my mind and I told him I wanted to take a bath.

He brought me with a little difficulty to the Grand Hotel of the Three Dauphins. But he couldn't resist letting it out that he was personally in charge of an American in uniform.

I reached the privacy of the hotel bathroom, but even there solitude was only comparative. Chambermaids rushed in to pour water over my back in small scalding squirts as I sat hunched in a tub of nice cool water. A porter borrowed a razor for me, but a woman rushed in to say she had lent me the razor of her husband who was a prisoner of the Germans. She insisted she be permitted to wring my soapy hands and kiss my ashen cheeks.

Another Frenchman got past Jean, who was standing guard, to demand: "Will you have dinner with me tonight?"

And the cashier came in to say she was sorry she had forgotten so much of her English.

No Roman emperor ever had such a bath.

When I was dry, Jean came and said there was a problem. The people were trying to break in the doorway of the hotel, and the only way to satisfy them was for me to make an appearance.

Thereupon, I made my first and only balcony appearance. What I saw below may not prove what the war is all about, but it was an experience that could tell the dictators a lot on the subject of what people are all about. Frenchmen and Frenchwomen looked up.

I saw a group of people suddenly feeling the thrill of being their own masters—suddenly experiencing the sensation of being liberated and whole again.

They saw a tired, embarrassed, wind-burned correspondent who never has killed an oppressor in his whole life and, according to his Selective Service board, is too old ever to hope to kill any in this war.

I heard the cheers, looked into those faces and then raised my arm, giving the "V" for victory sign.

Someone started the "Marseillaise" and on the second bar the whole crowd joined in, until that great, wide, peopled square was ablaze with the gusto of that fine, masculine, unanswerable challenge of Frenchmen to their oppressors.

I stood at attention until it was over—and then yelled something like "Vive la France!" or "Viva la liberté!" But I didn't feel like yelling. I felt like praying—or something.

. . . .

EDD JOHNSON

In 1954 Edd Johnson and twenty-five other passengers were killed in an airplane crash in Mexico. Johnson was living in Puerto Vallarta while on leave from the San Francisco *Chronicle*, where he had been a reporter and rewrite man since 1951. During the Second World War Johnson was a correspondent for the Chicago *Sun*. He had also worked for the United Press, the San Francisco *Examiner*, the New York *Journal-American*, *Collier's* magazine, CBS, and NBC.

Salute to the Men of the Maquis

. . . .

by

DUDLEY ANN HARMON

UNITED PRESS WAR CORRESPONDENT

[Editor's Note: The writer of the following dispatch is one of the few women war correspondents accredited to the Allied Armies and is an authority on the French Underground movement, having covered its representatives in London from the early days of the war.]

WITH THE FRENCH FORCES OF THE INTERIOR SOMEWHERE IN BRITTANY, Aug. 23, 1944—Down the street in the driving rain proudly march the men of the Maquis—a gallant little army in rags.

I have been given the honor of reviewing them because I am the first American correspondent to visit this town, in the heart of Brittany, where they have their headquarters.

They march proudly but they are a tatterdemalion lot. One is 16, another 64. One wears the jacket of a German naval officer and peasant trousers. Another tops an American blouse with a blue beret. There is a former industrial leader. That scholarly-looking trooper in shabby garb is a professor.

Only one in 100 has a helmet. Their guns are German, English and American.

"Eyes right," snaps their colonel as they march past. They come about smartly and stand before me.

"Won't you give them a message from America?" whispered the colonel.

It is hard to find words for men who have lived like animals, hunted and hunting, battling an enemy overwhelming in numbers and armed with every modern weapon. I cannot speak to them of what is most in mind and heart—the tortures which I have learned were inflicted upon the men of the Maquis. But they know these things from bitter experience. That is a message for America—not from America.

I stand in the rain and tell them America has heard of their exploits and is proud of them. The words are simple but they square their shoulders and smile at one another.

How can they smile? I have just toured the Maquis country and have seen what it meant to fight Germans. I have seen the charred remains of cottages which were burned to the ground with their owners roped to their beds inside. I have talked with the people of Bois de Bosegalo, where the Germans killed 45 Frenchmen—gradually. First they began by breaking their bones, one by one. First the arms. Then the legs.

At Locminé I inspected the Gestapo torture chamber where originated cries at night that kept the whole neighborhood awake. The walls were spattered with blood. The French doctor who treated many men whose bodies were black from having been beaten with chains told me, "One of my comrades had his eyes torn out." And a French parachutist asked: "Why did they have to burn my brother before they shot him? They could just have shot him outright. But I saw him burned."

A 22 year-old girl carried messages for the Maquis until the Gestapo caught her. She said: "They tied me in a special position with my arms under my legs and my head hanging down. I fainted several times. They beat me and questioned me for 12 hours but I would not give my comrades away. When they could do nothing they set me free. But four of our men were tortured before being shot so that I could only recognize them by their clothing."

These were the things which raced through my mind as I stood fumbling for a "few words from America" for the men of the Maquis.

I hastily saluted them and heard with relief the command of the colonel: "Dismissed."

Von Rundstedt's Fantastic Underground Quarters

· · · · · · · · · · ·

BY

H. R. KNICKERBOCKER

CHIEF OF THE CHICAGO *SUN* FOREIGN SERVICE

WITH THE AMERICAN ARMY IN NORTHERN FRANCE, Aug. 31, 1944—
The American Army today overran the "Grosse Hauptquartier fuer
den Westen"—the "Great German Headquarters for Western Europe"—at the town of Margival north of Soissons.

Your correspondent was the first to put foot in the bedchamber
and offices of Field Marshal Karl Gerd von Rundstedt, former commander in the west, and to explore a small fraction of the German
army installations covering one hundred square miles underground.

This German position was organized, dug and built about two
years ago. This was the German second line of defense after the
beaches and before the Siegfried Line, or West Wall. It is on a scale
so stupendous that it is almost incredible.

Maj. Paul Gayle explained to me as we began to climb down into
one underground habitation capable of holding one thousand men:

"When the Germans built this place two years ago they knew
they had lost the war. They built this knowing they would have to
fight the Americans here in northern France. If they believed we
could get to northern France, they must have known that they
would lose the war."

We were able during five hours this morning to explore only the beginning of this interconnected series of fortifications starting just outside the city of Soissons and extending away up north of Urcel, which was Von Rundstedt's personal headquarters.

Very little of this immense installation had been occupied. Hundreds of garrison bedrooms and barracks were fitted with new furniture, beds, rugs, electric fixtures and had never been used.

Von Rundstedt's apartments were behind concrete walls twenty feet thick. They were camouflaged by screens of grass. The entrance of the headquarters of the German General Staff was a city street, fifty feet wide.

We drove our jeep into it and down several city blocks under camouflage. All the French had been driven away from the vicinity three years ago and nobody but the German staff had been within many miles of Margival since 1941. We met a dozen young riflemen of the French resistance movement on the outskirts of Margival. They told us that this was the most forbidden place in France and that for Frenchmen to come anywhere near it was punishable by death.

The actual headquarters of the German army was in a great railroad tunnel about half a mile long with four tracks. The Germans ran their headquarters' trains into this tunnel, lived in their coaches and were able, any minute, to move on. Thus they had a superb mobile command post completely protected from any variety of enemy fire.

No airplane bomb nor artillery shell could have reached them. In all France there is not likely to be found any town so undamaged as Margival and the German headquarters. The lesson from all this is that the Germans are not trying to halt anywhere this side of the Siegfried Line and actual German territory.

This position along the ridge north of Soissons was one of the best lines conceivable. As one professional observer put it, a single platoon here could hold out against an entire armored division. Two-thirds of the German forts were underground, averaging a depth of fifty feet.

None of us had time to go through the whole system but we did go through about twenty miles of it, partly by jeep and partly by foot.

It was an interesting experience. From the height of the ridge one could look from Soissons to Vauxaillon and almost to Alon. All along the ridge were built fake farmhouses, barns, pig pens and even groves of fake trees.

As we walked mile after mile through the gun positions, barracks, officers' casines, emplacements for heavy cannon and observation posts, we observed that, compared to running the Germans out of this place, the capture of Paris was nothing.

Another observation that occurred to our party as we pushed through scores of rooms, never before entered by anyone, except the Germans, was the Germans had contradicted their own military reasoning. They had gone back to fixed, passive defenses instead of relying upon a mobile army.

One American officer remarked that it was the German army which in 1940 broke through fixed French defenses and proved that such defenses were no good. Yet the same German army spent billions of dollars building the same type of permanent defense as that of the Maginot line.

It was an interesting experience to go first into German headquarters deep underground in completely black corridors and chambers. Maj. Gayle went ahead with his pistol in hand, and I followed directly behind him, holding a candle over his head.

We went through an endless garrison of rooms each equipped with five bunks, five chairs, one table, an electric light, a washstand with hot and cold running water, and a next-door bathroom with showers. Many rooms had heavy carpets on the floors. In the officers' casino were large apartments with furniture which would grace a millionaire's residence.

A menu which I picked up from the casino floor listed for breakfast coffee with milk, butter and marmalade; for lunch, pea soup with veal: for dinner, cabbage, potatoes and coffee.

Another scrap of paper found on the floor revealed that no German officer could bring a guest to dinner without the consent of his commanding general. In the kitchen we found tons of German army bread. It was dry and tasteless, apparently made of rye. There were also tons of lard and canned meat.

Going along the four-tracked railway leading into the German headquarters tunnel we noticed the real refinement of camouflage. The Germans had painted the rails rust colored and also painted the ties gray in such fashion as to make the whole thing look as though it had been unused for many years.

"Ah, ha," exclaimed one of the French boys, brandishing his rifle, "the pigs planned to be defeated. Think of it, monsieur. So many years ago, they said to themselves, 'We shall have to fight around Soissons and we shall have to have many, many men and feed them many, many years in order to delay our enemies.' But they knew their enemies would only be delayed, not stopped."

In one of the biggest German kitchens our French friends began cooking lunch. A peasant woman did the cooking. They used German provisions. From the heaps of many tons of potatoes, they cooked pommes frites in excellent German lard. They went out and shot two rabbits and roasted them deliciously.

It was a perfect meal, but the French complained bitterly at having to drink water in the midst of rooms containing literally thousands of champagne bottles emptied by the Germans.

One section of the German headquarters streets under camouflage were lighted by regular street lights such as used in Berlin. The French boy showing this item, said:

"The Germans built this in order to escape from Paris. They knew that someday something would happen in Paris just like what did happen; that its people would rise and kill the Germans. It is fine to be alive, isn't it?"

And he fired a shot into the air for joy.

. . . .

H. R. KNICKERBOCKER

Hubert Renfre Knickerbocker was born and raised in Texas. He attended a number of schools, including Southwestern University, Columbia University, the University of Munich, the University of Vienna, and the University of Berlin.

His newspaper career began with a series of brief stints at such various papers as the Newark *Morning Ledger*, the New York *Evening Post*, and the New York *Sun*. In 1924 he went to Germany as a correspondent for the *Evening Post* and the Philadelphia *Public Ledger*, taking an additional position as traveling reporter for the International News Service. In 1931 he was awarded the Pulitzer Prize for correspondence. While covering the Spanish Civil War, he and two other journalists were abducted by rebels and were declared missing for several days. In 1941 he became the chief of the Chicago *Sun*'s foreign service. Knickerbocker covered every development of the war as it happened. He was the author of seven books dealing with the effects of World War II.

He died on July 13, 1949.

Escape from the Nazis

· · · · · · · · · · · ·

by

GAULT MAC GOWAN

STAFF CORRESPONDENT OF THE NEW YORK *SUN*

LONDON, Sept. 14, 1944—I am now able to tell the full story of how I escaped from the Germans and joined the Maquis in what is now liberated France.

I was being taken from the stalag in Châlons-sur-Marne to Germany. I was put into a third class compartment of a train which the German soldiers were using as a guardroom. Soldiers were sleeping all around me and there was a guard, always alert, changed every two hours.

It was shortly after 2 A.M. when a new guard had just come on and the train was pulling out of a wayside station that I succeeded in opening the carriage door unseen by the guard in the blackout and falling out between the tracks on the side away from the platform.

The guard, whose back had been turned for one providential moment, shouted as I jumped or fell, and in a few moments the train came to a bumping, jerking stop and a fusillade of bullets swept the scenery, hitting everything but me.

The train door through which I had escaped wasn't under my hand but was on the observation platform at the end of the car. To get out, I had to walk past the sentry, recumbent Germans who

226

were off duty, and others who were waiting their call for duty else-where on the train.

There were fifteen sentries posted on each side of the train, and it was they who gave me the fusillade when the alarm was sounded.

The sentry must have turned his back to look out the window on the platform side at the moment I chose to leave, but I couldn't see just what he was doing. It was too dark. I just knew that he wasn't seated beside me as his predecessors had been all night.

He had his flashlight switched off and the moment he heard me slip past, he must have switched it on and found me gone. He came after me, but it was too late. It was a fast moving job; I had gone. That's all there was to it.

Once sure that the fall hadn't killed me, I jumped up and hared it across the tracks, over the barbed wire fence surrounding the sta-tion, across the station approach and into a cow pasture, crossing another barbed wire fence.

The fences tore my clothes to pieces. I found that they had sev-ered my webbing belt and torn off all the buttons of my trousers. So I ran for shelter holding up my trousers, a ridiculous situation which wasn't funny for me until afterwards.

Once across the field, I flung myself into a bed of nettles to regain my breath and lay there panting while the Germans searched the nearby woods and the station approach. The place where I had es-caped was somewhere between Châlons and the river Meuse, and we were just entering the woody and hilly country.

The Germans tried to pull a fast one. They pretended to abandon the search and the train whistled and went on. But they had left a search party behind to look for me. Happily, they gave themselves away and while they were vainly searching through the wood, I made off in the opposite direction.

Throughout the night I traveled, the moon and the stars my guide and the flash of our guns toward the southwest a general indication of the war zone. I knew that Gen. Patton's Army was between Paris and Châlons, and I estimated that it would be possible to reach him.

But although I traveled all night, the dawn found me footsore and weary still in enemy-occupied country and Gen. Patton still a hundred miles away. At dawn, I made inquiries as to where I could find the nearest Maquis outpost for Allied France.

The French girls, in a donkey cart, taking home a load of faggots from the forest, were the first human contact I made after traveling all night overland.

I asked them the direction of Troyes, which I understood to be in Allied hands. They confirmed that I was headed in the right direction.

The girls started giggling and I found the reason was my strange attire. For I was no longer wearing trousers, having discarded them, but the pajamas which I had providentially put on beneath the trousers.

I decided it was best to tell them the truth to prevent their reporting me for outrageous behavior in broad daylight. So, in the interest of convention, they showed me a wood behind a village where they promised to meet me with more respectable garb.

They kept their promise; afterward they brought iodine for my wounds and a bandage for the sprained wrist I had sustained when I fell. They also brought me the most delicious omelette I had ever tasted. They seemed like angels to me.

After two nights of hiding in the outhouses of farms, I succeeded in reaching the Maquis, becoming the first accredited Allied correspondent with them.

· · · · · · · · · · ·

GAULT MAC GOWAN

Gault MacGowan had an immense passion for travel and adventure, which he sought in both his personal and professional life. After MacGowan served in World War I, he became a reporter and editor for several European and American newspapers, including the *Times* of London (Trinidad), the Paris *Daily Express*, and *The New York Times*. He joined the staff of the New York *Sun* in 1934, subsequently covering developments in the Spanish Civil War, the war in France, and Nazi infiltration in Europe, among others.

During his lifetime he was awarded many citations, including the Croix de Guerre for injuries he received while reporting on French forces in Tunisia. In 1956 MacGowan founded the magazine *European Living*, which he published until his death in 1970.

Return to Dieppe

· · · · · · · · · · · ·

BY

ROSS MUNRO

CANADIAN PRESS WAR CORRESPONDENT

DIEPPE, Sept. 14, 1944—It was just the way it should have been. The Second Canadian Division came back to Dieppe today, back to this town and these beaches where the original Second Division of this Army fought for eight terrible hours in the raid two years and thirteen days ago.

It came back in triumph. It came back without a single soldier being killed or wounded in the 40-mile advance from Rouen.

Troops of the Second Division stormed up that long straight road determined to settle the score with the German garrison of Dieppe. But the Germans fled.

They blew up ammunition dumps, static guns and harbor installations. Before the Canadians reached town this morning the Germans were scurrying east along the coast roads. Dieppe was empty of the enemy.

Dieppe's people crowded the streets to give fitting welcome to the division. It even eclipsed the acclaim they received at Rouen. There were flowers for the victors, endless cheering.

It was just as it should have been. I came back with the Second Division and if I had one last story to write I would want it to be this one.

Our entry marked a complete cycle. It was the climax of this war for thousands of our soldiers. You could see triumph in their faces as they whirled along the roads in Bren carriers, trucks and jeeps. This was their greatest day.

Yesterday, when Rouen was cleared of Germans, Gen. [Sir Henry] Crerar directed the Second Division on Dieppe. Through Rouen the Division poured after heavy fighting for several days in the Forêt de la Londe south of the city.

Its armored cars sped up the highway from Rouen and by evening were more than halfway to Dieppe. Leading the advance was a squadron commanded by Maj. Dennis Bult-Francis, of Montreal, who had been on the original raid, and was wounded on the beaches.

The reconnaissance had two clashes with small German forces on the way. It caught a German ack-ack party trying to escape to the east and wiped it out. It mopped up another group of stragglers.

During the night they stopped just short of Dieppe and this morning at 10:30 the regiment entered the city.

Behind them came the infantry regiments that fought at Dieppe before. Leading were an Ontario formation of the Royal Regiment from Toronto, the Royal Hamilton Light Infantry, and the Essex Scottish from Windsor.

Their carriers were covered with summer flowers and nearly every vehicle flew the tricolor.

Following the Ontario troops were the Cameron Highlanders of Winnipeg, the South Saskatchewan Regiment, and the Fusiliers Mont-Royal, three other Dieppe battalions. Behind them came the Black Watch of Montreal, the Calgary Highlanders the Regiment de Maisonneuve and the Toronto Scottish, all of which had some troops on the raid.

I caught up with the Royals, the R.H.L.I. and the Essex five miles from Dieppe and rode along in their column. There were about 25 in each regiment who had been to Dieppe before.

Farmers and their families stood by the highway to wave us past.

The colonel of the R.H.L.I. shouted to me: "Hop along ahead and see our recce. They are in Dieppe now, we hear." So I hopped along at sixty miles an hour.

Suddenly, there was Dieppe, spread out on the flat ground below at the mouth of the Arques river between two big headlands.

The eastern end of the town was smoking, but there was no other sign of war.

Yet I was awed by the sight of Dieppe. Those headlands from which the Germans brought down such hellish fire on our beaches two years ago held no scenic beauty for me.

I drove along down hill into the center of town and stopped beside a recce unit armored car. In ten seconds we were surrounded by laughing, smiling civilians. An old lady shook my hand with tears of joy in her eyes. Another pressed a bouquet of flowers into my hands. A pretty girl tossed another into our scout car. A little boy stuck the tricolor into the gun rack. Soon the car looked like a mobile floral display.

It was the same with every other vehicle that came into Dieppe today. It was like the happy ending to an improbable story to see this happening to our troops. But this was no fiction.

I walked around town, looking at what were the Canadian objectives in the raid. The harbor area along the eastern side of town had been demolished by the Germans before they left. Debris covered the streets in this sector.

Exits from narrow streets out to the Esplanade and mean beach in front of the town were blocked off by 12-foot concrete walls as they were two years ago. A Frenchman led me through a fortified house that had been a German strongpoint and we walked out onto the Esplanade.

The enemy had fortified the entire line of houses along this Esplanade. The tobacco factory in the middle of the line was a gaunt skeleton. It was set afire during the raid and gutted. The Esplanade, 200 feet wide, was covered with barbed wire from which hung German signs warning of minefields. Mines had been sown along it from one end to the other.

We walked cautiously down to the harbor end of the Esplanade where a jetty goes out into the channel and there was more wire, more mines. At no point could you get down to the beach where the fiercest action took place and where hundreds of Canadians, pinned down for hours, suffered terrible casualties along the sea wall.

Pillboxes dotted the Esplanade and there were several new gun-casements covering the beaches and harbor entrance. The Germans had added to defenses on the sea front since the raid.

In the face of the cliffs on the west headland we saw German machine-gun positions. It was these cliff guns that caused as much trouble as any. And more had been added since the raid.

The sloping main beach with its loose shale on which many of our Churchill tanks foundered is cluttered up with all sorts of iron and wood obstacles to prevent landing craft from beaching. They had not been there before. Underwater obstacles had been set up off-shore too, as they had been on the Normandy beaches where Canadian invasion troops landed.

The Germans had been taking no chances at Dieppe. They had strengthened their defenses a great deal. Eric Bell, of Regina, who was on the raid and saw heavy action on the main beach, was there looking at it. It must have revived a hundred vivid memories. He didn't say anything.

On that beach the R.H.L.I., Essex, F.M.R., and Calgary tanks had their roughest time. Around the west headland was Pourville, where the S.S.R. and Camerons landed. The road had been blown up and we couldn't get there. Sappers also said the bridge there was blown. It was over this bridge that Lt. Col. Cecil Merritt had led his men with the heroism that won him the Victoria Cross.

To the east of Dieppe the Royals landed during the raid and we could see the narrow beach where they were caught by murderous German machine-gun and mortar fire. The enemy had not left many guns at Dieppe. They hauled away what mobile ones they could and blew up others in pillboxes and casements.

Back in the center of town, crowds were still thronging around every Second Division man they saw wearing the blue battle-patches remembered from two years before.

Dozens of people wanted to talk to every Canadian, including about a dozen English people who had been in Dieppe all through the war, unable to leave. Mrs. Jean Touzon, of London, England, said: "I was here when the Canadians came on the raid and we were all terribly saddened by their losses. But the German losses were very heavy too. There were from 600 to 800 killed alone and the wounded numbered over 1,000. The raid shook them to their heels. There was nearly a panic in the middle of the morning."

She said the Germans became very nervous yesterday morning at the progress of the Canadian and British forces to the south around Rouen and began to blow up ammunition dumps, continuing their demolitions all day and during the night.

The last parties of Germans left about dawn, going east.

"Cripes, There's the Old Man Right Up Here Himself!"

· · · · · · · · · · · ·

BY

JOHN M. CARLISLE

STAFF CORRESPONDENT OF THE DETROIT *NEWS*

WITH THE 3RD ARMY, BEFORE METZ, Sept. 28, 1944 (delayed)—I went up to the front lines in a jeep today with Lieut. Gen. George S. Patton, Jr., commander of the 3rd Army. We ran a gauntlet of Jerry shells to get back over 5000 yards of open road that was under enemy observation. Four of those shells, and one in particular, came close—awfully close.

I was half scared to death. The general sat there very calmly in the little jeep, never moving a muscle, never turning his head, never ducking, while I crouched low behind him. He might have been driving down Woodward avenue in Detroit on parade.

For at least 45 minutes I wished I was back home but I am glad I went up to the front with the general. I found out something I had always wondered about. I found out why GI Joe in the 3rd Army respects, admires and loves this fighting general.

GI Joe in his foxhole likes to see his commander under fire and he admires robust courage, like his own, in other men, especially in generals. Gen. Patton has a robust courage that knows no fear.

Incidentally, I must apologize for writing only my own impressions. That is all I can write about. Some of the general's remarks were just priceless, but they cannot be written here now.

I met Gen. Patton in a little French village on the west side of the Moselle. I was coming from the medical tent, where I had been lying on a litter while a medical aide sprayed my angry throat and tried to relieve the cold that had turned my chest on fire for three days.

The general was feeling very chipper. He had been up to the front, had discovered three great fighting sergeants and had promptly made them second lieutenants right on the spot. The general now was going up to the front in our sector.

I had not been up there in a week before I knew the front was very rugged in our sector. Sharp fighting was going on, infantry action with a lot of heavy shells coming in. In a weak moment I asked him if I could go along, so I hopped into the backseat of his jeep with Maj. Al C. Stiller, of Tucson, Ariz., one of Gen. Patton's aides.

Sergt. John L. Mims, of Abbeyville, Ala., was driving the jeep, which took off behind the commanding officer of our immediate fighting force. My good friend, Capt. William W. Clarke, of Warsaw, Ind., was riding in that jeep with Corp. Leo A. Glotzbach, of Battle Creek, Mich., a very good fighting soldier who is a crack rifle shot, driving it.

We crossed the Moselle River over one of our treadway pontoon bridges. The combat engineers were working at the bridgehead in the mud with their bulldozers and their heavy cranes. Bareheaded GI Joes paused in their work. They all snapped to attention, saluting Gen. Patton smartly. Their uniforms were muddy and dirty, their faces were caked with mud, but they rose and saluted. Many of them were smiling.

I distinctly heard a buck private say: "Cripes, there's the old man right up here himself!" I heard another GI remark:

"It's good to see him, pal, up here."

The guns were booming everywhere—the big guns. Gen. Patton sat there returning the salutes, smiling, nodding at his men. I got a very definite impression that he is very proud of these fighting Yanks.

We went to a great fighting regiment's command post. This officer said we had to go a long way down a road that was under direct enemy fire. He said that every day we lost some vehicles hit by enemy shellfire on that road, but we went on anyway, with this officer getting into the other jeep. I get the impression that the general thought his regimental commanders were too protective, too anxious for his safety, and that he could go anywhere GI Joe was fighting.

As we drove down this open road, without any trees, without any cover, with the enemy on the high hills in front of us, our jeep opened up to open throttle. We just drove hell for leather. Our big guns were roaring all over the place and we reached a forward observation post, parking our jeep in the protective cover of a farmhouse.

Pvt. Donald J. Brady, of 454 Midway Avenue, Pontiac, Mich., was standing alongside the wall near his jeep. He showed me a dozen holes in the jeep where enemy shell fragments had hit the night before. He was untouched.

We walked into a little orchard. Gen. Patton is fond of pears, so Maj. Stiller knocked some down, with an expert aim. We ate them just as some Jerry shells came over. They were high, hitting on the hillside across the road from us.

The general never took a look. I took several good looks and stopped eating. I thought it was not much of a place to eat pears, but the general ate a lot of them with relish.

He walked through the orchard and through a clearing. As he came up to it, I saw a captain run across the clearing, crouching to reach a building. Gen. Patton walked into the open as if marching, met a battalion commander and talked there with him. Then they walked out on the road.

The general walked up the open road to high ground with his field glasses. Capt. Clarke and I stopped alongside the last fringe of trees. The Jerry shells were dropping below us and above us. They had a wicked whine as they turned over us in the air. Once I ducked low, and my helmet came off and banged me in the nose, but Gen. Patton was standing on the open road under enemy observation looking through his field glasses.

Gen. Patton stood there a long time with a battalion commander, a regimental commander and the commanding officer of the combat force in this sector. They got out a military map and they studied it together; then they walked slowly down the road. Gen. Patton was eating another pear while he talked with his field commanders. I talked with Pvt. Brady.

"It gives us guys a lift to see the old man up here," he said. "It has been rugged up here. It's nice to know he is thinking about us enough to come up himself. He's one helluva swell soldier, the old man."

Then we got into the jeep with Gen. Patton. Capt. Clarke had just told us:

"We'll have to run for it. The Jerries are really zooming those shells in. They are coming closer."

He didn't have to tell us that.

Then we went on to a bridge on a canal, where our jeep halted. The general took a camera shot of a canal barge the ingenious Yanks had turned around and got into position for the original fording of this canal.

"That was a sweet piece of work under fire," Maj. Stiller said.

Then we drove on, with the Jerry shells whining nearby. We came back to the little town and Gen. Patton drove away.

For the first time I was glad I had gone up front with him. I had heard him talk to his commanders, I had seen him never bat an eyelash under fire, never even duck. I got the definite impression that he was interested in how his GI Joes were getting along up here in the front lines of this sector. I got the impression that he just had to find out for himself, and then I knew for myself why the GI Joes of the 3rd Army will follow his leadership anywhere. He is that kind of a fighting general.

I am completely sold on Gen. Patton but I don't think I'll ever ask him for another ride.

MacArthur Fulfills Pledge
to Return

. . . .

by
WILLIAM B. DICKINSON
UNITED PRESS STAFF CORRESPONDENT

WITH GEN. MACARTHUR IN THE PHILIPPINES, Oct. 20, 1944—Fulfilling the pledge he made two and one half years ago, Gen. Douglas MacArthur returned to the Philippines today.

He came ashore in brilliant sunshine on the island of Leyte only a few hours behind the assault waves of American forces—the avengers of Bataan and Corregidor.

With him on the barge that carried him ashore from the cruiser in which he had traveled from his New Guinea headquarters were Filipino President Sergio Osmena and Brig. Gen. Carlos Romulos, resident commissioner of the Philippines.

They were returning to lead their countrymen as soon as the enemy invaders have been driven from the islands.

Lt. Gen. Richard Sutherland, able American chief of staff, who left the Philippines in the black days of 1942 with Gen. MacArthur, and Lt. Gen. George Kenney, the tough, competent commander of the Far East Air Forces, also accompanied the 64 year-old General in the fulfillment of his solemn vow to return.

Gen. Kenney, boss of the 5th Air Force, directed blows which Gen. MacArthur himself has said made possible the push to the Philippines.

As a representative of the combined American press, I accompanied Gen. MacArthur aboard the cruiser Nashville and landed with him.

As we entered Leyte Gulf this morning, a destroyer detected a submarine and later dropped several depth charges far off on the horizon.

Floating mines were reported at various times but none anywhere near the ship. At 8:20 A.M. today, the navigator was able to report that no enemy planes had been sighted.

Soon after dawn American planes were overhead and from that time on several almost always were within sight.

At the beginning of our voyage, the cruiser and its destroyer escort zigzagged along in the bright sunlight. At mid-afternoon scores of transport and warship masts rose above the horizon and we rendezvoused several hundred miles from Leyte.

Aboard ship Gen. MacArthur was completely relaxed. His plans had been made. There were no further decisions to be taken until his troops were ashore.

Incoming reports were tabulated and assembled so that the General was constantly in touch with developments and progress. Even as the hour of landing drew near he was unruffled. He slept well, ate a hearty breakfast, then went briefly on deck smoking his familiar corn-cob pipe.

After talking with several officers he returned to his cabin and lay down. He promptly fell asleep and napped for about an hour.

About 15 minutes before the scheduled landing at 10 A.M. the cruiser moved in toward the beach where Gen. MacArthur was to land.

Then the General went to the bridge, where he stood as the ship moved slowly toward its anchorage.

The roar of the preliminary bombardment filled the air. We could see shells from the battleships exploding in the hills behind the prospective beachheads.

At 9:58 the bombardment moderated and the first waves of landing craft hit the shore one minute ahead of schedule. The warships lifted their fire and shelled behind the advancing troops.

Reports from the landing forces were received almost momentarily. By 10:08 A.M. the report arrived that we were 500 yards inland

and advancing through open country without opposition.

Our ship anchored at about 11:10 and about the same time the first reports of opposition were received. The beaches were hit by some heavy mortar fire.

Our ships got the range on Jap positions and the bombardment continued at intervals.

Satisfied that everything was going according to schedule, Gen. MacArthur went into his cabin for an early luncheon preparatory to going ashore.

Talking informally over a chocolate soda—his first since an earlier trip aboard this ship—Gen. MacArthur expressed complete confidence in the success of the Leyte operation.

"We have achieved complete surprise in the fullest military sense," he said. "The Japs expected an attack on Mindanao or the northern Philippines. Their best divisions have been concentrated in Mindanao and their reinforcements have been sent there.

"Our air strikes were made there and Adm. Halsey's strikes were to the north. There are about 225,000 enemy combat troops in the Philippines. Our Leyte landing will cut them in two. We will have losses, but they will not be large."

The Japs have little more than one division on Leyte, the General said, and American naval and air power will make it impossible for them to reinforce the island.

Gen. MacArthur said tough fighting may lie ahead before the Philippines are freed of the enemy, but he left no doubt that the Leyte operation seals the fate of the Nips on that island.

Throughout the voyage Gen. MacArthur, as usual, scorned precautions for his personal safety. He was asked if he wanted a life-belt.

"No thank you," he replied. "I have too much faith in this ship for that."

Military men closest to the General believe his disregard of personal danger stems from an implicit belief that it is his destiny to liberate the Philippines and that nothing can happen to prevent it.

He sat upright at the stern of the barge with Gen. Sutherland. The General remarked with a broad smile:

"Well, believe it or not, we're here."

38 Days and Nights
on Dawson Ridge

· · · · · · · · · · · ·

BY

W. C. HEINZ

STAFF CORRESPONDENT OF THE NEW YORK *SUN*

ON DAWSON RIDGE, GERMANY, Oct. 22, 1944—If you want to go to Aachen now, you can drive in and out at will and there is nothing to stop you, for since Saturday Aachen has been ours. And yet on this ridge the guys who held the key to the city are still dug in—here in the mud and cold and wet and amid the dead, where they have been for thirty-eight days.

This is an ordinary-looking ridge here, this ridge that they have named after a gangling, 31-year-old son of a Texas Baptist pastor. But it happens to be the highest ground in these parts, and so from here you can see Belgium and Holland and just about everything except the way off of this ridge, which is lost in the fog and mist that [are] Germany.

This ridge is 883 feet high, and 400 yards long in its highest part, and it runs southeast of Verlautenheide toward Stolberg, which are two places the guys who fought and died here had never heard of before. This ridge had been divided into pasture lots and farming ground, but the sides are torn now and the three red-brick houses are shattered and broken, and only the skeletons of two steel towers still stand at the top, their power lines dangling to the ground.

They have been here for thirty-eight days and thirty-eight nights, these Americans, and the nights have been longer than the days and yet today they tell you that if you go fifty feet further and show your head over the top of this ridge you will draw fire down upon them all. Besides, there is no need to go any further because it is here, two miles east of the city, that the gates of Aachen were hinged.

This is where the gates of Aachen were hinged because this is where one forward company—"one lousy little old G.I. company," as Capt. Joseph T. Dawson of Waco, Tex., calls it—stopped the three best divisions that the Germans had to offer. This is where they stopped them with everything from artillery to rifle-butts and that other thing that is still called guts, and that is why they never reached the streets of Aachen, these three divisions, and why the gates of Aachen were hinged here.

They came up on this hillside here, these guys in this G.I. company, on September 14, and they dug in where you can find them now. They took this hill easily, because then the Germans were still on the run, but the next morning as they looked down they could see the German buildup starting to develop. All day, as they watched from above, they saw the Germans moving up in the woods about one thousand yards to the northeast, and in patches of rough ground in between. And they dug in.

On the morning of the 16th, that German infantry division attacked and when it hit, it hit, as the captain says, "one lousy little old G.I. company." It hit first with artillery and mortars and then it attacked with at least two companies.

"The intensity of the attack carried the enemy into my positions," the captain said, "and I lost men. They weren't wounded. They weren't taken prisoners. They were killed. But we piled them up."

They piled them up, that day, one upon another, as they have piled them up since, for they have taken three major attacks here and there have been very few prisoners. That one lasted from 7 to 11 A.M. And at 1:30 P.M. Lieut. John D. Burbridge of La Grange, Ga., took a platoon and physically drove them back from where the sheer weight of their attack had carried them in.

From then on until October 4, nothing fell on this position here except five hundred rounds of artillery a day, from everything from 150's up. And at night it was the same only worse.

"On October 4," the captain said, "that other infantry division hit us. We had had constant shelling for eight hours, and we had twelve direct hits on what was our command post then, because we were taking it from 270 degrees on the compass. When they stopped coming we could count 350 that we ourselves had killed—not those killed by our artillery or planes, but just by one lousy little old G.I. company all by itself."

On October 15 an SS Panzer division moved into position below, and struck at 11 o'clock that night. They struck with artillery and they struck with tanks, and behind them came the men, and the first tank that penetrated the position here was an American Sherman that still had the Allied star and insignia of the Fifth Armored Division on it, and had been captured on the Third Army front.

In the darkness of that night, split only by the flash of guns, the spitting of rifles and the cries of men—for the Heinies still holler when they are hit—the gates of Aachen almost swung open here, and for two days they groaned on their hinges.

Those were nights and days when men killed one another with rifle-butts, because it was too close to bring rifles to bear. At one machine-gun position a German toppled dead over the barrel of our gun, and in one foxhole an American fought off death and waited until the German who had shot him came up and looked down upon him, and then the American emptied his Tommy-gun in the enemy's face and the two men died, side by side.

Then there was this captain who, they tell you at headquarters, is as good a fighting man as there is in the American Army, and who called for artillery ten yards beyond his own position. But on that 17th of October the gates of Aachen, here on this hillside, were shut for good.

So down in Aachen they have won the city, house to house, and here on this hillside they have won only the right to stay another day, because they are still digging in. In those moments when the artillery shells aren't falling here you can see a G.I. running, bent over low, and under one arm he has a piece of timber and under the other a square of corrugated tin. They tell you he is improving his position, something that always goes on in these rare moments because this is where he lives and fights and this is where he doesn't want to die.

And in the piles on the hillside, where they stopped them, the Germans lie. They still lie here because the Germans don't bother with their dead, and when we try to move them, the Germans kill the men who go out to do the job. So they lie here, these Germans, some of them whole and many of them in parts, and the smell is bad.

It is so bad that some guys get sick, but there is one guy in here who, though he was sick when he said it, asked them not to try to move the Germans too far away from the foxhole where he lives day and night.

"Just move the ones that are within ten feet," he said. "I don't think those krauts have got guts enough to try to come at me if they have to climb over their own dead."

Meanwhile, down in Aachen now, you can drive in and out at will and there is nothing to stop you, for they held the key to the city here, these guys who, if you ask them about it, will tell you that they didn't fight for Aachen, but just to stay on this ridge for another day.

Back at headquarters they'll tell you that Capt. Dawson is as good a fighting man as there is in the American Army, and they won't be talking about his DSC or his Purple Heart with clusters, but about how he led his company first off the beaches in France and about why they named this ridge here after him.

"I've never seen anything like it before," he was saying. "This is the worst I've ever seen."

The captain is a tall man. He is 6 feet 2, but he is thin and his clothes fit him loosely, because he has lost twenty-five pounds over here. His face is bony and he has large ears and very brown eyes, long straight black hair and his nose doesn't stick out of his face, but runs straight along down through the middle.

"Nobody," the captain was saying, "will ever know what this has been like up here. You aren't big enough to tell them, and I'm not big enough to tell them, and nobody can tell them."

This is where they closed the gate to Aachen and where G Company stopped the best that three German divisions had to offer.

In this command post here they had lighted one white candle and one small kerosene lamp, which stood on a table, with maps and magazines around them. On another table against the far wall, dance music was coming from a small shiny radio, and outside in the night would be periods of quiet and periods of great noise.

When there was a period of quiet it was hard to realize that the Germans were 250 yards away. Then there was only this room, and soft dance music coming out from against the wall, and men sitting around straddling chairs, with their chins on the arms and their arms on the backs of chairs, and a small tan dachshund rubbed against your ankles and shoes.

"That dog is Freda," the captain said. "She was here when we came up on this hill and she's never gone away."

When there was a period of noise you could hear machine-guns outside cutting the night in geometric parts, and the whine of our own guns and the crump of theirs.

"Just one lousy little old G.I. company," the captain said when you had got him to talking about his guys. "Just G.I. privates, corporals, sergeants, and nobody will understand."

The captain said that nobody would understand because you had asked him to tell you about their thirty-eight nights here. He told you about it right from the start, the first day he had had a chance to talk like that in thirty-eight days. And now the rifle butts and hand grenades and the parts of bodies and the screams in the night—the Heinies still scream when they're hit—were with him again, and he knew that nobody would understand all that.

"And a kid says, 'I'll take that water to that platoon,'" he was saying now, and he had taken his feet down from the wooden table and was leaning forward. "And he starts out. He is about fifty yards from this doorway and I'm watching him. He is running fast; then I can see this 88 hit right where he is, and, in front of my eyes, he is blown apart."

The captain talked for a long while about things like that. He is a son of a pastor and his voice is soft and yet sometimes he uses strong words.

"What would you do," he said, "if a guy said, 'I can't take it any more'—just like that? If I lose that man, I lose a squad. So I grab him by the shirt, and I say: 'You will, you will. There ain't any going back from this hill except dead.' And he goes back and he's dead."

The captain was quiet for a moment now, as quiet as the room, for nobody spoke and there were no guns barking outside.

"He doesn't know why," he said, "and I don't know why, and you don't know why. But I have got the answer to those guys.

"I have got the answer to those guys," he said, and he was looking right at you, "because I wear bars. I've got the responsibility and I don't know whether I'm big enough for the job.

"But I can't break now," he was saying and you could see what was going to happen. "I've taken this for thirty-eight days and I'm in the middle of the Siegfried Line and you want to know what I think? I think it stinks."

And then the captain put his head in his hands and his elbows on his knees, and Capt. Joe Dawson, fighting man, sobbed.

There wasn't a sound in the room. You think now that nobody even moved and it must have been for about fifteen seconds. And then suddenly the captain raised his head and did a peculiar thing. Without looking at anybody, he said, "Shut up!

"Shut up," he said, "I want to hear this. It's the 'Bell Song' from 'Lakme.' "

The radio was clear and the soprano's voice was soft and so was the string music.

"Puccini," somebody said.

"No," the captain said, "not Puccini. Not Puccini, but I can't remember the name of the guy."

. . . .

W. C. HEINZ

Wilfred Charles Heinz worked at the New York *Sun* as a copyboy, reporter, feature writer, war correspondent, and sports columnist in turn. After 1950 he contributed to nearly every major American magazine, including the *Saturday Evening* Post, *Cosmopolitan*, *Collier's*, and *Esquire*. An article written for *Life* magazine in 1961 about a lung operation is still used in medical texts today. He was the author of three books, including *The Fireside Book of Boxing*.

Japan's Fleet Destroyed

. . . .

by

EMMET CROZIER

STAFF CORRESPONDENT OF THE NEW YORK *HERALD TRIBUNE*

BY TELEPHONE TO THE *HERALD TRIBUNE*

PACIFIC FLEET HEADQUARTERS, Oct. 26, 1944—Japan has been reduced to a third-rate sea power and her entire defenses have been gravely impaired as a result of the disastrous naval defeat administered by United States fighting planes and ships in the Philippine Sea and the central Philippine area.

In a series of three engagements beginning Oct. 23 and extending through yesterday the enemy's main carrier force was completely destroyed, several battleships were sunk and others severely crippled. What remains of the Japanese fleet is so badly damaged as to render it virtually impotent for months.

[The Associated Press reported from Pearl Harbor that twenty-seven Japanese ships were sunk or damaged in the Philippine engagement. Incomplete returns showed Japanese losses included ten battleships sunk, probably sunk or damaged, with two definitely sunk. The score also showed five cruisers sunk and five damaged, two carriers sunk and one probably sunk, three destroyers definitely sunk and one damaged, and "several" other destroyers sunk.]

One result of this great naval victory, which is shared by the 3d Fleet of Admiral William F. Halsey, Jr. and the 7th Fleet attached to General Douglas A. MacArthur's expeditionary force, and commanded by Vice-Admiral Thomas C. Kinkaid, is to give impetus and assurance to the Philippine invasion. Another is to advance the day when American forces may be expected to land on the China coast and join forces with the hard-pressed Chinese.

In its present condition the Japanese fleet can scarcely hope to prevent the complete realization of both these projects.

In addition to the loss of the light carrier Princeton reported earlier, one escort carrier of the 7th Fleet was sunk and several others were damaged. Other than these, we suffered no major loss.

(The 10,000-ton Australian cruiser Australia also was lost in the battle, the British radio said Thursday night, as heard by the National Broadcasting Company.)

The victory, which must be regarded as the most important naval achievement of the war, ranking above Midway in damage inflicted on the enemy, was secured at extremely low cost in personnel and ships. Again American seamanship and training demonstrated clear superiority over those of the enemy.

It is believed here that the Japanese sea lords mustered their maximum naval fighting strength for this test. Apparently they had two objectives: to break up MacArthur's amphibious operations around Leyte and to take the 3rd Fleet by surprise. They counted heavily—much too heavily, it now appears—on land-based air support by the Japanese Imperial Air Force operating from Luzon.

Some of this air strength did materialize, but it was too little and too late. The official communiqué issued here early this morning tells the story.

Chronologically what happened was this:

Early Monday, Oct. 23, an American submarine caught sight of a Japanese surface force moving eastward through the Sulu Sea, southwest of Mindoro. Search planes of the fast carrier task force verified this report, and a short time later spotted another and larger force moving southwest in the Sibuyan Sea. Both these forces came from the West, possibly from Singapore or Indo-China.

Waves of dive bombers and torpedo bombers were sent up to strike these two enemy forces. While these aerial attacks were in progress, word came that a third and still larger Japanese force had been sighted moving down into the Philippine Sea southeast of Formosa. This force, which included the main Japanese carrier group, had been spotted by long-range search planes from the Marianas and almost at the same time by the aerial patrols of the 3rd Fleet.

When the major force was spotted, Admiral Marc A. Mitschener's force recovered its planes from the minor league activities over the Philippines and headed north. His planes maintained contact with the approaching Japanese fleet during the night, and at dawn our attack was launched.

Instead of the Japanese surprising us, we surprised them. We had more carriers, tougher planes, better pilots. We beat them to the punch. Some details of the battle, which raged all morning long of the 24th, are still obscure, but this much is certain: not one single Japanese carrier left the scene of action. There were at least three, possibly four, in action against us and every one was sunk.

Meanwhile, the Japanese force first sighted in the Sulu Sea had steamed eastward through the night, traversing the Mindinao Sea, and at dawn headed for MacArthur's transport, landing craft and miscellaneous vessels in the vicinity of Leyte. Elements of the 7th Fleet, including escort carriers, moved into Suritao Strait to meet this threat, and as related in General MacArthur's communiqué, stopped it cold.

The middle enemy force, which consisted of two battleships, ten cruisers and thirteen destroyers, had by this time arrived in San Bernardino Strait, where it was in position to either dash to sea to join the battle there or move southward to attack the invasion area. It was too big a job for the 7th Fleet units which had been dispatched to meet it. Admiral Halsey, having the siutation in the Philippine Sea well in hand, dispatched a strong carrier task force which hurried down San Bernardino Strait and there again the enemy was stopped and routed, but not until we had suffered the loss of an escort carrier and damage to some of our other ships.

Here at Pacific Fleet Headquarters reports are still coming in on the last phase of the battle. Early yesterday our carrier aircraft and fast cruisers and battleships were still pursuing crippled remnants of the Japanese fleet. It was thought possible the score would be even larger when the final dispatches are analyzed.

Summing up the practical results of the engagement, it may be said that the damage done to the Japanese ships remaining afloat exceeds the known repair capacity of the Japanese shipyards; and it may be added that the enemy repair facilities will receive concentrated attention in the near future.

· · · · · · · · · · ·

EMMET CROZIER

Emmet Crozier, correspondent and founding member of the American Newspaper Guild, began his newspaper career at the Kansas City *Star* in 1912. After leaving the *Star*, he worked at the New York *Herald Evening World* and the *Globe* before joining the New York *Herald Tribune*. During this time he also worked briefly as a scenario writer for Paramount's Astoria studios and as a director of public relations for the Radio Corporation of America for three years. As a correspondent for the *Herald Tribune* he covered the Pacific campaigns during World War II. He retired in 1949 but founded a small community newspaper, called the *Heritage Villager*, in Connecticut in 1967.

He was the author of three books: *Yankee Reporters: 1861–65, American Reporters on the Western Front: 1916–18*, and *Thirty Years of Billiards* with Willie Hoppe.

Crozier died in 1982 at the age of eighty-nine.

Target of a Suicide Bomber

· · · · · · · · · · · ·

BY

JOHN GRAHAM DOWLING

CHICAGO *SUN* FOREIGN SERVICE

ABOARD U.S. DESTROYER IN MINDANAO SEA, Dec. 13, 1944—The columns of ships left the dubious shelter of San Pedro Bay, turned their backs on the distant blue mountains of Samar, and slipped southward down the rough, terrible coast of the Island of Leyte, making for Surigao Strait.

The agile, slim destroyers moved lightly along the flanks of the convoy. The screech of the bosun's pipe over our ship's announcer was followed by the brittle announcement. "This is the captain speaking. On this operation we can expect enemy air attacks."

That was all. The eyes of the men met in the passageways, over the tables and across the guns, and wan smiles were exchanged. Lt. (jg) James Clay Hunt, Lexington, Ky., torpedo officer, leaned on the rail, making a slapping motion with his hands and grinning. "The big foot has come down on us three times now and just missed us each time," he said.

He held up his crossed fingers. You do not reply, but you could not forget what happened during the one day at Ormoc, and this was to be five days of the same thing.

The ship's executive officer, Lt. Commander John C. Matthews, of Santa Monica, Calif., appeared on deck to smell the wind and said: "The reinforcing convoy over at Ormoc is catching hell today. They're screaming for air cover. I know how they feel."

"Have you got any more good news?" asked the ship's doctor, Lt. Charles K. Dilley of Marlinton, W. Va., medical graduate of Northwestern University.

"Sure," said the exec. "They sank a Liberty ship full of Christmas mail on its way here."

"How? Air?"

"No. Torpedo."

"Well, don't say anything about it to the crew."

"No, of course not."

In the wardroom later you became acquainted with Maj. Maxwell MacCloud Cooch, an artillery officer of the Australian Imperial forces. He is a bombardment observer. The two of you played acey-deucey and without malice discussed the merits of American and Australian manhood in regard to the military and of American and Australian womanhood in regard to matrimony.

Then suddenly, Lt. Leonard O. Scott, a Californian, appeared at the wardroom door and said quietly and without excitement: "They just attacked one of our ships."

You did not for a second believe Scotty because there had been no alarm and no general quarters sounded, and not a shot had been fired. But Scotty insisted and you followed him reluctantly out on deck, half expecting to be made a fool of.

Scotty was right. There in the Mindanao Sea, on the right flank of our convoy and against the rising green masses of the mountains of Bohol, a ship was firing heavily, the thin gray streamers of smoke piling upon the wind behind her.

Your force had been expecting this, but not this way, not without warning. The convoy even now was not on the alert. It appeared that half the ships in it were not aware that one of their number has been attacked. The Jap plane had apparently reached the convoy undetected. He hit without hesitation.

Now your ship's detectors picked up something else and the call to battle stations sounded. You went carefully to your cabin with your heart hurting a little bit and that going-to-the-dentist feeling in the pit of the stomach.

You put on your kapok life jacket and your tin hat and stepped out onto the deck. Doc Dilley was standing there, trying to take in the whole gray sky at once.

"I was afraid this was going to happen," he commented.

"If anything happens, where do you work? In the wardroom or the sick bay?" you asked.

"We take the bad cases to the wardroom," the doc said. "But I hope I don't have any work to do this trip."

"So do I," you said, but you didn't believe it for a minute.

The ships had crowded in tight for defense and the convoy pushed ahead in the choppy sea. Suddenly, you felt the vibration and heard the new pitch of the ship's hum. The wind in your face became stronger and the destroyer's roll was more noticeable. The speed-up was a sign of impending action. It brought you to attention. Finally, there was no sound except that of the wind.

Pharmacist's Mate 3rd Class Robert Irwin Lebin, of Chicago, passed among the waiting repair party, giving them cotton for their ears. Suddenly, from the bridge came a sharp order and the talker near you repeated: "Action port!"

All eyes swung apprehensively to the left and then, with a soul-shaking sound, your 5-inch guns opened up. You followed them frantically in an effort to determine what they were firing at, and then you saw it and the tension partly eased. It is always easier to face something you can see.

There was the Jap, a twin-engined bomber high and distant off the port beam, moving between the black bursts of our 5-inchers.

Then from nowhere two P-38's appeared and each made a short, quick pass at the Jap. You watched his left engine go into orange flames. This was the delicate part. The Jap was hit and knew it, but he still had the plane under control and you watched him weave from side to side as though he was looking over the whole fleet for a target.

You watched him bank around in a slow circle. Then came the horrible certainty that he had chosen his target and you were it.

While you started to tremble so badly you could hardly see through the glasses, the silhouette of the Jap plane changed from a side view to a head-on picture. The guns of your little destroyer opened up rapid fire.

The situation was perfectly understood. The Jap was hit and burning and was already as good as dead, and he had chosen to put his bombs on your ship before he died. As for your people, they faced the problem of blasting him out of the air before he could finish his run.

He was coming toward our ship at better than 200 miles an hour and you could see now that he was one of the biggest bombers the Japs have. If his bombs hit us, it would be as if a freight car loaded with dynamite was dropped upon the deck.

Up in the fire control our comedian, Claude Napoleon Sapp, slipped his eyes to the rangefinders and yelled over the phones:

"Get that——!"

The 5-inchers snapped while the young gunners at the 40s sat frozen in their places, waiting for their turn. The boys at the 20s stood with their cold and bitter young eyes on their sights, also waiting.

Nobody had to tell them when to fire. There was no time for orders, and they would know when the Jap was within range.

The 40s came into the fight, their white tracers going past the Jap at first and then into him. Bits flew off the wings and off the fuselage, but he was coming on. Then the 20s joined in, so that everything on the ship was firing at him except the torpedoes.

You felt that you were losing your mind in a high-explosive nightmare of concussions and fireworks. The deck was slapping you on the feet.

The Jap was no more than 75 yards off and still coming toward the ship, growing more monstrous with each split second.

You were feeling wobbly. "Well, well—so this is how you go out."

There seemed to be nothing to do, no way to get out of the way of this. You just stood there and watched it, remembering vaguely how good it was to have been alive.

Then, in an instant, the Jap wavered. The dipping tip of his left wing was almost imperceptible, but at this horrible point you felt that you could detect it if he blinked his eye.

The wing wavered, dipped a trifle more, first a port tip and then a starboard tip. You were aware of the steel from your ship's guns simply eating into the cabin of the oncoming Jap, simply putting so much fire into it that even a mouse in it could not stay alive.

In a moment of time, engulfed in a steel well of shocking sound and unbearable light, the Jap's wing tipped lower and touched the water, and in a flaming smash it was over as a pillar of orange fire and black smoke rose upon the water just 40 yards from your bridge.

The Jap plane had vanished and your ship's fire had stopped, and your ears were ringing like the bells of St. Patrick's on Easter, and your heart was like a piece of meat in the ice-box.

Dimly, through the cotton in your ears, came the vague cheers of the gun crews as their eyes went back to the skies to look for the next one and you, the observer, went down to the captain's cabin to the captain's washroom and threw up your lunch.

• • • • • • • • • • •

JOHN GRAHAM DOWLING

John Graham Dowling was born in Philadelphia, the son of actor Eddie Dowling and comedienne Raye Dooley Dowling. After graduating from the University of Notre Dame in 1934, he worked for the Chicago *Times* and the Newark *Star-Ledger*. In 1941 he was hired as a correspondent for the Chicago *Sun*, covering the Asian war fronts.

After the war he went to work for *Time* magazine, for which he was the Singapore bureau chief, then bureau chief in Buenos Aires.

On June 16, 1955, a plane carrying Dowling and twenty-four other passengers crashed in Paraguay, killing him and thirteen others. He was returning from Brazil after working on a story for *Time*.

The Bayonne Bitch to the Rescue

. . . .

BY

HOMER BIGART

WAR CORRESPONDENT OF THE NEW YORK *HERALD TRIBUNE*

SOMEWHERE IN THE PHILIPPINES, Dec. 20, 1944—The PT boat Bayonne Bitch, piloted by Ensign Lew Thomas of New Orleans, returned safely to its base this morning after snatching from Japanese-held Cebu an oil-well driller from California and a sugar plantation manager from Hawaii, who had been living like Robinson Crusoe throughout the long enemy occupation on mountain lookouts above the Camotes Sea. Also rescued were nine members of a Liberator crew shot down off the west coast Dec. 1.

The escape was timed for melodrama. While the fugitives scrambled aboard, a Japanese patrol tried to crack the thin guerrilla line a mile down the beach. Just before we arrived, a Japanese boat attempting to land was taken under fire, killing six and forcing the others to leap into the sea. The nightmarish howls of the drowning Japanese pursued us as the Bayonne Bitch plunged northward through the Camotes Sea.

I had gone along under the impression this was just a normal patrol—part of the tightening blockade of western Leyte, where several thousand Japanese face annihilation. Ensign Thomas, a husky blond former halfback of Tulane University, predicted a quiet night.

On two previous missions not even a Japanese barge had been sighted.

We left anchorage late yesterday afternoon and shot through the winding vent between the green palisades of Leyte and Samar. It was still daylight when we cleared San Juanico Strait. Halfway across the Samar Sea we watched the sun dip behind the verdant headland of Biliran, splashing a mackerel sky with fiery carmine, as if the dead volcanic cone had come to life.

This night before the longest night of the year closed in abruptly. Clouds rolled back, revealing a young moon and stars bright enough after moonset to cast phantom paths across the tranquil sea. We sat on the bow completely relaxed while someone hummed Christmas carols and Wildried Jorge, bantam-sized Puerto Rican, of Brooklyn, recalled his youth passed in Brownsville, N.Y., during the reign of Murder, Inc.

"Two gangsters were buried out of my church," he recalled. "Their pals sent big bunches of flowers shaped like an electric chair. I guess they were trying to be funny."

Far off the port beam we saw occasional flashes of light. Lieut. (J.G.) Chester Ray, of Allegan, Mich., executive officer of the PT boat, said it was the reflection of an artillery duel on northwest Leyte.

Now we were in the direct path of Japanese shipping. For two hours we cruised southward with the black wall of Cebu visible against the western sky. Occasionally we observed small, slow-moving craft near the shore, but always they turned out to be native sails and we let them proceed unchallenged.

Thomas did not mind. He kept scanning the dark shoreline. Part of his job was to pick up survivors of shot-down planes or sunken ships and Cebu and adjacent islands were likely havens for men awaiting rescue.

Near midnight we spotted a flashing light. It was clearly a signal, but a "Possible trap." Thomas brought the PT boat around and headed cautiously in. All machine-guns were manned and pointed against the somber littoral. Southward, off the port bow, we could see the dim, low outline of land. If this were an ambush, we were set up beautifully for enfilade fire.

You did not have to be psychic to feel clammy apprehension, such as comes from finding a letter from the Bureau of Internal Revenue. Lieut. Ray, a small-town lawyer, gave a terse summation: "I don't like it. It smells."

A ghastly howl came from off the starboard quarter. From a spine-chilling yawp it descended to a low, piteous, sustained wail. A badly wounded man lay in the water, perhaps a half mile off shore. He had to be helped or put out of misery—and quickly.

The night was bright above, but on the water surface we could not see two hundred feet. We could not find him. For twenty minutes we searched up and down the coast. Thomas would head off slowly in what he thought was the direction of the cry, then, when he halted and silenced the motors, the wail would come faintly from another quarter.

All this time lookouts watched the light on the shore. Suddenly, they saw flashes of gunfire a short distance up the coast. Quickly, Thomas put out to sea. The shooting stopped and now the cry was heard again. He was calling us and the words were not English.

Having a Japanese aboard would be too risky. We drifted down coast, alert for any boats putting out from shore. It was nearly 1:30. Unless we started back in thirty minutes we would lose our race with the sun and daybreak would catch us still in the Camotes Sea.

Thomas decided to risk a signal. He flashed a message. His men crouched over their guns ready to answer any fire from the shore. Several seconds passed. Then a faint light flickered on the beach. Minutes passed before two outriggers appeared. We heard someone call, "Ship ahoy."

As the boats drew nearer we saw some of the men were wearing cast-off civilian clothes. Many were barefoot and all had that vague, beaten-down look that comes from living in subtropical rain and forest.

The Liberator crew, led by Pilot Lieut. George G. Dandridge, of Paris, Ark., had walked one hundred miles in twenty days. Four scuffed off their shoes when they landed in the strait between Cebu and Negros. Ashore, they found small Japanese shoes and got into them by cutting off the front end and letting their toes stick through.

"They hurt so much we threw them away after the second day," said Second Lieut. Seymour Sobel, bombardier, of Queens. "Funny thing, I used to walk all over New York and think nothing of it, but these mountains went up three thousand feet and the trail was brutal."

Sobel did not suffer from leeches, which fastened on the ankles of the others. Staff Sgt. Irving Hoffman, of Chicago, discovered a way to remove the leeches. "I put tobacco on them and they dropped off," he said.

"We lived on raw eggs, rice and bananas," said Lieut. Dandridge. "There weren't any malarial mosquitoes and all we caught were colds. One of the men suffered a slight foot infection and had to be carried the last twenty miles, but he's all right now.

"We didn't see a Jap until tonight. Four were shot landing in what appeared to be a lifeboat, and the others jumped into the water. We also had trouble from a patrol coming up from the south."

Dandridge's Liberator was jumped by a Zero during a raid on Fabricano Airfield at Negros. A direct flak hit had exploded a bomb in the bomb bay, smashing the hydraulic system and control cables and knocking out the No. 1 engine. Then the Zero dived on the crippled plane, wrecking the No. 3 engine.

Dandridge rang the bail-out bell when the ship cleared land. They parachuted down off the southern tip of Cebu.

Others rescued were Second Lieut. Richard E. Phillipson, of Milwaukee; Tech. Sgts. William A. Hare of Leesville, S.C., and William H. Carlin, of Seattle, and Staff Sgts. George P. Door, of Marcus, Iowa; Willis C. Andre, of Los Angeles, and Joseph Pietrosky, of Penn Craft, Pa.

The crew's ordeal was short enough, compared with the prolonged trials of Jerome E. Stone, 52 year old oil-well digger, of Long Beach, Calif., and Allister Forbes, plantation manager of Honolulu.

Trapped in Cebu after the collapse of American resistance in the Philippines, Stone and Forbes took to the hills separately and did not meet until last August. Each built himself a nipa hut, acquired chickens, planted a vegetable garden and learned to eat rice three times daily.

"Pop" Stone, short and sturdy with a leathery neck and a tanned, deeply lined face, said he fought despondency by hiking several miles daily on secluded trails, watching cock fights from a distance and occasionally eavesdropping on the natives.

"When Bataan fell we thought help would come in six weeks at least," he said. "Then months passed without our seeing even one American ship or plane. But we never gave up hope."

There were many Americans on Cebu, he said. Most of them went to Cebu town and put themselves voluntarily into a concentration camp, awaiting the Japanese invaders. They urged Stone to join them, but "Pop" had other ideas and finally they dismissed him as a stubborn old fool.

The Japanese did not occupy Cebu until the following April. According to Forbes, they kept the Americans interned on the island until the following December, then they shipped them out.

"During that time the local food situation was good and the prisoners weren't treated too badly," Forbes said. He looked wan and haggard and said he had lost considerable weight. In recent months the food situation had worsened, he explained, and the island was almost entirely out of medical supplies.

Forbes said the worst period of tension came when the Japanese set up a Quisling government.

"For a time we didn't know how the people would react," he said. "Had the Japs been smart and treated the people squarely, it might have gone badly for us. Fortunately, they behaved like heels and there was a strong reaction in our favor. Now they are one hundred percent with us."

Both Stone and Forbes are married and have not heard from their wives for three years. They seemed quite calm over their deliverance, and, as the PT boat raced through the safe waters of the Samar Sea, they already were planning an early return. "Pop" said he wanted to finish an oil well now down eight thousand feet, and Forbes said all his interests were bound up in Cebu sugar.

"But first I want some beer and ice cream and a look at my wife," "Pop" said.

The crew of the Bayonne Bitch included Frank A. Melchionne, of Newark, N.J., and John Pizzoferrato, of the Bronx.

. . . .

HOMER BIGART

Homer Bigart, a two-time Pulitzer Prize winner, covered World War II, the Korean War, and Vietnam for the New York *Herald Tribune* and later for *The New York Times*. Educated in architecture at the Carnegie Institute of Technology (now Carnegie-Mellon University) and in journalism in New York University, he began as a copyboy at the *Herald Tribune* and retired from the *Times* forty-one years later after winning many journalistic honors. Bigart remembered "life [as a war correspondent] . . . as being either grimly exciting or painfully boring . . . and I don't want to relive a minute of it."

He died of cancer in 1991 at age eighty-three.

One-Way Ticket to Berlin

· · · · · · · · · · · · ·

BY

LOWELL BENNETT

INTERNATIONAL NEWS SERVICE WAR CORRESPONDENT

[Editor's Note: When the following dispatch was carried over the wires of the International News Service, the late Barry Faris, then editor in chief, in an accompanying message to clients, described it as "a remarkable story that will rank as one of the greatest of World War II." Bennett, he explained, had first smuggled a letter out of Nazi-held territory to the London office of International News Service under the date of December 11. The dispatch, he said, was written twelve days later.]

INSIDE NAZI EUROPE, Dec. 23, 1944 (delayed)—This is the story of a one-way bombing mission to Berlin, my parachute jump from an aerial bonfire in a flak-filled sky down toward the burning city, and the action which followed.

It begins at an RAF Lancaster bomber base in the Midlands of England on the afternoon of December 2. It ends—for the time being—with my escape some days later from a war prisoners' camp in Germany.

At the base, I had been assigned to one of the 4-engined bombers to ride as an observer on the next heavy night attack on the German capital.

We were briefed during the afternoon and took off toward the dying winter sun.

I had inspected our two-ton block-buster and hundreds of phosphorus incendiaries crammed into the belly of the bomb-bay before our takeoff, so I breathed easily only after we had cleared the runway and were wheeling and climbing southeastward toward the heart of Nazi Germany.

The first Nazi defenses were encountered just off the Dutch coast. Ahead of us, flak sputtered and speckled the darkening sky, but our pilot reassured this worried reporter:

"That's nothing . . . wait until we get to the big city."

Our stream of bombers thickened as we penetrated deeper into enemy territory.

A sharp lookout had to be kept on the scores of planes which swept along below, above, and on both sides of us. Near Hanover, searchlights by the hundreds aimed straight up, illuminating the cloud beneath us into a thick white blanket.

"That's so we are silhouetted against the light for the night fighters above us," was the pilot's dubious reassurance this time. And as he spoke the flak fire became thicker, closer and more personal.

Almost immediately thereafter we were approaching Berlin.

The spectacular flak display—competing with the stars above in number and a hometown Fourth of July in brilliance—scorched and seared the sky ahead.

The Pathfinder planes had already arrived as target indicators, framed by waves of flashing vari-colored explosions which hung, beckoning-like, above the bomb-rocked city.

Four miles beneath us, fires were beginning to spread, blood-red patches splashing and heaving in a hell on earth.

We entered our bomb run right through the center of the shield of hundreds of shell and rocket explosions, scores of weaving, fingering searchlights, and dozens of fighter flares.

"Enemy fighter climbing toward us from starboard," our gunner shouted through the intercommunication phone.

We watched the interceptor plane clearly in what seemed almost daylight as he swung up towards us.

Our pilot swung the heavily laden bomber one way and another in violent evasive maneuvers. But in such a tight-packed stream of bombers, a night fighter could hardly miss.

I watched several clattering bursts of fire which spitted past us like aerial torpedoes and seemed to strike other bombers.

Disaster came to us with terrifying suddenness.

The world seemed to burst into an inferno of flame. Our plane shuddered and rocked violently. Cannon shells had ripped into the starboard wing and both engines exploded into a furious fire.

But to the panic and chaos the pilot's controlled voice "feather [cut off] starboard engines" brought momentary saneness.

The engineer switched off the motors.

But it was hopeless: the fire had flashed to the wing fuel tanks and flames enveloped us.

Dozens of searchlights coned us with blinding brilliance.

"Okay, boys, bail out, sorry," the pilot called—the grimmest words imaginable.

We buckled our parachutes as he struggled to keep the plane on even keel.

"Hurry, boys, can't hold it much longer," the pilot urged with cool restraint.

We followed each other into the bombardier's compartment, stumbling and fumbling our way through the passage, tearing off our oxygen masks, then dropping and spilling out into the rush of ice cold air.

I'm not a good soldier. For me, it was sheer panic and fright such as I had never before experienced.

I dove out clumsily. I pulled the ripcord of my parachute almost immediately, which is the wrong thing to do at a four-mile altitude.

Flak spangled the darkness around me. My ears rang with the concussion of explosions, my lungs ached for oxygen, and my head whirred with the wildness of a mad nightmare.

Beneath me, the fires spread larger and clearer; I was certain I was going to drop right into one of them.

Another burning plane swept past below, so close there was a momentary rush of hot wind across my ankles.

A nearby shell burst rocked the parachute and, for a moment, I thought it had been pierced.

In the space of a few short gasps of breath, I counted three bombers careening like flaming meteors toward the ground.

It was an experience defying description.

I remember shouting to myself, "You wanted a big story, well here it is."

The musette bag strapped to me was twisted around my throat and, with frozen fingers, I couldn't move it, so I couldn't look down easily.

Suddenly, however, I managed somehow to realize I was dropping into a river or lake.

I tugged frantically at the parachute to veer off toward land, but I was too cold. It had been forty below zero at the height from which I had jumped.

Then, suddenly, I hit, sinking waist-deep into mud and chest-deep into water.

I released the tangled chute, inflated my lifebelt, and tried to struggle out of the mud, clutching at the reeds for support.

But the mud was too thick, my trenchcoat too heavy, and my body too frozen to respond to mental commands.

What happened during the next few hours is not exactly clear. I believe I was temporarily out of my head for I shouted to myself to move and couldn't.

"Your wife and baby are waiting; fight to get out of this," I tried to tell myself.

But it was no use. My arms and legs were freezing.

What seemed like an eternity later, two men came out of nowhere in a rowboat, pushed their way through the reeds with a pole, and pulled me out. They dragged me into the boat and I fell flat on my face, my legs and arms numb and useless.

Ashore, they carried me to a cottage, rubbed my legs and arms back to life, and gave me coffee, bread and cigarettes.

Towards morning, I learned I was in a village on the outskirts of Berlin.

A woman neighbor, who spoke some English, came to see me. She brought a blanket and, while she knitted a sock I had torn, she told me about her home in Berlin.

Her husband was on the Russian front. She had been evacuated from the capital with her child.

One of the men who had saved me was a German army corporal on leave; the other a lumber merchant. Both appeared friendly and curious.

I had expected to be lynched because I figured I would represent to them the means by which their city was being destroyed.

But their friendliness was amazing. They fed me and stoked up the fire. They dried my clothes and we talked of the war—haltingly because of the language difficulties. The woman said one thing about the raids: "We will never capitulate."

Later, two sergeants came from a nearby searchlight battery and took me to their hut. I slept in one of their beds while they tried to dry my clothes some more.

During the afternoon, I was taken by truck to a camp near Berlin with other members of our crew who had been picked up and surviving crewmen of other crashed planes.

Some time later, during another transfer, I escaped.

But the details, my subsequent travels, and my present location, must remain secret until I have reached a safer point of dispatch.

For the moment, it is impossible to leave my present hiding place, but it is relatively safe. At least I can get some food, some warmth, and some rest.

In all fairness, I must say that since my unwelcome arrival in Germany, until I escaped, I was treated in a courteous manner I wouldn't have believed possible.

So was, from what I saw, every airman still alive who that same night had only a one-way ticket to Berlin.

· · · · · · · · · · ·

LOWELL BENNETT

Lowell Bennett was a correspondent for the International News Service during World War II, during which time he engineered daredevil escapes from two Nazi concentration camps. After the war he worked as a press officer for several military and civilian agencies and was named director of public information for the United States Information Agency in 1961.

The 101st Saves the Day at Bastogne: "Nuts!" to Surrender

· · · · · · · · · · · ·

BY

EDWARD ANGLY

CHICAGO *SUN* FOREIGN SERVICE

WITH AMERICAN TROOPS IN BASTOGNE, BELGIUM, Dec. 29, 1944— As the name of this battered Belgian town goes down in the martial annals of America, there goes with it the name of the 101st Airborne Division. That was the division that held this important road center, in the heart of the battlefield the Germans chose for their surprise offensive.

They held it for seven days in the face of complete encirclement by the enemy with five German divisions trying unsuccessfully to punch through the perimeter in the snow-clad rolling countryside. And it was these American soldiers who broke the back of Field Marshal Karl Gerd von Rundstedt's campaign.

Now that units in Lt. Gen. George S. Patton's Third Army have bored their way through to this area the way is open, and with good weather and with good luck they may succeed in the next few weeks in pulling off one of the great coups of this war.

But it should never be forgotten that it was the 101st that stood like a rock in the midst of the Germans when they streamed westward.

Now it may be told that the man who commanded this defense during the siege is 46-year-old Brig. Gen. Anthony C. McAuliffe.

His men call this five-foot-five-inch West Pointer "Tony" or "Gen. Mac," but he thinks they call him "the old crock" because 46 is rather getting on toward senility among troops who are air-borne.

In addition to his 101st, also known as the "Eagle Division," McAuliffe had with him through the siege some small units of the 10th Armored Division, others from a tank destroyer battalion and a few stragglers, including some Negro engineers.

Most of the stragglers got lost in withdrawals when the Germans cut a gash through the U.S. First Army on Dec. 17. At that time the 101st had but recently reached a rest camp in pleasant surroundings in France. It certainly deserved a rest, for it was the 101st that had been the first air-borne division to land in Normandy and it was the same division that subsequently fought its way out of encirclement in Holland.

The division's commanding general and his two stars, meanwhile, had been called to Washington for a conference in the Pentagon building and the division's one-starred assistant commander and two of the regimental commanders had gone to England for their period of rest.

The remaining officers and all the men had only begun to relax when the Germans broke through the First Army up here where Belgium, Luxembourg and Germany touch frontiers.

Von Rundstedt broke through on the night of Dec. 16 and 17— on the weekend, as is Adolf Hitler's habit. On the night of the 17th, McAuliffe was roused from his rest and told to be ready to move the whole division by 2 o'clock the following afternoon.

He got here at 3 o'clock the next afternoon through roads cluttered with withdrawing units of other American outfits. He had just enough time before darkness fell to pick out places to bivouac his regiments and select a likely terrain on which to put up defenses.

Through the night, his men rolled in against the traffic rolling out. Before the night was over, one battalion under Lt. Col. Ewell was attacked by Tiger and Mark IV tanks and was cut up rather badly.

But, meanwhile, as McAuliffe recalled when I got through the narrow corridor to his besieged perimeter yesterday: "Ewell's men killed a lot of krauts and we ordered him to go on the offensive."

From then on, the 101st kept on killing Germans.

From buck private to their top officer, they realize today something of the epic nature of the job they have done. But it was only last evening, amid shot and shell that still continue, that higher authorities far back of the lines in their infinite editorial wisdom decreed that the world could now be safely told what the Germans have known all along—that the name of the division that has held out all these encircled days in the Bastogne perimeter is the 101st Air-borne.

Against all the krauts they killed, their own numbers of dead are small and their wounded who had to get along without surgical care for so long have all been evacuated to the rear.

Ambulances rolled the night before last and all of yesterday down one snaky dirt road that was at that time the only path that been opened for them.

McAuliffe and every man under him give immense credit to the Air Forces for helping them hold out. For it was the Air Forces in five days of fine weather, beginning on Dec. 23, that pounded through every sunlit hour the German panzer and infantry units that kept assaulting the 101st's balloon-shaped perimeter only 14 miles around.

And it was airmen who dropped them food when they were almost out and ammunition when they had left only a few rounds for their artillery.

They seemingly didn't mind being surrounded. They say they were used to it from their Holland experience. And their commander says he never doubted their ability to hold this place.

Asked if his men now needed rest, McAuliffe without any touch of dramatics yesterday said:

"Though help has and is coming through to us, we are still holding our posts. We are ready for offensive action and we are ready to pursue. One outfit only is in need of rest and it is being pulled out.

"I don't know the big picture very much, for we have been cut off. But I know we have been in touch with a lot of German units and that we have cut them up a lot. Some people have been flattering enough to say that our holding up the Germans here held up their whole drive."

McAuliffe, whose father was connected with the Interstate Commerce Commission, was graduated with a West Point hurry-up class that got its diplomas just eleven days before the armistice that ended that other world war. His wife and daughter, Patricia, live in Washington, D.C. Their son is a buck private at Camp Bowie, Texas.

Of his own men and the stragglers with them, McAuliffe lost one unit during the entire siege. It was on Dec. 21 southwest of the town that the unit was overrun by tanks and asked for help over the phone. But there was no available help, to be sure for attacks were coming from all points. That was the last he heard of that unit.

Captured Germans were almost as much of a problem in McAuliffe's manpower shortage situation as were the wounded without surgical care. Men were rotated from different fighting units to guard the prisoners. One night a bomb hit close to the prisoners' corral and in the confusion some of the prisoners got away. All but one were recaptured.

Three times the division command post was hit. Every command post in the perimeter was slugged at least once by bombs or shells.

But just as the morale of the Germans who were captured seemed to be lowered each day, so that of the Americans sticking it out in the encircled area rose.

The wounded, though denied proper surgical care, begged that no surrender be made for them. One man suffering from trench feet said that although he couldn't get into his shoes, he could get into his overshoes and asked to be allowed to wear them and go back to his post on the firing line.

So high, indeed, has the morale of the 101st become that one colonel jokingly said to McAuliffe today: "Sir, these men of ours are sure going to be insufferable from now on."

They have a right to be. For instance, on Dec. 22, when the Germans put a road block across a highway in the northwestern part of the area, one company was sent out to reduce it. They reduced it—and in so doing killed thirty Germans and took twenty-six prisoners. The company suffered one casualty—one man's arm was broken.

When McAuliffe dictated the one word, "Nuts!" as his reply to a German surrender demand, a colonel said that he would like to handle the business of delivering it to the German commander's emissaries. He took a jeep to where they had been blindfolded and drove them to the line.

A German major, using an English-speaking captain as his interpretor, asked, "Is the reply favorable? If so, I have the authority to proceed with the negotiations for your surrender."

The American colonel told him that the reply was not favorable.

"That's too bad," said the German major. "Thank you very much for your kindness to us."

"I wasn't kind," said the colonel. "My general's reply is 'Nuts!' Do you know what 'Nuts!' means?"

When this had been translated, the German major confessed that in all truth he did not.

"Tell him," said the colonel to the captain, "that 'nuts' means the same thing as 'Go to hell.' You know what that means, don't you?"

The captain said he did, and the German major, when it was translated, said that he too understood that term.

. . . .

EDWARD ANGLY

Edward Angly was a correspondent for the Associated Press from 1920 until 1930, when he went to the New York *Herald Tribune*. He headed its London bureau and was its chief correspondent in the Middle East. In 1941 he joined the Chicago *Sun*, subsequently covering virtually every battlefront and every hot spot, often being among the first journalists at hand. For the *Sun*, he was the Far East correspondent, covered the developments in areas around the South Pacific, The Soviet Union, and Baltic states, and headed the Paris bureau. In 1945 he became a full-time free-lance writer, contributing to most major magazines and writing the book *Fifty Billion Dollars*. An earlier book, published in 1930, was *Oh, Yeah!*, cowritten with Jesse Jones.

Angly died in 1950 and was buried in his native state of Texas.

"Thus Far—and No Farther" in the Bulge

· · · · · · · · · · ·

BY

FRANK CONNIFF

INTERNATIONAL NEWS SERVICE STAFF CORRESPONDENT

WITH AMERICAN INFANTRY AT LA GLEIZE, Belgium, Dec. 29, 1944—The shadow of every storied place in American history where our fighting men have drawn a line and said "thus far, and no further" hovers today over this little town cradled on gently-flowing Belgium hills.

In the Valhalla where all good warriors go, the men of the Alamo, of Bunker Hill and Gettysburg must have prepared a special welcome for the gallant young initiates who joined their valiant fraternity during the past week.

They took their positions among the crooked contours of the Belgium hillside in an hour of utmost urgency. They were hopelessly outnumbered and they knew it. The sacrifice they were to make would be unsung and unrecorded. They knew that, too.

But the kinship that links patriotism of the past with deeds of the present boasts a continuity that scoffs at the caprice of passing years, a pliant strength that no sophistication ever will really sever.

La Gleize today is ours again. In this pocket we ultimately destroyed tons of Nazi material and annihilated thousands of Hitler's best soldiers. The lightening rapier of Field Marshal von Rundstedt became a blunt and rusty sword as it probed for a soft spot that simply did not exist.

The men responsible died to do it. They were men who battled 'til the last breath, the last bullet, before the Nazi tide washed over them in those dark moments a week ago.

This correspondent never really understood how we absorbed that first wild enemy lunge until he talked with Capt. Edward McBride, of Somerset, Ky., in the company command post. Outside, La Gleize was deceptively tranquil.

Bearded and weary, McBride had endured that initial agony. Dozens of his closest friends perished within arm's reach. He realized that courage was flaming its brightest in the darkness around them.

But it was not until the Nazi wave recoiled and we regained our original positions that McBride fully grasped the gallantry of La Gleize's expendables.

"When I would come to an American machine-gun position," he recalled, "I'd find all the ammunition gone. Then I'd see the gunners. They would have carbines and pistols still clutched in their hands. I'd pry a weapon loose and find all its chambers empty. Occasionally, there would be one or two cartridges left.

"All around them would be dead Germans. Our men kept fighting until everything was gone, using pistols when nothing else was left.

"Then I'd go to the mortar position and find the same story. I'd see dead GI's still holding rifles. Some had knives, but they just kept fighting till the last bullet. All around them would be dead Jerries.

"Everywhere I'd find dead Americans—lots of them—I'd find a dozen dead Nazis sprawled around each of them.

"Sometimes, an American would still be holding a Jerry as if he fought him with his bare hands. Once during the battle an ammunition carrier reached the depot, badly wounded. He started unloading and was so badly hurt I told him he didn't have to go back. I wanted to send him to the rear.

"He looked at me and laughed: 'They are still fighting in there; aren't they? Well, that's where I'm going!'

"And that's where he went."

McBride, lank and raw-boned, talks with the faintest drawl. His men idolize him. As a correspondent, that is a story I would like to "catch"—the quiet affection and easy kindness that exist among combat men. It is their sole recompense for the scourging hours they endure together. In future years when hoary Junkers weigh the imponderables of this blazing struggle, they might remember McBride and the men of La Gleize.

For not in maps or statistics will they find the answer to what happened here. It was something in our heritage. Something that happened a long time ago. Something only an American could understand.

. . . .

FRANK CONNIFF

Frank Conniff began his career as a copyboy at the Danbury (Connecticut) *News-Times,* in the city where he was born. After graduating from the University of Virginia, he returned to Connecticut to be a sportswriter until he joined the Hearst newspaper chain in New York. For Hearst, he traveled through Africa, Italy, and Germany as a combat correspondent during World War II, and later he covered the Korean War.

In 1955 Conniff interviewed Soviet Premier Nikita Khrushchev and other top leaders in Moscow with fellow correspondents Kingsbury Smith and W. R. Hearst, Jr. The resulting series won a Pulitzer Prize, one of many honors Conniff received.

Conniff became general director of the Hearst Headline Service in 1958. He also wrote a column called "Capital Corner" and a later column called "Conniff's Corner."

Conniff ran for a House seat in 1964, but was beaten. His last job before retiring in 1967 was editor of the *World Journal Tribune,* another Hearst paper.

The War Moves into Germany

· · · · · · · · · · · ·

BY

GORDON GAMMACK

DES MOINES *TRIBUNE* STAFF WRITER

GARZWEILER, GERMANY——, 1945—A smiling little girl about 3 stood in a doorway in this town as troops and tanks moved through the streets and waved her hand at the doughboys.

There was nothing unusual about that. Little children are the same the world over.

But the child's mother came to the door, took one quick look up and down the street, grabbed the child and jerked her away from the doorway.

Then the door slammed shut.

That was the only evidence I saw of outright bitterness in a German community where a considerable number of civilians waited in their homes while the war went swiftly by.

Most Germans just looked bland and indifferent even, when soldiers moved into buildings and occupied them for necessary purposes.

They even seemed indifferent to the din of our artillery batteries blasting away from positions not very far distant.

I had my first brush with the no-fraternization rule when in a small courtyard. A woman came from a house suddenly and smiled as she passed. Should I nod back or pay no attention?

I guess I compromised with a half-smiling nod, but I hear that even smiling is considered fraternization.

Everyone seemed to think the battle was going well.

A lieutenant came in to report he had found three 500-pound bombs wired for explosion in the path of our tanks.

Over the radio came reports from officers with attacking tanks. One report came in like this:

"Can you hear me?"

"Yes, I hear you. Hear you well."

"We had to reconnoiter a tank ditch, but we're on our way now. We're rolling."

"O.K., that's fine."

"Roger."

Beside the radio I was attracted by a small square piece of paper on which was typed, "My dearest Daddy, I love you, Daddy, and I want you. I would like you to come home when you can. Tell choo choo man to hurry the train for I want you. Bob."

How this note got on the window sill of a German home I don't know.

The command post had moved in only a few minutes earlier. The voice came on the radio again, "Bypass either way. Either way will be O.K."

The ruling placing a blackout on the progress of the Ninth army troops is wise because it is doubtful if the German command itself knows where we are, but just the same it makes reporting the war difficult.

Tracking down Iowans is equally hard because everyone is on the move somewhere or other and everyone is busy.

Even so, you can't stop soldiers just back of the actual fighting from going in for some buffoonery. I saw several soldiers parading around in high silk hats found in the wreckage of buildings and one group of doughboys located a supply of theatrical costumes—wigs and everything—and they are having fun with them.

Store window dummies are dressed up in uniforms with German helmets.

Beside an ordnance outfit was a sign, "We fix flats."

Soldiers were riding along roads on bicycles they'd picked up somewhere.

Soldiers even take time to look up correspondents now that the vogue has come in of advertising us with signs saying "Press" in big red letters.

Soldiers stare at us sometimes shouting things like, "Hey, how about taking my picture?"

They haven't forgotten Ernie Pyle, even if he has gone to the Pacific. "Hi, Ernie," one soldier yelled at our jeep.

But the boys really went wild as a jeep carrying pretty Ann Stringer, United Press correspondent, went by. Ann's husband, Bill, was killed in France last summer while reporting the war for Reuters and Ann's sort of carrying on.

Doughboys are amazed to see a pretty American girl up front and they really ogle her. You hear remarks like, "Hey, look at that," or "geez, a woman" and "well, for cripes sake."

Doughboys moving up in trucks leaned over to get a closer look. Henry Wells, of the Chicago Tribune, made a prize comment. "You'd think these guys had never seen a jeep before."

When Ann's jeep stopped in a German village, at least two dozen soldiers swarmed around to talk to her. They insisted on giving her their souvenirs so she wound up with a German helmet, a knife and a few other knicknacks.

It all goes to show how crazy American soldiers are about American girls. Just a chance to look at one was wonderful for them.

Epic of Los Baños

· · · · · · · · · · · ·

BY

GORDON WALKER

STAFF CORRESPONDENT OF THE *CHRISTIAN SCIENCE MONITOR*

MUNTILUPA, LUZON, Feb. 24, 1945—The rescue of 2,146 civilians from the Los Baños internment camp forty miles south of Manila was a highly coordinated land, sea, and air operation packed with all the drama and suspense of a Wild West dime thriller.

The rescue forces struck at dawn. Infantry, amphibious tanks and picked paratroopers plunged more than five miles into enemy lines to bring out the interned civilians. So successful was the operation that not a single civilian internee was hurt.

But the Japanese camp commander and the entire Japanese garrison of 243 were liquidated.

This all went on while not less than two hours away by road, an enemy garrison of a thousand troops was stationed, apparently ignorant of the daring rescue or else taken too much by surprise to make a countermove.

The rescue mission actually was divided into three separate parts. Two hours before the appointed landing time, a group of fifty-three amphibious tanks mounting heavy machine guns took off from Mamatid, a town on the shore of Laguna de Bay, to move south down a huge inland lake to where Los Baños lies at the southern end.

The amphibious tanks landed on the point of land nearest Los

Baños and then moved about 1500 yards inland to where the camp—formerly the Philippines Agricultural Experimental College—lies in the shadow of towering Mount MacQuiling.

The key to the entire operation was a small party of American scouts who landed from native canoes two nights earlier at a point northeast of Los Baños. This force contacted a group of Filipino guerrillas commanded by an American officer who had been sent to work with the Luzon guerrillas several months ago.

The guerrillas then moved in and took up positions around Los Baños and awaited the appointed rescue time.

Two minutes before landing time the guerrillas set up smoke flares to mark the landing field for the paratroops, who dropped from nine transports about 1½ miles northeast of Los Baños.

The paratroop drop, which was made out of Nichols Field by elements of the Eleventh Air-borne Division, was made simultaneously with a landing by amphibious tanks.

As soon as the first men had landed from planes, the guerrillas closed in on the internment camp and, using knives and grenades, liquidated the Japanese guards who had been billeted in buildings within the camp compound.

The Japanese did not put up any stiff resistance and before they knew what had hit them, the guerrillas had disposed of the camp commandant and his assistant—both of whom had made living conditions practically intolerable for the internees for many months.

By this time, the amphibious tanks and paratroops had closed in on the camp from two directions and after meeting no further resistance began the task of loading the internees onto Amtrac tanks.

While guerrillas and paratroopers stood guard to make sure that there was no enemy counter attack of any kind, the internees were loaded into the huge lumbering water-borne tanks and taken back to the point of landing on the south end of Laguna de Bay. There they began a two-hour water-borne haul to Mamatid where the tanks had embarked originally.

Still another covering force consisting of infantry, artillery and anti-tank destroyers was meanwhile fording the San Juan River which lies two miles northwest of Los Baños. This force was sent to divert any possible enemy force from attempting to thwart the rescue.

The entire operation required the utmost teamwork of guerrillas, paratroops and sea-borne landing forces. Altogether it probably was more audacious and fraught with more danger than either of the previous rescues of civilian prisoners at Cabanatuan or Santo Tomas.

Had the Japanese who camped in the foothills of Mount MacQuiling decided to attempt interception, the entire operation undoubtedly would have fallen through.

So tightly coordinated was the operation that at 6:58 the guerrillas sent up a smoke flare to spot the paratroop landing field. At 7 sharp, the first American paratroopers landed on the appointed field in a dry rice paddy.

The story of the internees themselves is the same story of rigid Japanese surveillance, malnutrition and most primitive living conditions that was found at Cabanatuan and Santo Tomas.

Los Baños actually was an annex of Santo Tomas and was set up by the Japanese in January, 1942, when eight hundred Santo Tomasites were sent down to build a new camp at the Agricultural College site.

The Japanese had promised that Los Baños would be a model camp with all the luxuries of mountain air, big vegetable gardens and modern conveniences. Why the Japanese chose to write something in the nature of a travel brochure on the Los Baños camp is a question, though it probably was intended as propaganda for world consumption.

After the first three hundred, who were chosen from single men of military age, had broken out of the camp, it was found that the Japanese did not live up to their promises. The camp was primitive and sanitary facilities [were] almost nonexistent.

The rescue was the fourth such accomplishment in the drama of liberation of the Philippines. The Los Baños camp was the most crowded. It included 1,589 Americans, 329 Britons, 56 Canadians, 33 Australians, 89 Dutch, 22 Poles, 10 Norwegians, 16 Italians and one Nicaraguan.

The camp was established by the Japanese in May, 1943. The liberated captives, though emaciated by hunger, were reported in better physical condition than their fellow sufferers in Santo Tomas.

. . . .

GORDON WALKER

Gordon Walker was chief Far Eastern correspondent for the *Christian Science Monitor* and was assigned to the Pacific theater in 1942. From 1951 to 1954 he was a news editor in Boston. He returned to overseas correspondence two years later and covered events in Communist China, Japan, Korea, Taiwan, and Southeast Asia.

Walker died of cancer in Boston in 1959. He was forty-two.

Big Business in the Pacific

. . . .

BY
KEITH WHEELER

WAR CORRESPONDENT OF THE CHICAGO *TIMES*

PACIFIC BASE, Feb. 26, 1945—A corporation of GIs of my acquaintance are equipping themselves with a beer refrigerator by methods that are standard operating procedure for this sort of transaction in this part of the world.

The refrigerator originally turned up in possession of an Australian. When the motor burned out the Australian swapped it to an American colonel for a gasoline stove.

The colonel traded it and two quarts of whiskey to another colonel for a kerosene-powered refrigerator that worked. The second colonel loaned the crippled refrigerator to the corporation on condition they got the motor repaired.

Conniving to obtain this result has now proceeded for two months and is nearing an apparently successful conclusion.

First they took the machine to an ordnance shop with request for a rewiring job but the ordnance men said they couldn't do it, giving an obscure reason.

However, they discovered an Australian major who said he could accomplish a rewiring job. In return he requested permission to purchase an American wrist watch, which was granted. But before the watch was obtainable, it was necessary to fill the request of a post exchange officer, who had the watch and wouldn't sell it until his needs were met. The PX officer wanted a date with a nurse which was arranged by obtaining for the nurse a half-soling job on her last pair of shoes.

An amateur cobbler agreed to half-sole the shoes in return for a bit of native carving which was obatined from a Melanesian artist for two packs of cigarettes.

The Australian major turned the motor over to his driver who knew an electrician whose services he solicited in consideration of a pint of rum. At the cost of an old pair of shoes the electrician rewired the motor whereupon it was installed in the refrigerator.

When the juice was turned on it became evident that it was a direct-current motor and would not function on AC. Meanwhile, the ordnancemen discovered the refrigerant gas had leaked out of the machine. They tried replacing it with fluid used as an insect killer, finding this a satisfactory substitute.

A man in the engineers was discovered who knew the location of an alternating current motor for which the direct current job could be traded.

However, the AC motor's owner required as booty a certain make of cigaret lighter in workable condition. After some investigation, a satisfactory lighter was discovered. To obtain it, however, it was necessary to trade a Jap pistol which in turn was traded for a carved lion of native ebony. The lion was swapped for a mechanic's vise and the vise for the lighter.

Negotiations have now reached a state where the corporation considers it advisable to obtain a case of beer to put in the refrigerator. They know where a case of beer may be had in return for a box of pistol ammunition which can be had in return for twenty feet of 35-millimeter camera film whose present owner will part with it in consideration of sufficient lumber to build a table in his tent.

Meanwhile, the ordnancemen who will install the electric motor are running the refrigerator with a gasoline washing-machine engine, employing it to manufacture ice cream. That's why they couldn't fix it in the first place.

. . . .

KEITH WHEELER

Keith Wheeler, a native of Carrington, North Dakota, was a war and foreign correspondent and columnist for the Chicago *Times* until 1951, when he became a writer and correspondent for *Life* and *Time* magazines. He was the recipient of the Sigma Delta Chi Award in 1942, the National Headliners' Club award in 1945, and the Overseas Press Club Award in 1956. He was the author of six books, including *Peaceable Lane*, published in 1960.

What a General Does in Battle

· · · · · · · · · · · ·

BY

VICTOR O. JONES

WAR CORRESPONDENT OF THE BOSTON *GLOBE*

WITH THE NINTH ARMY IN GERMANY, Feb. 27, 1945—When the Allies opened the big push (for the Roer River and Cologne) I had the unusual opportunity of watching the opening hours of the attack from Maj. Gen. Alexander R. Bolling's office in the basement of a railroad station in a German border town. I had met the general the afternoon before the attack and was surprised when he said: "Come back any time, or maybe this would be the best place for you during the opening hours when it will still be dark and nobody will know what's going on."

So at 3 o'clock, while the artillery was thundering away, I returned and stayed with the general until after breakfast, just as light was breaking. The general's office was like a fort with walls four feet thick in the cellar and ceilings reinforced with steel beams. There were steel doors which dropped down instead of closing.

"Yes," the general said. "We inherited this place from the Germans. It was built long before the war, but like all public buildings in the town, and not a few private ones, it was built with a war in mind. When we moved in it took but a short time for the men to set up all these phones and lights."

Gen. Bolling is a scholarly looking man with a thin face and flat stomach, wears horn-rimmed glasses and may be 50 years old. He comes from Philadelphia, but has made the Army his career since being commissioned a second lieutenant at the outbreak of the last war. His father was a doctor who died of wounds in that struggle and only a few days ago Gen. Bolling was informed that his own son was missing in this one.

The general introduced me to his staff who were working in other bombproof rooms all around him—his chief of staff is Col. Louis W. Truman, first cousin of the vice president—and then chatted about Boston and things in general as though the war was millions of miles away instead of next door.

I commented on this between earth-shaking crashes of artillery which penetrated even here, and he said: "All our work is done. It is a poor general who has anything to do during the last few hours before an attack. We do all our work before that, and I am making it a point to keep away from regimental and battalion officers at this time. It's their show, and so that we would be relaxed the staff here went to the movies both last night and earlier tonight."

It was now just past 3:30 and I knew the fate of the Roer crossing was even now hanging in the balance a mile or so away. There were four field phones at the general's elbow and occasionally a sergeant or one of his aides would put a slip in front of him. These were copies of reports being received in other cellar rooms by the intelligence or communications divisions on phones or picked up on the radio, for headquarters was connected not only by various telephone lines, but also with an elaborate hookup of portable radios.

The general picked up one of the slips and frowned. "They've got the first battalion commander, but I don't know how serious it is," he told me. I had heard the soldiers raving about this young lieutenant colonel and figured this might upset the general, but he just laid down the note.

Another note was laid before him. "There is pretty strong artillery and mortar reaction at the crossing sites," he reported to me.

An aide came in. "I haven't been able to find out how badly the colonel was hurt, sir," he said, "but perhaps I can get it over one of those phones," pointing at the general's phones. "Go ahead, Joe," the general said, "but you've gotta have a nickel to make any calls in here."

But the aide couldn't get through and now the general went into action for the first time. There had been all sorts of testing noises from the radio room, next door.

"Tell that lieutenant out there to stop piddling on that radio and get busy on these phone lines," he said to the aide. Then he picked up one of his phones, cranked it up and asked for somebody. Streams of conversation came back.

"Keep your head, lad, and just get me that number, and no monkey shines. We've got a war to fight and Washington's birthday is over," said the general.

While he was waiting one of the other phones rang, and the general had two sets up to his face, just like city editors in the movies.

"The field artillery observer has phoned from the railroad tracks? That's great. That's fine. I guess he isn't there alone."

He looked at his watch and, turning to me, said, "That's twenty-four minutes since shoving off on this side—not bad. Some of the infantry at least must be up with him, though these artillery forward observers are pips."

The general laid down one phone just as somebody started talking on the other. "All of the whole company is across? That's fine. That's swell. Nice work. How about the wounded battalion commander? Not bad, eh? In the leg, eh? You say you heard his voice just now over the radio? That's fine. Keep going and keep me posted if you've got time."

He hung up. "The colonel was hit in the foot, but is still leading the battalion," he told me. "He's a tough fighter and I wouldn't be surprised if he was riding piggy back out there."

The phone rang. "The first and second wave completely over? That's fine. That's swell. What about the greenhouse and the slaughterhouse [these were two of the crossing sites]? They're getting over, too? That's good. And the boats are returning in good shape? That's fine. We may need them, if we can't keep the bridges up."

He called up and asked for an aide. "See how those foot bridges are coming." The aide reported they couldn't get through to the colonel of the engineers, but they were working on it. The general grabbed the phone and said: "Now look, Bill, I have got to have those wires in and I want them in quick. Put every man you've got on them and if that's not enough, I'll give you the 35th team, but I've got to get those lines."

Gen. Bolling picks up a slip. "The first footbridge is in," and reading from another slip, "and the corps reports that the 102d next to us has one battalion across further upstream. That's very nice."

It's now only a little after 4, but you feel as though it was maybe noon. The phones are never quiet, the aides come and go with verbal reports and with the little paper slips. Gen. Bolling asks whether you'd like to climb up to the top floor where he has an observation post.

"I'd go with you, but I don't dare. Earlier tonight, on my way up, I flashed my light downward just for a second to see where the banister is missing and the MP growled: 'Put out that light.' What did I do? I said, 'Yes, sir,' very meekly."

So the general calls an orderly and takes you up to the attic where you can look toward the river through all sorts of fancy lenses but can't really see much because daylight hasn't arrived and the valley is full of our smoke screen.

You return to the general's office and he's just watching his aides mark the latest positions on one of the maps covering the walls.

"That's right," he is saying, "only six hundred yards from Koerrenzig." He brought me up to date from slips of paper he had saved.

The leading infantry which was approaching Koerrenzig, the first objective, was receiving machine-gun fire. I used the expression: "Pinned down." "We don't allow that term here," he said. "Occasionally we get held up, but nobody ever pins us down. A company has reached the outskirts and is waiting for C Company to draw even. In five minutes the artillery will stomp down on the place."

Exactly five minutes later all hell broke loose. The artillery had never been quiet since it opened its barrage, but the volume rose and fell in intensity. Now, for a few minutes, the Army concentrated its fire on a town of half a dozen streets. Then the thunder abated and five minutes later the general had a slip on his desk which said that Koerrenzig had been occupied without opposition.

Then and later I was amazed at the close cooperation between foot soldiers and the gunners back of them, commanding the arc of the terrain in front of the advance. All the infantry had to do was to call a code number and target into a walkie-talkie and scores or hundreds of shells wiped that town off the map.

There was a lull and the general reached for a batch of Bronze and Silver Star citations to sign. One was for T5 David E. Anthony, of Boston, who had risked his life to bring up ammunition in action last November. I was amazed that the general should be doing such chores in the midst of battle and that a short time later he was asking the adjutant general why the division hadn't received any mail since moving up to the front.

That phone line to the engineer still wasn't working, but just as the general picked up another phone to do something about it, we heard the voice of Col. Truman in the next room taking the hide off someone about the same subject.

He wound up with "that's not good enough for me and if it is for you, you'd better turn in your suit." The general whistled softly. "Guess I couldn't have done any better," he said. A few minutes later he had that connection with the engineer.

Number one bridge had been shot away by mortar but was being retrieved. A pocket on the river bank which had been by-passed by the first battalion was still pouring small arms fire into the engineers who had suffered seven casualties, but they had foot bridges two and three almost over and were working again on Number One.

"Nice going, Company C. You're doing fine and we'll get those krauts out of there right away." The general told an aide to tell the regimental commander to clear out that pocket. "You're going fine already? Good boy. I knew you would," said the general.

The first casualty report was put before the general. He read off the figures. "Not nearly as bad as we expected," he said, "but this is only for this side of the river and I'm afraid of those mines—so afraid I don't dare ask."

An orderly asks whether the general wants breakfast brought in. "No," was the reply. "We'll go over to the mess, but let's wait until we take this next objective. There goes the artillery concentration and they will be walking into it in a few minutes. The general will enjoy his eggs better if he knows we're in there."

A five-minute wait and the expected happened. We walked across the street just as dawn was breaking. Gen. Bolling answered every sentry's salute along the way not only with one of his own, but with a friendly "Good morning" to which the sentries answered, "Good morning, sir." I commented on this. "It's not regulation," the general said, "but I like it and that's the way we do it."

At breakfast I found out that they have cockeyed rumors even at headquarters. One of the majors reported he had heard that five of our tanks had been destroyed. The general looked incredulous but picked up the phone which was next to his place at the head of the table and ordered a check made.

The call back denied the report and the general went back to his egg after kidding the rumor monger.

Then he told us about the recent visit of Pvt. Mickey Rooney with an entertainment group to his unit. "I don't think I like the little whippersnapper, but he's got something. Then Rooney sat next to me at the head table at mess and you know what he said to me? He said: 'You know, it's tough being a celebrity in the Army.' How do you like that for a buck private?"

. . . .

VICTOR O. JONES

Born in Wallingford, Connecticut, on September 14, 1905, Victor O. Jones was graduated from Harvard in 1928 and joined the Boston *Globe* as staff writer the following year. He worked his entire career at the *Globe*, retiring as executive editor in 1965. He spent the final two years of World World II in Europe as the *Globe*'s correspondent. He died in 1970.

It's Smoother Going
in the Newsreels

· · · · · · · · · · · ·

BY
LEWIS GANNETT
STAFF CORRESPONDENT OF THE NEW YORK *HERALD TRIBUNE*

GEREONSWEILER, GERMANY——, 1945—Technician Fourth Grade James Evans, of Lake, Miss., was hunched into a corner at the head of the cellar stairs. There wasn't room for him downstairs. The cellar had a solid concrete roof and even after the generator jeep had been hit, knocking out the lighting system, the cellar seemed cheery and comfortable. It shook when the 170's landed, but it didn't shatter.

One of those lamps you pump up by hand lit the war maps in the front room where the battalion commanders listened to the runners' reports and, poring over their maps and mosaics, tried to figure out what was what and where. The candle-lit back room contained a table littered with the refuse of K rations, an old foot organ, several rickety chairs and a score of muddy, solemn soldiers. The telephone lines had gone out as soon as the tanks crossed the road dragging wire with them as always; the radiomen in the hallway didn't need more than a flashlight to take down messages, and a coalbin was full of weary GI's sleeping in noisy darkness.

T-4 Evans had a magazine in his pocket which he could half read by the light coming through a shell hole in the brick wall. The hole was on the south side of the house away from the Jerry. Nobody stood near the window on the north side. Occasionally, someone quickly mounted the stairs, ducking as he passed the window, poised himself for a moment in the shattered attic trying to avoid silhouetting himself against the light and took a quick look toward the Jerry lines. No one stayed long. Jerry had that building, as the boys say, "zeroed in," and while his range was a little long, shell after shell carried bits of rafter with it into the field across the street and sent more broken tiles cascading below. Nobody knew exactly what was happening in the flat fields to the north.

"Bringing in the Jerries" was the heading on the magazine article and it showed pictures of eager Germans leaping out of their trenches to become American prisoners. I looked over T-4 Evans's shoulder and he looked up at me. "Say," he drawled, "when you look at the pictures in the book or see a newsreel, it sure don't seem like it seems like here."

Another shell whooshed overhead as he spoke. Evans huddled tighter into the corner. I, as a privileged character, a war correspondent, ducked downstairs to the maps and light and safety below.

The lieutenant was explaining to the captain something he had just heard over the walkie-talkie radio.

"As near as I got it," he said, "our company has got this pillbox here [pinpointing the spot on a map] except there's a few live krauts in it. Then they've almost got this pillbox except somebody—I think it was a tank commander, but I'm not sure—said he had a ditchful of krauts in front of him and he wants the infantry to move up, but they say they are pinned down."

"What about Able's company?" asked the captain.

"It's got the pillbox there [pointing again] practically surrounded and we've got a tank up there—I don't know where he came from but he's there ready to shoot the stuffing out of it. But two men crawled up on the pillbox with a bazooka and got hit and they're still lying there and Cass is telling the tanks not to shoot until they get those wounded men out of the way."

"Where's Brown?"

"Hell, he's crazy," the lieutenant reported. "He's up there somewhere and he says he sees troops moving on the Linnich–Lindern road, which he can't possibly see, and he thinks he's heard Tiger tanks down on his left, and he wants artillery fire, but he don't say just where he is or just where he wants it, and we ain't firing until we find out where he is and what he wants and he tells us right."

The cellar shook a score of times while the lieutenant was talking.

"What the hell's the matter with our artillery?" the captain wanted to know. "Haven't we got any Cubs in the air? Can't someone find out where these goddam shells are coming from and blast the hell out of Jerry? Call 'em up and tell 'em I said so. If you can't call 'em, get somebody on the radio who can get 'em. Or send a runner. There! I've clocked it. That's thirty-six rounds of heavy in ninety seconds, and it's too damned much."

The captain seemed a mite excited. Everybody in the cellar felt the strain of the incessant banging, and the mud-spattered boys who every few seconds came leaping through a shell hole in the straw-filled house and slid panting into the cellar didn't relax the tension.

"Captain says can you get us some litter bearers?" one demands. "We ain't going on until we get those wounded outa there."

"I'm from Fox company," another reports. "We're right here— most of those boys spotted their positions with precision—but we can't move on our right and we don't know where I company is. Should we move or wait for them to show up?"

Sometimes it was:

"We think we're here, but we ain't sure. We're by those brown bushes. Can you tell us where that is?"

"Sure, we've got prisoners, but we ain't had time to send them back."

"We're 300 yards out. We've got the first pillbox, but we can't find the second. We don't think it's where you said it was. Who plotted these damnfool maps, anyway?"

It did not look at all the way it does on the newsreels, and it did not sound like the precise schedule of operations outlined to the correspondents the night before. It was a muddy, muddled war, not the kind of war that makes headlines, but the kind of atom battle of which eventual headlines are actually composed.

The only part of the battle that went according to schedule was the first ten minutes. Those boys—some of them had landed in Europe less than a month before—had crawled out of their foxholes in the grim, cold, wet, pre-dawn dark. (I thought it an ordeal to ride through the dark in a dry jeep to reach the jump-off place before daylight, and I had slept in a warm, dry cellar when those boys were dozing in slithery, sloping foxholes.)

They had surprised Jerry, and then Jerry had reacted with vigor. He had sent up rocket flares and tracer bullets, which from my observation post looked very pretty. Then he poured it in. A dozen boys that day bitterly asked if I were one of the correspondents who had written that Jerry was short of ammunition. Jerry did not have many duds that day and he was not sparing anything. He knew that bit of land was tactically important, and he knew he had commanding positions.

By dawn our infantry was pinned down in trenches that Jerry had dug for his own defenses and several of our tanks were smoking. We had advanced in some places as much as two miles; in others hardly half that, and when orders arrived to move out again in broad daylight in the face of Jerry's guns, some of the boys' comments were not quite printable.

By noon, however, the man at the maps knew precisely where every unit was. Wires had been mended under fire and most of the telephone lines were working. A first-aid post down the street had been filled and emptied and was filling up again. Timidly peering out of the shattered attic I had seen those litter bearers moving out steadily to the front, not quite sure whether the German infantry would respect the Red Crosses on their helmets and the bands on their arms, and very sure indeed the German artillery could not see the Geneva symbols.

Out of the chaos had come a little cosmos. Plans which had been made at a higher level had been altered by the men on the job, and when the briefers at headquarters had pieced together a dozen such fragments of the battle, correspondents would have another headline: "9th Army Advances."

The only things I had ever read that seemed at all like it were John Hersey's "Into the Battle," and Harry Brown's "Walk in the Sun."

I had been as thoroughly scared as I ever had been in my life. Earl Anderson, of "Yank Magazine," who had driven up with me in the dark, had decided to stay at the battalion post overnight to watch the next phase of the operation, so it was my job to get the jeep out and drive away. I went out and looked at it. It had six shrapnel holes in it, but the motor started. I cleaned the windshield and removed the bricks and wires from the punctured top. Then, as a shell whistled overhead, I leaped back into the cellar. It took me half an hour to screw up enough courage to sit down in the jeep and drive.

I was a mile back from the front line, behind a line of houses, and all over that flat unprotected country, GI's were matter-of-factly going about their business, stringing wires, carrying wounded, digging trenches, running messages and fighting.

Any of them would give his eyeteeth for a chance to drive back to a hot supper and a warm bed. I wondered whether I would ever be able to put together words to give any impression to the people living normal lives in New York, Cornwall or Rochester of the daily routine of those scared, brave boys on "limited operation."

. . . .

LEWIS GANNETT

Lewis Stiles Gannett began as a newspaperman in 1916 at the New York *World* and then wrote for the *Nation,* the Manchester *Guardian,* and the New York *Herald Tribune.* His column, "Books and Things," ran for twenty-six years, until 1956. He was a member of the Harvard Alumni Association and a director and vice-president of the NAACP. He was also the author of *Young China* and *Sweet Land* and edited the well-known series of books *The Mainstream of America* and *The Family Book of Verse.*

Lewis Gannett died in 1966.

Yanks Cross the Rhine

· · · · · · · · · · · ·

BY

JAMES L. KILGALLEN

INTERNATIONAL NEWS SERVICE STAFF CORRESPONDENT

PARIS, March 9, 1945—American troops in overwhelming strength surged across the Rhine today to build up a gigantic assault force already five miles inside the heart of Germany.

Gen. Eisenhower's spokesmen, ending the Supreme Headquarters' silence on the location of the 1st Army's Rhine crossing, announced that the Americans captured intact the Ludendorff bridge across that river at Remagen, and have been storming across it.

First Army troops have captured the town of Erpel and surrounding high ground on the east bank of the Rhine in the Remagen sector, headquarters also announced.

Berlin admitted American capture of the bridge. It said that by chance the span had not been destroyed by Nazi engineers.

Remagen is 80 miles southeast of Cologne and about 275 miles southwest of Berlin.

German resistance disintegrated also on the front where the 11th Armored Division captured a Nazi general, commander of a division, and 3,200 other officers and men.

The Nazi DNB agency broadcast that American spearheads had reached Linz, a town three miles east of and opposite Remagen on the west bank of the Rhine. The Germans reported heavy fighting north of Linz.

Official spokesmen announced that the 9th Armored Division of the 1st Army captured the Remagen bridge.

The Division's push to the Rhine came "after an amazing cross-country dash from Euskirchen," in which Rheinbach and Stadt-Heckerheim were captured. The division pushed southeastward out of these points to the vicinity of the Ahr River above Bad Neuenahr.

Driving east, it then pushed into Remagen and captured the bridge.

The German radio said the bulk of the Nazi forces below Cologne retreated across the Rhine, but reported heavy fighting still raging at the Bonn bridgehead.

American troops are now in possession of one-half of the town of Bonn. The Germans blew up the main bridge over the Rhine at this university city and units of the 1st Army Division of the 1st Army are pushing through the city to the river.

Three-quarters of Bad Godesberg, the resort town where Adolf Hitler "received the late Prime Minister Chamberlain in the days preceding the Munich agreement, have now been occupied by American forces, but fighting continues in that area.

An unsubstantiated DNB dispatch said the Americans were striving to achieve crossings in the Cologne area against heavy German resistance.

Gen. Eisenhower lent emphasis to the growing surge of Allied conquest by disclosures officially that in the last nine months of combat 1,000,000 German soldiers have been taken prisoner.

The bag included two field marshals, 55 generals, five colonels and five admirals. Fifty-eight Nazi divisions were destroyed including four parachute divisions. Ninety-five per cent of the prisoners were combat troops.

. . . .

JAMES L. KILGALLEN

Born in Pittston, Pennsylvania, James Kilgallen moved to Chicago, where he went to college. He worked on the Chicago *Tribune*, the Chicago *Farmers and Drovers* Journal, and the Laramie (Wyo.) *Daily Boomerang*, became the managing editor of the Indianapolis *Daily Times*, and was a reporter for the Associated Press and for the United Press International. He joined the International News Service in 1921 and, as a correspondent, covered the major events of World War II. After his retirement he continued writing from his home in New York City until his death.

The Corpse That Was Coblenz

· · · · · · · · · · · ·

BY
AUSTEN LAKE
WAR CORRESPONDENT OF THE BOSTON *EVENING AMERICAN*

COBLENZ, March 19, 1945—This ancient Prussian capital resembles a prehistoric ruin of cliff dwellers. It is a smoking shell with scarcely a habitable house. The only sounds were the hammering of American artillery against the granite face of old Ft. Konstantine where a handful of suicidal Nazis were making silly theatrics.

It is over now, but then I could see our demolition shells chewing away heavy stone work like a chisel in the hands of a giant mason.

The fort suggested the high hillside face of a Tibetan Lamasary.

It is twenty-six years since I was in Coblenz last as a soldier in the U.S. Army of Occupation. Coblenz was a beautiful prosperous city then, a wine-growing metropolis with well stocked shops, pleasant sidewalk cafes and a mania for spotless order. There is little left—only a nest of rubbish-filled hollow walls that stink and smoulder, houses with frameless windows like sockets in a skull, avalanches of fallen masonry that make morbid valleys in streets, shattered shade trees and acres of dumpland waste.

I walked through Kaiser Wilhelm ring, which in that older time was much like the shop side of lower Boylston street in Boston, but walked is hardly the proper word. It was Sunday afternoon and snipers were still picking off unwary stragglers from hideouts in ruins, so I joined a doughboy patrol as it picked its way gingerly over the rubble, eyes on windows, fingers on triggers.

"Gives you the creeps," said Pvt. John Leoncello, one of the sniper hunters. And it did. It was like hunting spooks in a ghost town.

We passed slowly through the wreckage of Hertz Jesue, the ancient Gothic cathedral from which the roof had collapsed, stained glass windows had disappeared and in which the chancel was an unrecognizable tangle.

A few holy figures stood in their niches, a gargoyle grinned from the transept. A body of a young German soldier lay face upward in the gutter, blue eyes open, wax-like features calmly composed. Our doughboys ignored him as part of the rubbish. "Sniper," commented Lieut. John H. Nolan, of Portland, Maine. "We got him in the church ruins this morning."

A lean cat slunk into the wreckage of an apothecary shop, stopping to sneer over its shoulder. "Mind your head," warned Pvt. Tom Keith, Manchester, N.H., pointing the muzzle of his rifle toward the tottering chimney, adding "worse than bullets might knock your brains out."

There used to be a cozy little restaurant in Clemens Platz at the corner of Lime Tree Park called Schloss and where an old Milwaukee German repatriate named Max Hennecke was famed for Wiener Schnitzel and heady Moselle wines. The fat bald patron used to babble happily with our occupation soldiers and treat them to Pilsner in seidels large as butter churns, but there is no restaurant there any more. The entire side of the street is gone. Just piles of pulverized stone.

A platoon of Heinie prisoners was being checked at the corner while a youthful rifleman pointed his Garand with the same impersonal negligence a suburban householder might direct a hose nozzle preparatory to watering his lawn.

A German-speaking sergeant was shouting "Haende hoch" to prisoners who linked fingers behind their necks.

Pfc. Robert Martin, of West Hartford, Conn., laughed over capturing two krauts this morning by means of a cheese sandwich. He was eating his K ration near the municipal museum when a couple of war-weary Boch climbed out of the cistern. In his surprise Bob pointed his cheese sandwich instead of his gun and they yielded with "haende hoch." "I guess they thought I had a secret weapon," he said.

I have an old guide book which delineates pre-war glories of this museum. It says, "The rooms are decorated regally and remain in their original splendor with handsome furnishings by Januarius Zick." Januarius should see them now. It looks like an excavation for a subway.

A magnificent mess, was the way Pfc. John Spillman, bazooka man—learned in the lore of sudden destruction—put it.

There may be other civilians in Coblenz, but I saw only three women in tattered overalls and two swarthy-skinned slave laborers. The rest of the original 60,000 are evacuated or dead, but there was a curious collection of men in street clothes marching at the end of a prisoner column—Nazi soldiers who tried a quick change, but not quick enough. They didn't have the nerve to destroy their army identification papers. When searched, they grinned sheepishly. As they strode along, one in white waiter's coat, another with Tyrolean hat, there were no answering grins from watching GI's who are deadly serious men.

I have seen hate in the eyes of many of these German townsmen, sullen smouldering accusation from under heavy brows, phlegmatic stolid animosity from eyes that burn like sealing wax. There is no joy of deliverance from Hitler's furious philosophies. They are un-reconstructed and full of potential menace. But I have never seen such whole-souled hatred as burns in the faces of dispossessed refugees of the town of Metternich, suburb of Coblenz.

Small wonder that they glared wishful murder as we moved past, for they have lived under an incessant rain of U.S. bombs and shells for many months. Their houses and factories are reeling, charred hulks, their only possessions were what they salvaged on hand carts or shapeless bundles on their back. No war guilt there, no consciousness that surrounding chaos is the price of war and just retribution for maniacal mischiefs of "furor germanicus."

Several women spat viciously as I passed. An elderly crone screamed "Schweinhund."

The trooping bands of little tots, for there seems to have been no lapse in Nazi propaganda, looked on with wide-eyed reproach, sensing, without understanding, their elders' animosity. There will be no democratic re-education here. These are essentially the same peoples with whom American occupation troops fraternized after the 1918 armistice, when our soldiers and local citizenry chummed together like affiliated lodge members of the Loyal Order of Moose. Many a U.S. doughboy of that elder period married a Rhineland fraulein, either took her home or managed to remain, indeed, until war came again.

There was a fair sized coterie of Germanized doughfeet living as expatriates in the Coblenz area, men who became Germanized and lived the cordial, lazy life of the vineyard country. Where are they now? But between them and us of this later war generation there is nothing but deep-seated spite and mutual animosities.

There will be no fraternization this time; no sitting cordially in Rhein Hall and weindorf and exchanging prosits with native neighbors. Our soldiers have seen too many of their buddies killed by Nazi fanatics and citizens have lost too many of their families and most of their property.

Coblenz is like occupying a morgue. It is a sprawling junk pile and for our troops policing the area it is life among hobgoblins, fetid stink-tainted air. Only moon, owls and slinking alley cats provide our soldiers with night time society. Coblenz is a corpse.

. . . .

AUSTEN LAKE

Born in Buffalo, New York, Austen Lake was an accomplished athlete at Lafayette College and later played professional football in Buffalo and Philadelphia. In World War I he drove for the French Ambulance Corps and joined the U.S. Tank Corps, commanded by George S. Patton. After studying at the Beaux-Arts School in Paris, he was a sportswriter for the Boston *Transcript*. Lake then went to the Boston *Record American* and *Sunday Advertiser* in 1933. He was a combat correspondent during the Second World War and a columnist. He died in 1964.

Three Yanks Storm Berlin

. . . .

BY

ANDREW TULLY

WAR CORRESPONDENT OF THE BOSTON *TRAVELER*

[Editor's Note: Tully's story was delayed and did not appear in print in America until May 8, the day President Truman announced Germany's unconditional surrender.]

BERLIN, Apr. 27, 1945—I arrived in Berlin a few minutes ago.

I am one of the first three Americans to enter Germany's capital, at this moment a crashing battleground.

With me are Virginia Irwin of the St. Louis *Post-Dispatch* and my driver, Sgt. Johnny Wilson of Roxbury, Mass. and the 26th (Yankee) Division.

To get here, we drove seventy miles through Russian lines—from the town of Torgau on the Elbe river, where American and Russian troops made official contact.

Tonight, we are the guests of a Russian artillery guards major, Nicolai Kovaleski, in the German house he requisitioned just within the Berlin city limits and within easy earshot of both artillery and small arms fire.

Germany's capital city is a dirty, shattered, smoking shambles.

Although we have not yet tried to go any farther than this command post on the south end of the city, Major Kovaleski has assured us that the battle is at its height in the center of the city and that to proceed further in the growing darkness would expose us to possible danger from both sides.

Still it is difficult to believe that we are in a city for which a battle is being fought. The noises of the war are present, especially the shattering crash of artillery, and outside the atmosphere is heavy with smell of cordite. But here, inside the CP, there's an air of festivity. The Russians are welcoming the first Americans to enter Berlin.

In this upstairs room converted into a dining room, we are now going to eat a late dinner. We have already drunk several tremendous toasts in vodka to Stalin, Roosevelt, Truman and Churchill and Major Kovaleski is beaming in a paternal manner at his new American friends as he contemplates the next toast. I do not know how long I'm going to stand up under it, for when you drink a toast with a Russian you drain your glass and vodka is something akin to distilled dynamite.

The meal promises to be a gargantuan one. The two German women requisitioned as cooks already have set smoked salmon on the very white table cloth and there is a soft cheese and black Russian bread as well as both vodka and cognac to go with this first course.

But what I want to do most on this wild night dash after the wildest of days—is go to bed. This is the most fantastic, craziest thing I have ever done, and now that there is time to relax, I am just beginning to realize what has happened and where I am.

I am more than slightly scared. I am worried about getting my story out, about getting thrown into the brig by the Russians, and about whether I'll ever get back to the American lines.

It seems days since this afternoon when, at the fabulous Russian feast celebrating the juncture with the American forces, we decided to take off for the German capital.

We had gotten our jeep over the Ele river by showing the Russian soldiers operating the ferry our SHAFF identification cards, shouting "Jeep" in their ears—and making swimming motions.

The feast was about over, and Russian officers had begun to dance with the pretty Russian women soldiers when I remarked jokingly to Virginia:

"Let's keep going to Berlin."

She didn't blink an eyelash. "O.K." she said. So we started—just like that.

We knew we had to go east for some distance before we could strike north toward Berlin. We had a map which took us as far as the city of Luckenwalde, about twenty miles south of here. After that, we had to follow signposts and keep our fingers crossed.

We made it here in about five hours—I think we started around 3 o'clock in the afternoon. It was the maddest five hours I ever expect to experience.

Our position was at least bordering on the illegal. Although there had been no direct orders forbidding American correspondents to go to Berlin, we also had no permission to do so. We had our SHAFF cards and other identification papers, but none of us spoke Russian and on such a fluid front it was entirely possible that, because we presented the unusual, we might, if apprehended, be summarily treated as spies.

Our precautions were two-fold. First, we appropriated one of the home-made flags which the Russians had put up on the road to Torgau for the celebration and tied it on the side of our jeep. Second, we stayed away from Russian headquarters and avoided as much as possible encounters with high Russian officers. This worked. But there were bad moments all along the road.

For about the first thirty miles we had no trouble at all. Whenever we encountered Russian soldiers we slowed down, saluted, yelled "Americanski" and pointed to the flag. And the average Russian seemed to think it quite natural that we should be prowling about behind his lines.

We got our first scare in the town of Herzberg. There, as we drove down a street lined with Red flags and lithographs of Stalin, we were flagged down by a unique MP—a Russian equivalent of the American WAC.

She was very stern, very stern. By signs, she demanded our papers. We had none, of course. But we grasped at a straw and showed her our SHAFF cards. After scrutinizing them carefully, she waved us on and we almost collapsed with relief.

We drove over roads at times deserted and at other times jammed with the most widely assorted military traffic I have ever seen. American made trucks rubbed their fenders against homemade wooden farm carts drawn by horses and driven by mustached Russian non-coms. Several times we saw ox-carts carrying ammunition. Refugees lined the road going in the other direction—refugees driving horse-drawn wagons, bicycles and all manner of sulkies and carriages, or dragging small handcarts or pushing antique baby carriages.

We drove through dark forests and heard occasional sniper fire. We drove over partially demolished bridges, took detours through fields and shallow river beds. Several times we got tangled in Russian convoys and sat in the jeep sweating out the moment when a Russian officer would become suspicious and demand that we explain our presence.

In another town we were stopped again—this time by a Russian sergeant with a Mongol face. But he didn't even ask for our papers—not after Johnny had yelled "Americanski Americanski" and Virginia had smiled her most charming smile.

"Keep on smiling," I told Virginia fearfully. "Toss that sex of yours around like you never did before."

She tossed it around.

Then we had a flat tire, within perhaps fifteen miles of Berlin. While Johnny groaned and sweated to change it, we stood there on the road and tried to talk to and placate a group of Russian soldiers who gathered around us fondling wicked-looking riot guns. Somehow, Johnny got that tire changed before the soldiers had quite made up their minds that we were suspicious characters and they let us drive off.

Artillery was booming all around us now and the time had come to try to get a guide into Berlin. We drove on for about eight miles more and stopped in a fairly good-sized town—don't ask me its name—and asked a knot of soldiers for their commandant. We just kept yelling "Commandant" and "Americanski" and pretty soon about a hundred grinning Russians had gathered around our jeep. We talked for awhile, using motions mostly, but finally, a young lieutenant who stepped forward motioned that he would take us to the boss.

We left Johnny with the jeep and Virginia and I started down the street with the lieutenant. We never found the commandant, which is perhaps fortunate for us. We were stopped instead by a major— our good Major Nicolai Kovaleski—who demanded of the lieutenant who we were. When the lieutenant's explanations failed to please him, he directed a stern eye at us two bedraggled Americans.

"Parlez vous?" he asked.

I could have kissed him. My French is pretty poor, but I can understand a Frenchman and can also make myself understood. I told him, "Nous sommes correspondents de guerre. Nous desirons aller Berlin."

Well, he was suspicious as hell. He had a look at our SHAFF cards and he asked us where we had come from and where the American Armies were and if we had a vehicle. Then, all of a sudden, he told us curtly to get our jeep and follow him in his car.

We did, thinking to ourselves: "Well, bud, this is where a couple of Yanks get slightly shot up."

Major Kovaleski, bless his now-white hair, didn't shoot us. His car, apparently driven by a madman, led us the remaining few miles past the big sign which says "Berlin" and finally up a long winding driveway to his CP.

With the air of a man herding condemned men to their death, the major had us escorted upstairs, ordered us to remove our coats, and then sent each one of us, one by one, to the bathroom to wash. When we were all seated around the table again, the questioning was resumed, but in a more friendly manner. I showed him clippings of some of my stories I had in a pocket and he seemed satisfied.

And just now Major Kovaleski has instructed his orderly that the American woman journalist is to have fresh flowers in her room tomorrow morning.

This is Berlin. These are the Russians. If I can forget to be scared, I think I'm going to be happy here. At any rate, I'm going to eat some of that wonderful-looking salmon and some of that good black bread.

• • •

Running a gauntlet of bursting shells, seemingly falling in aimless fashion throughout the city, I got to within sixteen blocks of the famous Unter den Linden today (April 28).

I was within ten blocks of the historic Wilhelmstrasse, where a little man named Hitler once ruled the Third Reich.

Specifically, I was in the Schöneberg section in the southwest part of the city, about two hundred yards up the Eberstrasse, which leads to the Kolonnen.

Unless I wanted to form a one-man task force I could go no farther, for the entire center of the city was a no-man's land. With shell fragments spraying the air and buildings collapsing under the force of a thunderous artillery attack, the air was a permanent bluish gray from the numerous pitched battles which went on all around. The reek of gunpowder was almost stifling.

It was the most desperate fighting I have ever seen—surpassing for pure violence and desperation the battles for Metz and Frankfurt and Nuremberg. At least it seemed that the German military automaton was heeding his mad dictator's orders to fight to the death.

Almost every square inch of city seemed to be the scene of fighting. On rooftops, snipers peppered the streets with automatic rifle and machine-gun fire. Russian soldiers, with a cold, magnificent courage, were mopping up road blocks and street barricades of huge fir logs. Houses and apartment buildings were being cleaned out one by one.

In the Eberstrasse the buildings are wrecked, but not as badly as would be supposed. Near the intersection of Alberstrasse, for instance, is a structure that apparently housed a department store. The only damage to this building is a huge shell hole in the center of its front. But the buildings on either side are mere shells, one of them with only two walls standing.

As our jeep drove up the Eberstrasse and stopped, two Russian soldiers were herding a half dozen members of the Wehrmacht from this department store building. These Nazis were lucky, for their comrades lay dead on the sidewalks and in the hole which was the entrance to the building. German dead were everywhere. I counted at least fifty bodies sprawled in assorted positions along our route.

The fighting was so uncontrolled today that one never knew when he might run into the middle of it. Virginia Irwin and my jeep driver, Sgt. Johnny Wilson, and I were the only Americans in Berlin and because none of us speak Russian we were like innocents lost in a black wood. We had a map of the city, but had no way of knowing where the lines were and all we could do was to drive along until we could go no farther and then try another direction.

It took us four attempts to get to the Ahoneberg. Three times we were turned back by fighting ahead, but on the fourth attempt, by making careful detours, we got fairly well into the heart of the city.

Coming in from the south, we drove up the wide, well-paved Berliner Strasse until we were balked by a road block at the southwest corner of the Tempelhof. A Russian MP also made his appearance here, but our crude Russian-made American flag, lashed to the jeep's windshield, allayed his suspicions, and when we pointed to the road block and shrugged our shoulders, he directed us to take a left turn down a ringbahn. We took off, made an oblique right turn down the Sachsendam and then we hit another road block. We turned right again down the Naumann.

It was getting hotter, but there didn't seem to be any point in stopping while streets were open, so we continued a short distance down the Naumann and then took a left turn down the Tempelhof weg and made our last stop—persuaded by a sudden burst of machine-gun fire a few hundred yards up the street.

We saw very few civilians, and most of those we saw were peering from paneless windows of their wrecked homes. Twice, when civilians in the street saw our American flag, a flame of hope lighted their faces. "When are the Americans coming?" they asked. We told them the Yanks weren't coming; that Berlin "belongs to the Russians," and their faces fell.

We had no desire to be seen talking to the civilians for fear it would make the Russians suspicious. But we didn't have to talk to them to see the cold, desperate fear in their eyes. The man in the street in Berlin is well aware of his crimes against the Russian people and he is horrified by the fact that retribution is at hand.

One civilian, a woman who spoke English, told us two American airmen, liberated prisoners, had been seen in the neighborhood but, although we drove around for almost an hour looking for them, we never found them. By that time, too, we were getting a little bit nervous about things. Besides, I was weary after last night's welcoming feast staged by our Russian hosts.

That feast is something I'll never forget. It was the most magnificent hospitality I have ever enjoyed and our host, Major Kovaleski, is one of the finest soldiers I've ever met.

Bathed and refreshed after being escorted by the major to the house he was using as a command post, we sat down to a fabulous meal. Besides the smoked salmon and cheese, there were both mutton and pork fried in deep fat with generous touches of garlic, mashed potatoes, wonderful black bread and two high trays of Russian pastries. And the beverages were vodka, cognac and a mysterious yellowish liquor the major described as "spirits."

Besides the three of us, there was the distinguished, white-haired Major Kovaleski and six officers of his staff at that table. The major insisted that Johnny, "the brave American sergeant," sit at his right hand and throughout the meal he paid lavish attention to the first Yankee GI to get to Berlin. When the Roxbury soldier, still dazed at the thought of where he was, lagged behind in his eating, the major would put an arm around him, pat his revolver with his other hand, and roar with mock severity: "Mangez!"

Johnny, not quite sure of what was going on, would gulp a couple of times, look at me anxiously—and eat.

The drinking was terrific. For awhile, I kept up with the Russians in draining my tumbler of vodka for every toast, but after three or four toasts I could do no more than sip my drink.

Major Kovaleski and I certainly are pals. I was at his other hand, and after each toast we would rise, stand at attention, and then shake hands warmly. As the meal progressed, the major frequently put his arm around me and announced to the table that "Le Capitaine André est mon camarade." His officers couldn't get his French, but they got the idea, and smiled upon me paternally.

Then there was dancing. Poor Virginia, being the only woman present, had to bear the brunt of this terpsichorean marathon. She danced at least twice with every officer, and when she finally pleaded exhaustion a couple of young lieutenants dragged Johnny on to the floor and put him through his paces. I escaped by devoting myself to intense conversation with the major.

It was one o'clock before we could go to bed. Then, with the same flourish he did everything, the major escorted us to our rooms. I don't know how Virginia fared, but I had one of the biggest feather beds I've ever seen. And Johnny perhaps was paid the greatest tribute of all. He had a bed while Major Kovaleski, an officer of the great Russian army, went to bed on the floor.

. . . .

ANDREW TULLY

At the age of twenty-one, Andrew Tully was the youngest newspaper publisher in the country when he bought the Southbridge (Massachusetts) *Press*. He was the author of more than sixteen books, wrote a column called "Capital Fare" for more than twenty years, and was a correspondent for the Boston *Traveler* during World War II. He also reported for the Worcester *Gazette* and the *World-Telegram* in New York before settling in Washington, D.C., as a writer, then columnist for the Scripps-Howard Newspaper Alliance, the Bell-McClure Syndicate, and the McNaught Syndicate.

He died in 1993.

End of the Sawdust Caesar

. . . .

BY

MILTON BRACKER

NEW YORK TIMES CORRESPONDENT

MILAN, Apr. 29, 1945—Benito Mussolini came back last night to the city where Fascism was born. He came back on the floor of a closed moving van, his body flung on the bodies of his mistress and sixteen other men shot with him.

That is not a pretty way to begin the story of his final downfall, his flight, his capture and his execution. But it is not a pretty story and its epilogue in the Piazza Loreto here this morning was its ugliest part and will go down in history as a finish to a tyranny as horrible as ever was visited upon a tyranny.

At 9:30 this morning, the former Duce's body lay on the rim of the mass of corpses, while all around surged a growing mob, wild with the desire to have a last look at the man who once was a Socialist editor in this same city.

The throng pushed and yelled; partisans strove to keep them back but largely in vain. Even a series of shots in the air did not dissuade them.

Mussolini had changed in death but not enough to be anyone else but Mussolini. His close-shaved head and his bull neck were unmistakable; his body seemed small and a little shrunken but he was never a tall man.

At least one bullet had passed through his head; it had emerged some three inches behind his right ear in a sickening protrusion of brains and bone. There was another small hole nearer his forehead where another bullet seems to have gone in.

As if the dictator were not dead or dishonored enough, at least two young men in the crowd managed to break through and aim kicks at his skull.

One glanced off, but the other landed full on his right jaw and there was a hideous crunch while it wholly disfigured the once proud face.

Mussolini wore the uniform of a squadrist militiaman. It was comprised of a gray-brown jacket and gray trousers with red and black stripes down the sides. He wore black boots, badly soiled and left one hanging half off as if the foot was broken. His small eyes were open and it was perhaps the final irony that this man who had thrust his chin forward for so many official photographs had to have his yellowing face propped up with a rifle butt so as to turn it into the sun for the only two Allied cameramen on the scene.

When the butt was removed, the face flopped back over to the left. Meanwhile, I crouched over the body to the left so as not to cut off the sun from his turned face. A group of us had been thrust by enthusiastic Milanese, who had not yet seen any Americans, right into the circle of death. It was naturally one of the grimmest moments of our lives, but it will at least serve to give absolutely authentic eyewitness accounts of this terrible ultimate moment in the history of an era.

If there is comfort in such a death and such an aftermath, it could only be observed in the fact that Mussolini lay with his head on the breast of his mistress, Clara Petacci, who had sought to rise to movie fame through him.

Only 25, younger even than his daughter, she had been executed with him in the suburb of the village of Como on the shore of Lake Como—and now she lay in ruffled white blouse, her dark hair curly and her youth apparent even now.

The other bodies, lying in the same circle, only a few kilometers from Piazza San Sepolcro, where Fascism actually began and where fifteen Italian patriots were executed by Fascists a year ago, included those of Alessandro Pavolini, puppet regime secretary; Francesco Barracu, ministerial official; Paolo Zerbino, interior minister, and Gofredo Coppola, who was rector of the University of Bologna and who had fled there ten days before the Allied entry.

The last chapter in the life of the man who led a phony march on Rome in October, 1922, began last Wednesday, April 25, when, following the transport workers' strike the previous Sunday, a general strike of all Milanese workers tied up the whole city of more than a million people.

Mussolini was still chief of the puppet Fascist republic government. He appealed to Ildefonso Cardinal Schuster to intermediate at meeting with leaders of the Committee of National Liberation and this—in which Mussolini made his last appearance where he had any authority—took place at the arch-episcopal residence, just off Piazza Fontana.

At this meeting, the Duce appeared more tractable than Marshal Graziani.

Told that the Germans in Milan had already indicated a desire to surrender to the Allies, however, the Duce in the waning moments finally turned on his Axis partners, declared they had "betrayed him."

According to an account in the Il Popolo of Milan, he went on: "They have treated us as servants, and harshly—for many, far too many years. Now we have had enough."

Returning to his quarters after asking an hour's leave to discuss terms, Mussolini then sent word back that the terms were not acceptable and he would leave.

He arrived at Como at 10 P.M. Wednesday and made efforts throughout the night to arrange passage across the Swiss frontier. First reports said his wife, Rachele, was with him, but it would appear now that it was not she at all but Petacci.

Sometime Thursday morning in a caravan of some thirty cars, Mussolini headed north up to the west shore of the beautiful Lake Como. He was wearing a black coat over his uniform. It was near Dongo, a sheltered village about three-quarters of the way up the shore of the lake, that a sharp-eyed young partisan named Urbano Lazari spotted him.

. . . .

MILTON BRACKER

Milton Bracker was born in Cincinnati in 1909 and joined *The New York Times* staff in 1931 after receiving a bachelor's degree from Columbia University. In 1943 he was assigned to the London bureau and was a foreign correspondent for most of the rest of his career. He covered the Mediterranean theater from 1943 to 1945 and followed that with stints in Rome, Mexico, South America, Africa, and Western Europe. He settled in Rome, where he was the *Times'* bureau chief when he died in 1964. He won numerous journalism awards, including the George Polk Memorial Award in 1952, and was an avid fiction and poetry writer.

The Masters Bury Their Slaves

· · · · · · · · · · · ·

BY

JOHN R. WILHELM

CHICAGO *SUN* FOREIGN SERVICE

WITH THE U.S. THIRD ARMY ON THE DANUBE FRONT, GERMANY, Apr. 29, 1945—Under a bright blue sky with the spring sun slanting down on the green shrubbery of Nuenberg cemetery, several hundred of the most prominent citizens of this German village today buried 204 battered bodies of Polish Jews who had been beaten and shot to death near here by their SS (Elite Guard) overlords.

I watched as these German burgers, clad in their best Sunday clothes, some with stiff white collars and neat black ties, picked up these emaciated, mutilated corpses and placed them side-by-side with their own German ancestors in the village cemetery.

Several women were weeping. Many shuddered. Others turned away in a faint. But the burial went on. It continued under the watchful eyes of American infantry guards who were ordered to see that the pitiful victims of Nazi savagery and sadism were given decent interment by members of that self-styled super-race that violated all codes of humanity in killing them.

These 204 wasted corpses were found on a pine-studded knoll near Nuenberg. They were a tiny portion of the five thousand Poles the SS men shot in what was one of the bloodiest marches in history—the evacuation of prisoners from Buchenwald concentration camp to Bavaria.

Eleven thousand prisoners in all took part in that forced march. The almost unbelievable story was revealed today by Americans of the Ninetieth Division, who overtook the last remnants of the column of death.

Of those who started in the procession on March 8 from Buchenwald, only six thousand are now alive. It was said that one man was left for dead every ten yards of the 125-mile march.

Their bodies are actually to be seen—a line of grisly shrunken corpses sprawled in ditches and hedges along the highway. They were shot and killed as, starved and unable to keep up, they fell by the wayside.

The village people toiled all day long this spring Sunday not only to give these victims proper burial but first, to exhume the bodies from the two shallow pits where the SS had sought to hide the 204.

Going about the grim business was the burgomeister, who has held that office here for thirteen years. He and the others gently lifted these bodies. Some of the others were Josef Probst, the village banker; Hans Sollner, the local town clerk, and even the priest.

There was shame in most of their eyes and they were silent. There was one exception, a woman who giggled. An American soldier, Pvt. Steve Rudish of Blairsville, Pa., walked over and rebuked her.

I talked to some of the villagers and they said this was an unerasable blot on the German history. They said they had heard of these concentration camps, but this was the first time they had ever seen such things with their own eyes.

On the surface they appeared ashamed of the killings, but they also plainly felt that their little village was connected with the massacres only by accident—by virtue of the prisoner columns trudging through it when the SS killed the 204 Poles.

The story of the procession of death was told by one of the survivors. He is Marcel Cadet, an English-speaking Frenchman who was thrown into a concentration camp by the Germans after he was arrested in Paris in 1941. His wife, he said, now lives in New York.

"On the morning of March 8," he said, "we were told that we would leave Buchenwald. That was because the Americans were coming close. Of course, none of us wanted to leave then, but the SS cleared the camp with clubs and rifles and rubber truncheons.

"I saw fifty men beaten and pounded to death by the guards before we even left. One man was killed this way on the ground two yards from me.

"We were loaded on a train at Weimar with eighty-five men to a car. We were given two-day rations of a pound and a half of bread and one hundred grams of margarine. When the train arrived at Dachau on the fifth day, four hundred or five hundred of the already starved men had died from hunger on the train.

"There were about four thousand of us who left the train for an unknown destination. Another column of five thousand followed.

"We started up a hill and before the head of our columns reached the top we heard shooting. That was the beginning of shooting throughout the trip.

"During the march, if we tried to help comrades, SS men would push us away and shoot them. The guards never aimed especially but shot two or three times until the man died. The guards seemed to do it with pleasure. They shot one man when he stopped to tie his shoe laces.

"Once I saw bodies of my fellows piled ten-high in a heap after our group had halted. Once again we heard the Americans were coming even here and we were so happy we cried. But then the shooting started again and men were dropping every five yards."

When American tanks finally caught up with the column, Cadet said, the SS shot some two hundred men hoping that their bodies would make a human roadblock. The majority of the SS escaped, he said.

It was some of these victims that the German villagers were giving a proper burial today. One by one, the bodies of the dead slaves of the Germans were lifted into the coffins by the Germans—a small gesture of decency in a crime beyond human comprehension or atonement.

. . . .

JOHN R. WILHELM

John R. Wilhelm was born in Billings, Montana. He was a reporter for the Chicago *Tribune*, then worked as a manager in several United Press offices. As tensions grew in Europe, he was a correspondent for Reuters of London and the Chicago *Sun*. After the war he served as bureau chief, foreign editor, and director of news for McGraw-Hill World News in Buenos Aires and Mexico. He became director of the Ohio University journalism school in 1968 and later was founding dean of its College of Communication. He wrote or contributed to several books, mostly travel guides. He retired in 1981 and died in June 1994 at age seventy-eight.

The Graveyard That Once Was Berlin

· · · · · · · · · · · ·

BY

SEYMOUR FREIDIN

BY WIRELESS TO THE NEW YORK *HERALD TRIBUNE*

BERLIN, May 3, 1945 (delayed)—Over the rubble that remains of the most bomb-leveled city in the world, the red banner of Soviet Russia flew triumphantly this afternoon as exultant Russian soldiers swept into the hedgerows of the Tiergarten opposite the Reichstag and subdued the last of the Nazi defenders.

A chilling rain fanned by a northeast wind slanted across the smoking vestiges of the dead capital, converting the crater-pocked streets into huge pools of brackish water, while the Red Army men advanced into the park congratulating each other and promising extermination for the fanatical S.S. (Elite Guard) troops making their last stand for Fuehrer Adolf Hitler.

The steady downpour provided the remaining mournful note for the passing of Berlin. This once-great capital, whose decisions frightened the world a few years ago, is a charred, twisted, unrecognizable graveyard.

Nothing is left in Berlin. There are no homes, no shops, no transportation, no government buildings. Only a few walls—and even those are riddled with shellfire—are the heritage bequeathed by the Nazis to the people of Berlin.

Beside the historic Brandenburg Gate—the German symbol of

military glory, now blocked by concrete, its strident chariot of victory drawn by four horses twisted beyond recognition and with three red flags entwined about the driver—this correspondent joined a wave of the Russian mopping-up party driving into the last enemy pocket.

Once a magnificent zoological park, covered with heroic statues and monuments to men who played leading roles in German history, the Tiergarten had become a shell-shredded no-man's land, with paths and lawns chewed up by fires and trees interlaced with toppled statuary.

Crawling behind the upright statue of Moltke, because the Russians do not wear helmets and mine might be mistaken for a German one, I watched the Russians overrun the dug-in enemy positions. With speed, efficiency and terrific fire power born of long battle experience, the Russians rooted out the defenders in jig time, and it was 3:08 P.M., according to my watch, when the resisting Germans ceased firing. (Moscow announced the fall of Berlin officially the day before.)

Berlin can now be regarded only as a geographical location heaped with mountainous mounds of debris. The air power with which Hitler threatened to destroy all opposition boomeranged with a vengeance on Berlin. And Russian artillery finished off what was left standing in the German capital.

Moreover, this late metropolis, which once had a population of 4,000,000, has been virtually deserted by civilians. Apparently those who were unable to flee the ghost city have remained hidden in cellars.

Those who emerged were bent over picks and shovels under guard. They were engaged in clearing the main thoroughfares of the cascades of debris. They were dazed and fear-ridden. Their arms and legs moved like the limbs of puppets, without direction, spasmodically and uncoordinated.

As the civilians picked at the rubble, they had a first-hand opportunity to view for themselves the problem of reconstruction which confronts Germany. 'Round-the-clock air attacks have reduced all the buildings to powdered brick and teetering walls, very little of which can be salvaged. Only a perimeter of homes in the outskirts is habitable.

From such famed streets as Unter den Linden, once proudly described by Berliners as the most beautiful avenue in the world, Wilhelm Strasse, Friedrich Strasse and Wall Strasse, to those as relatively unimportant as Berg Strasse, is the mute testimony of the efficiency of the Allied air assaults. Much of the wreckage is old, indicating that the Nazis were never given the opportunity to clean it up because the raids never ceased.

In Wilhelm Strasse, which once boasted stately government edifices, there is nothing but crumbling masonry. The Reich Chancellery, where Hitler plotted with his cronies, is a shell of four broken walls encompassing a heap of rubble thirty feet high in some spots.

Russian soldiers singled out the Reich Chancellery for special attention. The Red flag fluttered over it. The Russians had hung a huge photograph of Marshal Stalin on the east wall, while by accident or design an oil portrait of Hitler lay face down beside the south end of a dead horse.

A German prisoner in Berlin told me the Wehrmacht communiqué announced that the Fuehrer died in the Reich Chancellery, pistol in hand, with some of his closest friends dying with him. So with the aid of three Russian soldiers I poked around the rubble in an effort to find some signs of Hitler's body, but it would take a crew of bulldozers about a week to get to the bottom of the debris.

Getting to Berlin through the Red Army lines and a stay in the city was a combination of exuberance and warmth shown by the Russians for Americans. Russian officers did not hinder us in any way, but were helpful and guided us practically the entire distance from the American front.

John Groth, the artist and war correspondent, and I started out for the German capital yesterday (Wednesday) when I rejoined him after a three-day junket with a Russian tank outfit, which treated me in magnificent style. Our jeep was accompanied by three United States Army photographers, who had their own vehicle.

The photographers were Bob Boyle, of Los Angeles; James Killian, of Highland Park, Ill., and Frank Preciade, of San Diego, Calif., who kept up a running chatter all along the route with passing Russian soldiers, although the only understandable words were "Americanski" and "Russky."

We left Wittenberg at about 2:30 P.M. and followed a convoy of Russian trucks. There were no German signs. Everything was in Russian. Darkness was falling, we knew no password and were well aware of the fact that Russian guards are quick on the trigger at night.

Fortuitously, the column of trucks we were following stopped for some repairs on the vehicles. The convoy commander came up to us and wanted to know who we were and where we planned to go. In German we told him we were curious about Berlin. He smiled and replied that as far as he knew there was nothing to hold us back.

We exchanged insignia as souvenirs and were invited to follow the convoy to Blankenfelde, a suburb of Berlin.

At 3 A.M. today we arrived in Blankenfelde after taking so many detours it appeared impossible that we could ever find our way back. There, the convoy commander suggested that it might not be healthy to enter Berlin in utter darkness and offered us billets in a German home. There was little sleep, however, for any of us because streams of Russian officers and soldiers poured in to give us the once-over.

We took off for Berlin according to directions given us by some officers who had left the capital a couple hours earlier.

Speeding toward the heart of the city, we passed the Tempelhof Airport. The field was ripped by mammoth bomb craters and most of the buildings and hangars were a collection of walls, with rain pouring through the gaping roofs.

At Bluecher Platz, road blocks had been thrown up, and scores of dead Germans, four light tanks and a dozen vehicles were strewn about an area of two blocks. Abandoned German equipment running from such personal effects as socks and underwear to rifles, shells and mines were scattered about the streets, forming a trail of the defenders' retreat through the city as they were pounded back by the Russians.

Nearly all the street signs had been uprooted, but the Russian soldiers were everywhere in great numbers, on foot and on horses, and we asked them for directions to the Wilhelm Strasse, the first street that came to mind.

Gleefully explaining that Berlin was "kaput" ("finished"), a German-speaking Russian pointed out the way.

Every street was covered with live grenades lying loose among the cobblestones. Butterfly mines, either abandoned by the Germans in their haste or left behind deliberately, showed in the torn sections of the pavement.

Despite the steady downpour, flames licked brightly in hundreds of ruined buildings, and the crunching collapse of structures could be seen and heard on every block.

Streets within the immediate vicinity of Wilhelm Strasse were choked with wrecked tanks and guns, the majority German. Dead horses beyond count lay in grotesque positions, many covered with the debris of battle.

Everywhere reverberated a cacophony of falling buildings, shouts of soldiers, the staccato bursts of machine-gun fire and loud explosions. Paying no attention to the noise, a Red Army soldier, his tommygun slung over his back, was perched on a sign which indicated that Dr. Paul Hentsche once had offices in the vicinity. The soldier was playing an accordion and singing what sounded like a folk song.

When we reached Wilhelm Strasse—it was leveled beyond recognition except for a few street signs that drooped loosely from shattered posts and a plaque indicating that the Finance Building had once stood not too far from the Reich Chancellery—twelve heavy and light German tanks were piled up around the first three streets.

We parked the jeeps and prowled around Wilhelm Strasse and Wilhelm Platz, picking our way through eviscerated buildings.

The palace where Dr. Paul Joseph Goebbels lived in high style after his oratory carried him to a position of power is as dead as he is reported to be.

After my search for Hitler's body proved futile, we drove the jeeps down to Unter den Linden. The first sight of the former majestic boulevard was rubble and Russian soldiers scrambling to get to the Brandenburg Gate to finish off the Germans holding out in the Tiergarten.

At the west end of Unter den Linden a pretty girl M.P. directed traffic with brisk efficiency. She never batted an eye when an occasional bullet whistled overhead. The only time she shifted position was to transfer her tommygun from one hand to the other.

The Adlon Hotel, which had been suggested as a place for correspondents to stay upon the occupation of Berlin, would be better suited as a stable now, if the horses could take it.

Our party broke up and I wandered over to the Reichstag, which had been gutted by fire twelve years ago, and watched the Russian soldiers photograph each other unmindful of the fighting going on a few hundred yards away in the Tiergarten. The Red flag, soaked by rain, hung over the dome, and inside the hollowed building I picked up a smoke-blackened guide book to Berlin.

Returning to the Brandenburg Gate, I joined the Russians entering the Tiergarten, and then retraced the way back to our jeeps. We bounced along Unter den Linden, passing the ruined Tomb of the Unknown Soldier and the thoroughly destroyed War Museum. The Berlin Cathedral and the palace where Kaiser Wilhelm II declared war in 1914 were all a shambles.

On Berhen Strasse there was a rallying cry painted in rough letters saying: "Heil Werwolf!"—the only reference to the Werewolf underground I have seen in Germany.

But in departing from the city we saw that many of the blackened and bombed walls bore the inscription: "Mit unser Fuehrer zum Sieg"—"With our Fuehrer we will be victorious."

. . . .

SEYMOUR FREIDIN

Seymour Freidin was born in 1917 in New York City and educated at Columbia University and the University of Vienna. As a reporter and foreign correspondent for the New York *Herald Tribune* he covered the U.S. forces in Europe, Asia, and Africa. From 1949 to 1961 Freidin was a columnist for the New York *Post* syndicate while simultaneously contributing to *Collier's* magazine. He returned to the *Herald Tribune* in 1962 as executive editor for foreign affairs. In addition, Freidin was the author of the books *Fatal Decisions* and *The Forgotten People*.

The German Women Haven't Quit

· · · · · · · · · · · · ·

BY

CATHERINE COYNE

WAR CORRESPONDENT OF THE BOSTON *HERALD*

WUERZBURG, GERMANY, May 3, 1945—There probably isn't a more badly destroyed large city in Germany than this ancient capital of Bavaria, nor is there a more fitting monument than these ruins of a once pleasant civilization to the folly of the German dream of conquest. In the morning sun this area seemed to summarize the end of that dream turned nightmare.

To Americans it is a complete summary. Those who travel across conquered Germany have seen the disintegration of the German army. They have seen thousands upon thousands of soldiers standing on acres of barbed wire enclosed ground, so many figures in gray-green that at first they looked like a great field of waving corn.

Past destroyed buildings along streets cleared of rubble today are roaring big American trucks filled with more surrendered soldiers being taken to captivity by American Negro soldiers, who slow down to inquire excitedly whether peace has been declared yet.

Factories and cities are in ruins. White flags fly from damaged homes. German women stand by the road to smile and wave at captured soldiers, children toss cakes and flowers to them. When the smiles are questioned, women always assure us it is good these boys, at least, will be safe.

Yet, the smiles are not echoed in their eyes. Instead, it is possible to see there the dawn of terror, the same terror French and Belgian women, the same terror girls in Poland and the Ukraine sought to hide when those men in gray-green uniforms, now riding like cattle in trucks, flowed in a tide of death over their countries.

German men appear to have no pride. Many have arrogance, but they lack pride. Arrogance cracks easily, and so do these men. But not German women. They may fawn on Americans in pleading for favors, because they fear Russians and French more than Yanks, but they still have pride, a fanatical pride in the early accomplishments of Hitler. It seems to me, at least, that German women here do not see in these ruins the end of the Nazi dream.

You can see their pride in the way they look at their men being taken away. They put up a great front, waving and smiling, but there is pride and something else in the way they stand up straighter, in the way they hold up their children to see evidence of the disintegration of the mighty Wehrmacht.

Even the sweetfaced nun, whose black robes billowed out fantastically as she bicycled up to us, displayed a fierce pride in her German background, though it was obvious she detested Hitlerism.

She struggled to keep back tears when we confirmed news of the death of Hitler and Goebbels and agreed their end was a prelude to the end of the war.

In excellent English, she said she had been a teacher before the rise of Hitler. "That man closed our schools," she said bitterly, "because we were Catholic sisters." She clutched the rubber ends of her bicycle handle until her knuckles went white.

"A happy day for my sisters and me?" she echoed. "It is good the regime is ended. That is very good. It is good the war is about to be ended. That means two evils ended." She turned her face, stained by dust raised by racing American supply trucks, toward me and continued: "The end of the war is one thing. But military defeat— don't you realize I am a German? Military defeat is bitter for a German."

I was amazed. A Franciscan mother superior at a hospital in Muenchen Gladbach made the same remark to me a month ago.

Another woman said to me: "We were misled. We should not

have had war with America. That was a mistake. I don't believe the fuehrer wished it, for he loved German children."

She had a 5-year-old son by the hand and a 9-year-old son stood by her side. "I remember," she continued, "when I was a little girl I had bad teeth and I was weak. We were poor and my mother couldn't get proper food for me. The fuehrer changed all that. We are poor people but see, my children are healthy and strong. The fuehrer did that."

We were standing by the shell of the residence, once beautiful palace of Bavarian rulers. I pointed to it and said: "The fuehrer did that."

She shrugged her shoulders and tightened her hold on the smaller boy's hand. Ninety-five percent of this city is destroyed. Most of it was wrecked in less than thirty minutes on a single March night after Hitler spurned an Allied offer to spare the city on condition two army corps be moved out of here. The raids took her home. She returned here this morning from a haven across the river to search in the rubble for preserves.

"The war is lost," she said excitedly. "We Germans were misled." For a few minutes she watched in dreamy silence as trucks made the sharp turn in the road. Then she said defiantly: "I still have my children and they are strong and healthy to face the future your people will plan. The fuehrer did that much for them."

"Where is your husband?" I asked.

She spoke so softly the interpreter had to ask her to repeat. She nearly screamed: "I don't know. Perhaps in one of these trucks." She paused, then said softly: "Perhaps—"

I said: "Hitler did that too."

She blushed, then she looked at me and smiled. I don't know why she smiled. I felt that there before me stood one far more dangerous than any soldier in the trucks or in those gray-green masses imprisoned along the roadside. Those men have quit, but, terrified though she is of retribution, that woman—and there are others like her—hasn't quit yet.

. . . .

CATHERINE COYNE

Catherine Coyne Hudson was born and raised in Portland, Maine. After graduating from Boston University, she became a reporter for the Boston *Herald*. During World War II Coyne was one of the few female correspondents in Europe, reporting from England, France, and Germany. After the war she covered the Nuremberg trials and later staffed the Time-Life bureau in Boston.

She died in Massachusetts, at the age of eighty-five, in 1992.

The Horror of Dachau

· · · · · · · · · · · ·

BY

E. Z. DIMITMAN

EXECUTIVE EDITOR OF THE CHICAGO *SUN*

MUNICH, GERMANY, May 3, 1945—Please take a little walk with us this bright but chill afternoon—through infamous Dachau. It won't be a pleasant five hours you will spend.

A group of American newspaper and magazine editors and publishers didn't enjoy it. Neither will you.

It is our responsibility to invite you to join us in touring the Nazis' No. 1 concentration camp. And it is your responsibility to accept— your responsibility if you don't want a third world war 25 years hence.

Only by seeing and hearing and smelling—and realizing—will you understand the Germans and the German philosophy. Only in this way will you feel the same way as the members of our armed forces feel—from the highest officers to the privates.

Only in this way will you realize the urgency of world peace and world security.

You will be shocked, you will be shamed and you will be nauseated.

You will see, but hesitate to believe your own eyes; you will hear from the prisoners, but you will be unbelieving; you will smell and you will become ill.

Join us in this tour of Dachau and its 32,000 political prisoners and then pray for the success of the San Francisco conference.

The jeeps, finally reaching Dachau about three days after its liberation by the Yanks, slow up as we pass a string of railroad cars. They look somewhat like American coal cars. Actually they are freight cars with open tops.

The center doors are open. Before we see, we can smell death.

Finally we look in. Grotesque forms sprawl on the floors of the twelve or fifteen freight cars. We look closer. You, too, come a little closer, hold your nose and look carefully.

These strange forms are the bodies of men. Men who, once upon a time, wanted peace. Men who loved life. Men who lived more or less freely. Men who had homes and wives and children; men who had sweethearts and mothers.

Now, they are dead—victims of the German government. They are dead because they did not agree with the German philosophy. Or they are dead because they took up arms to protect their native land against the aggressions of a self-proclaimed race of supermen.

There are about 2,000 corpses in these cars. We don't stop to count them. Neither do you.

By German reasoning these men died natural deaths. That's how they were recorded on the books kept by the SS (Elite Guards) who ran the camp.

By decent human standards—by American standards—they were brutally and systematically murdered.

But let's leave the bodies for awhile. We will come back later to learn how they were slain. We can't stay any longer, or all of us will become ill.

We enter the camp. Of course, we have had typhus anti-toxin injections. You will want them; in fact, the American officers of the Allied Military Government, who are now conducting the camp, will insist upon it. Typhus is quite widespread inside, as you will learn as you plod with us along the muddy paths.

Before we cross the threshold, medical corpsmen use a spray gun to cover us, head to foot, with D.D.T. powder, to kill the insects that will infest you on this tour.

Join us in entering a close barracks. The hundreds of men assigned to this barracks are enclosed by barbed wire. These are transients not yet assigned to work squads, men too ill or too weak to work the twelve and fourteen-hour shifts required, and some recalcitrant inmates.

They get even less food than the others. The others get about one-fourth of the amount of food necessary to sustain life.

Most of the men you see don't look like human beings. Many of them no longer are. Their faces seem to have shrunken in size. Their eyes are dull and staring. Their minds and their wills are already dead—victims of German design.

Physically they are thin and emaciated. If you will listen as we talk with these men you will find that the average loss of weight in a concentration camp is between thirty and fifty pounds.

How would you look that much thinner?

Listen to the hacking coughs of so many of the prisoners! It is tuberculosis, you will learn later.

Come on outside again; look at the blue sky and the smiling sun and there, in the distance, the green of the trees and the grass and newly planted fields.

Now, look alongside the barracks.

Those thin, bony forms are corpses. They are the bodies of Frenchmen and Belgians and Hollanders and Russians and Poles and Czechs and other Europeans.

What are they doing there, just outside the windows of the barracks?

We will ask some of the prisoners. Some speak English; for others we have interpreters.

Oh yes. Of course.

We understand, don't we? They just died. The SS and their stooges, the guards, didn't have time to remove them to the crematory.

Let's get away from this. Let's try another barracks.

Ah, here's a prisoner who speaks English fairly well.

He introduces himself. A Polish priest, Casimer Michelaski.

He was the head of the Catholic Action group in Poland. That, to the Germans, was a high crime. It was almost as bad as being a Jew or a liberal or an intellectual.

* * *

The good father tells us of an entire barracks nearby, assigned to clergy rounded up by the Germans since 1923.

He recalls, with irony, that only nine miles or so away is Munich, where Nazism first crawled from under a slimy stone.

Another prisoner, also able to express himself in English, wonders what was wrong with the world, its leaders and its people, to permit this foul thing to grow and develop and finally engulf the whole world in blood and bestiality.

By the way of an aside, my good friend, to take your mind off the little things you have seen and heard and smelled, you will feel a little better when you visit Munich later in the evening and see the retribution visited upon the home of Nazism. But that's later.

The priest tells his story—all of them are alike as they were at Buchenwald, the concentration camp we visited last week. Lack of food, brutal guards, dysentery, typhus, tuberculosis and, finally, welcome death.

He tells us of the crowded conditions and shows us the barracks. Tiers of wooden shelves—shelves is the right word, isn't it, my fellow American?

Let's measure one—32 inches wide, 2 feet high and almost seven feet long. Not too bad. It might do for one person. But two, and sometimes three men live in each shelf. There, friend, we can see three men in that bunk, on the other side. And here are seven bunks, each has two men.

Many of them, despite the chattering of their fellows at the unexpected visit of so large a group, are too ill or too disinterested even to lift their heads.

The will and the spirit are dead, my friend, killed systematically and by a set pattern.

But here is a man whose spirit is not dead. He is thin and not well. But he is still a man.

He is Peter Van Gestel, a Dutch Jesuit, he tells us.

Let's listen to him for a few minutes. His English is fair. He was taken prisoner by the Germans in September, 1941. Why?

For loyalty to church regulations. That's as good a reason as any.

He has been at Dachau since March, 1942. Three stinking years. More than enough to break most men. To kill them physically, if not spiritually. But not this Dutchman.

Several hundred clergymen, representing almost all faiths and twenty nationalities, are in the camp. Thousands have been here in the past.

"What happened to them?" we asked. You will join me in questioning these men, won't you? You may have some questions we might overlook, because we know the story—we heard it at Buchenwald.

Well, Peter Van Gestel tells us about 1,000 priests died here. Others were taken away and never came back.

He can't vouch for what happened, because prisoners naturally couldn't ask such questions—not if they wanted to live—and prisoners weren't permitted near the extermination, experimentation and executive departments. No sir, that fun was reserved for the SS under the heading of special privileges.

But the good father had heard stories which we could believe or not. He believed them. He had reason to, he explained.

They used priests and clergymen of other denominations as other nations use guinea pigs—for experimentation.

One hundred and seventy-eight Polish priests were taken to the laboratory and injected with malaria germs. Oh, no, not to kill them. Just to study the reactions. Only three died, but the others carried the germs thereafter and suffered from high fever at regular intervals, before they, too, died.

Other priests, mostly Polish, were subjected to immersion in sea water, after different diets, to determine the best type of food for German seamen and fliers likely to be forced to spend long periods in the water.

No statistics on the dead are available, he informs us.

Others were given various injections in an effort to develop a cure for phlegmon—a disease resulting in ulcers and brought on by malnutrition.

Forty were selected to become test tubes, all for the glory of Adolf Hitler, Nazism and a greater Germany. Fifteen died.

Let's visit the hospital, What do you say, my friend?

The hospital is a good one. Fine equipment provided by the Nazis when they established Dachau as soon as they came into power in 1933—not by a putsch or other armed rebellion, but by the votes of the people in a duly constituted election.

Always remember that, when you differentiate between Germans and Nazis. The German people elected Hitler and all his cutthroats, perverts, sadists, fiends and all-around killers.

The physicians and surgeons are splendid ones. But they are prisoners of the Germans too. The guards permit the prisoners who are medical men to care for their own. There always was a shortage of drugs, however.

Let's visit the patients.

Here are a lot of surgical cases. Arms and legs in all sorts of makeshift gadgets, raised above the body.

Those are fracture cases. You and I, my friend, were told how they received them, but we will tell about it a bit later, when we return for the dead in the boxcars. We will also tell at that time about the gunshot wounded who fill another ward.

The other cases are tuberculosis, dysentery, typhus and all the other ills that follow malnutrition, overwork, dirt, crowded, unsanitary conditions and the like.

What's that outside? Oh, just yesterday's hospital dead. Forty-four bodies.

And what's that across the street? One hundred and two bodies. Yesterday's dead in the camp barracks.

Just an average day for Dachau.

What's over there? Oh, now, that's something else the prisoners tell you. Those are the bodies of the SS guards who were shot or beaten to death after the Americans came in.

Let's just walk over to one more barracks. See those hundreds of men—just bones and skin. That's all. Eyes sunken, lacklustre. Are they dead or alive? They are alive, but not for long. They are dying. Some every hour. Not union hours, but 24 hours each day. Their story belongs with the boxcar dead. Wait.

Too much for you, my friend? But don't go. This is not for yourself. You have children, haven't you? You don't want them to face a repetition of a nation gone completely mad. Stick along, make the tour rapidly but completely, and then tell me Dumbarton Oaks is a hoax; that San Francisco is a sellout.

Maybe you are the wrong one for the trip. Maybe we should have Gerald L. K. Smith and Liz Dilling. Maybe former Senator Nye. Maybe Senator Wheeler. It wouldn't hurt Senator Vandenberg to be here.

Hold your nose, steel your heart, control your stomach. Let's go.

A big enclosure. A strong building. Enter at the left. Our guide is the Allied Military Government boss here, Col. Kenneth Worthing of Fond du Lac, Wis. A neighbor from the middle west, reputed home of isolationism. But that's not Col. Worthing. He knows better.

Here are four chambers, gas chambers, about six feet wide and possibly twenty feet deep. In the early days of Dachau, prisoners whom the Germans believed had lived long enough would be herded inside, the gas turned on and, presto change, there would be forty corpses in a chamber where there had been forty men before.

That was for the Jews—forty, fifty, one hundred a day. You couldn't kill the Jews fast enough.

Now there are no Jews in Dachau. There are few in any German concentration camp. They are all dead.

But that form of killing wasn't cute enough for the SS. It wasn't any fun. It was too simple. So the chambers were abandoned. The A.M.G. now uses them for disinfecting the clothes of prisoners. The Germans killed human beings; we kill lice and other vermin.

They have a better setup now, my friend. Come along. First, here's a large room with benches. Painted on a door in the room is the word "Brausebad" or shower bath.

Selected prisoners were picked for extermination, but not execution. There's a difference. Selected prisoners were invited to come for a shower bath. No one refused an invitation at Dachau. There was no R.S.V.P. attached to the come-up-and-see-me-sometime-baby invitation.

A rejection meant instant death by a clubbing, if the guard had indigestion, or by a shot in the back of the head, if the guard was happy and cheerful.

So, the group gathered for the shower. They stripped. Each was handed a bar of soap and a towel. The door to the Brausebad was opened. The prisoners looked in. They saw lights and apparent shower outlets studding the ceiling.

Once they were in, the door was slammed shut. But it was not water that shot through the opening. It was gas.

There is a peephole for the operator. Like a speakeasy peephole. He and his comrades could watch the death, one by one, of the thirty or forty hapless prisoners inside.

Simple. Efficient, too.

There's another door leading from the gas chamber right to the crematorium. It only took a few seconds to move the bodies, stuff them into large ovens, close the door, fix the fire and coal up.

Forty men were only a little heap of bone ashes.

What's that awful smell? That's in the next three rooms, sort of waiting rooms. But there are no six-month-old magazines for the waiting patients to read. Just several hundred bodies of prisoners stacked up.

There was a little shortage of coal for a few days before the Yanks crashed in last Sunday. There wasn't enough to set the furnaces going to dispose of these bodies.

Let's go? I agree. You have seen enough. There's no use going over to the execution department, where they shoot you, either for infraction of the rules or because you were a big shot and they wanted to honor you by shooting you to death—a sense of discretion or something.

Now we go back to the boxcars of death, the fracture and gunshot wound cases, the dying in the barracks.

It's a simple story. Early in April the Yanks penetration toward Weimar began to worry the officials in charge of Buchenwald. They decided to move the prisoners away before they could be liberated and tell their stories of organized bestiality and murder.

About 4,800 prisoners were loaded into these open freight cars. It was freezing cold. For twenty-two days this line of freights moved southward, toward Dachau. For twenty-two days there was a total of seven potatoes and four quarts of water. There were no toilet facilities. It was too crowded to lie down. So they stood for twenty-two days.

When Dachau was reached, 2,718 were able to walk or be helped off. These are the men in the barracks who are dying. These are the men whose bodies lie outside of the barracks wall, joined regularly by others.

The men in the hospital with the fractures suffered their hurts as the cars jostled about over the newly repaired roadbed after Allied fliers had bombed the lines. The men with the gunshot wounds made futile efforts to escape, only to be shot down by the armed guards.

We want to talk to two men before we leave, my friend—the head American doctor here and the only American Army officer liberated in the camp. Both are Midwesterners. Both as anti-isolationist as old Bertie McCormick is isolationist. These three should meet for cocktails some afternoon.

First, here's Col. George J. Hathaway of Superior, Wis., chief medical officer, 15th Corps, Seventh Army, Sixth Army Group. Let's listen to a few statistics, that's all. Don't be bored. They tell a story.

From 1933—when Nazism came into power—until the end of 1942, about 125,000 prisoners were quartered at Dachau.

Thirty-four thousand died "natural" deaths—that is, from starvation and disease. There is no record of the number exterminated or executed. Now listen, maybe you better write them down and drop a note to your senator.

In 1943, the "natural" deaths totaled 1,596.

In 1944, a total of 4,805 died "natural" deaths.

In January, 1945, the list grew to 2,888.

The February total was 3,977.

March saw 3,668 die "natural" deaths.

April's total was 2,626.

A little addition: in the first four months of 1945, a total of 13,159 prisoners died "natural" deaths.

There's a reason for the increase. Beginning with 1944, the Germans were being pushed around in earnest, and they shifted prisoners out of the way of victorious Allied troops. They came here in truck convoys and by train from camps that had been infested by typhus.

Prisoner physicians diagnosed the cases for what they were—typhus. The head German physician—a medical student and apparently not a good one—said it was only flu. Flu it was, therefore, and typhus spread through Dachau.

Col. Hathaway added, as a medical man, that the typhus, the tuberculosis, the dysentery and the pneumonia that were keeping the crematory so busy, were superinduced by malnutrition. That was a major factor.

By the way, my friend, did you notice that the bodies of the SS, both inside the camp and outside the barbed wire where they fell before American bullets or fists of enraged prisoners, were nice, plump bodies? No skeletons, no sir. There was plenty of food for them.

On your ride through the countryside in open jeeps today—we covered seventy or eighty miles—did you notice how well-fed and healthy the men, women and children were? They are all Germans. They have been fed on the fat of Europe. There was no starvation, no malnutrition, no "natural" deaths.

And now for the final visit. We talk to Maj. Rene J. Guiraud, son of Mrs. Marcel Pierkat of 3220 S. 54th avenue, Cicero, Ill. He was captured behind German lines eight months ago and brought here.

He worked in the hospital. He saw a prisoner clubbed to death by a block leader. The leader was promoted to prisoner camp leader. He had the stuff of which Nazis are made, although he was of a different nationality.

Maj. Guiraud helped to treat prisoners who suffered from dog bite. Guards walked about with trained dogs. When a guard wanted a little excitement he set a dog upon a prisoner or two and watched the ferocious animal claw and bite the prisoner into unconsciousness. Just for a little sport.

The major, who lost fifty pounds under the German diet at Dachau, told of a house of prostitution that was set up to encourage prisoners who worked. He gave some added details on the gas chamber and crematory.

He outlined the diet, about one-fourth of what is necessary to keep a man alive. He told of a visit by Heinrich Himmler—an inspection tour—last December.

Finally, he had a message to America.

"Let's realize what we are up against in the German race," he said. "Let's make sure there will be no more aggressor nations and no more wars. Let's assure peace and world security.

"Let's so treat Germany and the German people that we won't have to come over again 25 years from now and see and hear and smell the same things."

Did you say "amen," my friend?

· · · · · · · · · · ·

E. Z. DIMITMAN

Born in New York in 1898, Dimitman graduated from high school in Philadelphia and was soon working for a string of Philadelphia newspapers—the *Press*, the *North American*, and the *Public Ledger*—before being hired by the *Inquirer* in 1925. He became executive editor in 1939, three years after the paper was purchased by Moses Annenberg. In 1943 he became executive editor of the Chicago *Sun*, and in 1948 took the same post with the Newark *Star-Ledger*. He joined Walter Annenberg's Triangle Publications in 1953 and spent the remainder of his career as Annenberg's assistant. He died in Philadelphia in 1987.

Last Fantastic Battle in the Reich

· · · · · · · · · · · ·

BY

JAMES WELLARD

STAFF CORRESPONDENT OF THE CHICAGO *TIMES*

TANGERMUENDE ON THE ELBE, May 7, 1945—Today I saw the last battle in Germany. It was fought between thousands of disorganized, hysterical, screaming Germans and implacable, ruthless Russian tanks and infantry, two hundred yards from where I sat atop an American tank.

Had this tank opened fire, it would have slaughtered hundreds of Germans at point blank range.

I saw things so fantastic that they surpassed anything I have witnessed in four years of war.

I saw Russian shells burst in the middle of a blue-gray mass of German soldiers and civilians waiting to cross Tangermuende bridge onto the American side of the Elbe. Scores of men, women and children were killed or wounded.

I saw German soldiers pushing old women out of boats in which they were trying to cross the river. I saw a German officer stripped naked, paddling a rubber boat loaded with two German soldiers, three women, their baggage and bicycles.

Two German soldiers swam the river in their vests, climbed up on the west bank and were sent straight back to the east side, still in their vests.

I arrived at Tangermuende about 10 this morning. It is here that 50,000 German soldiers have passed into our lines as prisoners within the last three days.

They built themselves a catwalk along the blown-out bridge, which lies awash in the Elbe river. Across this catwalk they have been streaming night and day for five days.

Behind them the Russians have been steadily closing in. Today, about noon, the Russian tanks were only about 1,000 yards from the river bank.

Some German rear guards were still trying to hold off the Russians. That's why the war continued in this place.

I stood and watched as the Germans came streaming over the wreckage of the bridge, SS, paratroopers, generals, high-ranking staff officers, nurses, tankmen, Luftwaffe personnel, every description of Wehrmacht soldier, ran across wild-eyed. At the end of the bridge, they saw a huge sign in German which said, "This you can thank your Fuehrer."

American guards told them to throw down their equipment and run to a field, from where long lines wove down the road. The pile of Luger pistols, field glasses, rifles, cameras and wrist watches was nearly as high as the dome of St. Paul's Cathedral.

About noon, the Russians broke out of the woods. The fury and horror of the scene became indescribable. Russian shells and mortars cracked smack into the middle of crowds of Germans.

Out of the woods and the town across the river poured thousands of German soldiers, running every way, like ants coming out of a broken ant-hill. Russian mortars fell among them.

Down on the river bank, the scene was like something out of Dante's inferno. The Germans, men and women, kept leaping into the fast-moving river and kept being washed back on shore. Dead, dying and living were scrambled.

The Americans were permitting only those who could cross by the bridge to span the river. But hundreds would not wait. They pushed off into the stream on planks, rafts, amphibious jeeps and rubber boats, or swam.

Meanwhile, behind me, long lines of prisoners were marching up the road as far as I could see—whole units in battle formation, singing Nazi songs. They had forgotten their comrades on the other side, where a hell of fantastic proportions had broken loose.

A party of Russian tommy-gunners had fought their way out of the fields and almost down to the river bank, where they were ambushed by SS men hiding among parked trucks, hundreds of them. The Germans were burning the trucks as fast as possible and ammunition within them was exploding, sending cascades of flames skywards.

By this time, the German soldiers were for the most part safely across the bridge. They had precedence over the women and children. I myself saw that they were more concerned with saving their own skins than in helping even the wounded children.

The conclusion I drew was that the SS brought down upon their own people this fury of death from the Russian guns.

We could have massacred the whole mob, but we didn't.

. . . .

JAMES WELLARD

James Wellard was born in London, graduated with honors from the University of London, and received his Ph.D. from the University of Chicago. From 1940 to 1956 he was a correspondent and journalist for several U.S. and British papers. After the war Wellard taught at the University of Illinois and Longwood College in Virginia, and he was a Fulbright scholar at the University of Teheran in Iran. He wrote more than twenty-one books of both fiction and nonfiction.

Germany Surrenders!

· · · · · · · · · · · ·

BY
EDWARD KENNEDY

ASSOCIATED PRESS

REIMS, FRANCE, May 7, 1945 (AP)—Germany surrendered unconditionally to the Western Allies and Russia at 2:41 A.M. French time today. (This was at 8:41 P.M., Eastern war time Sunday.)

The surrender took place at a little red school house which is the headquarters of Gen. Eisenhower.

The surrender, which brought the war in Europe to a formal end after five years, eight months and six days of bloodshed and destruction, was signed for Germany by Col. Gen. Gustav Jodl.

Jodl is the new chief of staff of the German Army. It was signed for the Supreme Allied Command by Lieut. Gen. Walter Bedell Smith, Chief of Staff for Gen. Eisenhower.

It was also signed by Gen. Ivan Susloparoff for Russia and by Gen. François Sevez for France. Gen. Eisenhower was not present at the signing, but immediately afterward Jodl and his fellow delegate, Gen. Admiral Hans Georg Friedeburg, were received by the Supreme Commander.

They were asked sternly if they understood the surrender terms imposed upon Germany and if they would be carried out by Germany.

They answered yes.

Germany, which began the war with a ruthless attack upon Poland followed by successive aggressions and brutality in internment camps, surrendered with an appeal to the victors for mercy toward the German people and armed forces.

After signing the full surrender, Jodl said he wanted to speak and was given leave to do so.

"With this signature," he said in soft-spoken German, "the German people and armed forces are for better or worse delivered into the victors' hands.

"In this war which has lasted more than five years both have achieved and suffered more than perhaps any other people in the world."

. . . .

EDWARD KENNEDY

Edward Kennedy was chief of the Paris bureau of the Associated Press in 1945, when he broke the news of Germany's surrender to the Allies. As a result of the "premature broadcast," he was disaccredited until General Eisenhower reaccredited him in 1947.

A Brooklyn native, Kennedy worked for papers in Pennsylvania, New York, New Jersey, and Washington, D.C., before he started at the Associated Press in 1932. His last job was associate editor of the *Monterey Peninsula Herald* in California.

He died in 1963 at age fifty-eight from injuries suffered after he was struck by a car while walking home from his office.

Down Memory Lane

. . . .

BY

DREW MIDDLETON

STAFF CORRESPONDENT OF *THE NEW YORK TIMES*

PARIS, May 7, 1945—The old waiter that you liked best listened to the singing out on the Champs-Élysées and brought out a bottle. He filled his glass to the brim for himself and, gesturing toward the street, he said: "For those like Monsieur Lee, who will not return."

We drank. Listening to the singing on the street—they were singing old songs now from that other war—you thought back to Dickie Lee and all the others you had known in almost six years, good ones and bad ones, the ones who liked it and played it out to the end, the ones who thought it one kind of war at the start and, when it changed, got out; the ones who died, the ones who lived.

The intoxication of knowing it was over pictures in your mind, and there in the quiet of the bar in the Rue de Berri, all the people and the scenes came back. They were not much of the war, but they were something.

For one thing, in Paris now, at the end, there is always a curious feeling of having been here before, when the world was young, when there was a Maginot Line and a Gamelin and a Daladier and a naval blockade to rely on. You used to go to the bar then with Dickie Lee and other men from the same squadron of the Royal Air Force up near Lille. You think back to the world of 1939, and think of how it was and how it can never be that way again—there are too many things between us and the world of 1939.

Perhaps it started that next Spring, when we went into Belgium. All the girls came out and gave the soldiers of the British Expeditionary Force little cakes and pitchers of wine, and the sun shone hot in the hills beyond Brussels.

Then, beyond Louvain, you first came on the stupid horror that you have found war to be—dead Englishmen lying in the hot sun and, just beyond, dead Germans in their command car.

That was something very different from what you had expected life to be. Later you found that a couple of million other people felt the same way.

Anyway, they were there, and, from a ditch beside the road, looking across fields rich in spring, you saw a grotesque silhouette cross the skyline. Someone said: "There they are, there's the bloody Panzers."

The rest of that brief campaign is a succession of long drives, of moments of quivering terror in some roadside ditch when Junkers 87's came screaming down; the savage fight at Louvain and finally the long agony of evacuation. You got out at Boulogne and for one moment there was some hope.

We were in a hotel room above a square crowded with refugees who had just been machine-gunned by the Germans. Out of the loudspeaker at your elbow came that strong, reassuring voice: "What is our aim? It is victory. . . . I have nothing to offer but blood, toil, sweat and tears."

Then the Heinkels came in again, very low this time, and we fell on the floor.

You came back to France to watch a great nation die in seven days, from June 10 to June 17. They say now that France was not beaten then, but that is not the way you remember it. Infantrymen marched along the roads pitching their rifles into ditches and shouting: "Hurrah for peace." Often you saw officers' cars speeding southward. There were still British there and still some fighting, and somebody said: "They've got a chap named de Gaulle who's very good indeed. He did a very good show with some tanks a while back."

*   *   *

At a little place named Lisieux you saw the British hold for a few hours a great wave of German armor. Then it was all over and we were headed for Brest, stopping for the night in a village named St. Aubin d'Aubigne, where the priest and the Mayor came out and gave us food and lodging after everyone else had refused us a roof because of our uniforms, which were British.

There was never such a summer as that. They called it Hitler's weather, and every morning, when the haze lifted from the Channel, you could hear them coming over—Dorniers and Heinkels, Junkers and Messerschmitts.

Then from England came the high keen of climbing Hurricanes and Spitfires. Sitting on Shakespeare Cliff above Dover, you would see the RAF by threes and sixes tearing into the big German formations. No one knew until long afterward that he had been watching one of the decisive battles of the war. But it was.

The Germans were beaten, there in the high air over England, and although they smashed London that autumn, their air force could never do the job that it was designed to do—blast a path into land for the army by daylight bombing. A colonel from Washington named Spaatz was sitting in Rule's in Maiden Lane the night the first bombers came in.

"They're beaten," he said. "By God, the British have done it. They've made them bomb by night, they've stopped them."

It took a lot of men, among them Dickie Lee, but it stopped them. They never were the same in the air again, but there was a long period when, although they were stopped, we had not started.

Up in Iceland, on the edge of the Battle of the Atlantic, you saw what happened out there. Men lay in hospitals, men of America, men of Britain, of every nation. Mostly they looked down at their feet, or rather where their feet had been before they were amputated. They came in shivering and gaunt from life-rafts, and died.

There were Americans in Iceland now, pretty close to the war. First the Marines and then the Tenth Regiment of the Fifth Division of the United States Army. They were green, but they were young, strong and tough. They turned out to be a hell of a fine regiment in the Fifth Division. But all that was very far away then.

They kept coming in, saying: "Just where in hell is this war, Mac?" and: "Wait till we get a shot at these guys, we'll show them."

One night they heard about Pearl Harbor, and they knew they would have their chance. It did not come for a long time; then it was a long way away.

Transports swung in toward the black mass of Africa and you clambered down a net with kids from Tennessee, Georgia, New York and Rhode Island. You had been at Dieppe that summer and, remembering the way the dead looked as we drew off from that stricken field, the screams of men trying to get out of burning tanks, you shivered on the way in. But the kids talked about football and wondered whether they would see any elephants.

Fortunately it was easy, and they took the airfield very cleanly. In mid-morning the first Spitfires came sweeping in from the west and late that afternoon, when the Germans came over, they got twenty-two out of thirty. Anglo-American cooperation was born.

Africa was a long, bitter campaign, but never dull. All the bad things that had happened in France seemed worse because we thought it would be easy. There was a bad time in February at Kasserine and some trouble late in March around Kairouan, but by April everyone was pulling together.

You remember the last day at Tunis, when the tanks rolled down the hills with machine gunners cutting down the Hermann Goering Jaegers as they ran, and the rattle of rifle fire in the streets of Tunis.

After that, long rows of prisoners came in, and by nightfall it was all over. There was some fighting up on the Cap Bon Peninsula that next week, but at the finish there were a quarter-million prisoners; and a lean general named Bradley and a short, dapper one named Alexander, working under General Eisenhower, had beaten a German army in the field.

There had been a lot of bloody fighting at the end—Hill 609, Long Stop Hill—and the team that General Eisenhower was to build into the finest Allied army in the world had started on the long trail to victory.

Coming on the road to St. Lo two days after the battle, you saw the dead still unburied. Off beyond the town, General Bradley was trying to break out. For awhile there was confusion, and then suddenly this great elaborate machine that we call the United States Army began to move, tanks and planes, infantry and guns. When they stopped moving they were in Germany, halfway across a continent.

Dust rose from the tank tracks in the clear summer air and by mid-summer we had rolled through the lush heart of France. One afternoon in August, you went back to St. Aubin d'Aubigne and the same Mayor but a different priest were there at the church to bury three men of the resistance who had died freeing the town. The old priest who had been good to us four years before had been shot by the Germans.

Then one morning in the dawn you saw the Eiffel Tower, Sacré Coeur and all Paris lying in front of you. On a hill near St. Cloud you could hear people singing the "Marseillaise" and watch shell bursts off to the right.

It lingered on until spring, but the war really died just inside Germany last Autumn when the enemy tried to hold Aachen. He was stronger then than he has ever been since but he could not hold it. The First Division—tough, hard-dying men—went in and took it away from him.

Late on a Saturday afternoon, German civilians streamed out of Aachen and up the road to Brand, as so many other civilians had left their cities in the previous five years. Behind them, their city burned as so many non-German cities had burned. A German woman said: "I have a son in the air force, but I never wanted war." When the last strong-point in the town fell, Elite Guards tried to remove their badges from their uniforms. The fires that burned in Aachen burned more briskly in a hundred other German cities.

And now tonight they were singing the old RAF song, "Bless Them All," in the streets. You paid for your drinks, walked home and hoped that someone would bless them all, American and British, good ones, bad ones, all those who did the fighting and the dying.

. . . .

DREW MIDDLETON

After brief stints as a sportswriter and reporter for Poughkeepsie, New York, papers, Drew Middleton landed at the Associated Press, where he covered the European theater as a war correspondent. In 1942 he moved to *The New York Times* and worked as chief correspondent in most European offices. Middleton wrote more than fifteen books and received many journalistic honors, including the Headliners Club award for foreign correspondence, the U.S. Medal of Freedom, and the U.S. Navy Certificate of Merit. He retired as military correspondent in 1984 and died at age seventy-six on January 10, 1990.

All Is "Kaput" for Adolf

· · · · · · · · · · · · ·

BY
JACK FLEISCHER
UNITED PRESS WAR CORRESPONDENT

OBERSALZBERG, GERMANY, May 15, 1945—A man who was a stenographer at Adolf Hitler's headquarters in Berlin said today that
the Fuehrer decided on April 22 to meet his end fighting the Russians from an underground fortress behind the Reichchancellory.

The man is Gerhardt Herrgeselle, who was summoned to Hitler's
headquarters last July to do stenographic work after another stenographer had been killed in the attempt of the German army generals
to assassinate Hitler.

Herrgeselle said that Hitler, his sweetheart, Eva Braun; Martin
Bormann, deputy leader of the Nazi party; Field Marshal Wilhelm
Keitel; and Col. Gen. Gustav Jodl, who signed the German surrender
at Reims, were living in the underground fortress.

"Around 10:20 o'clock on the morning of April 21," Herrgeselle
said, "the Russian artillery fire became heavier and obviously they
were seeking to concentrate their fire on the government district.
Later, Russian planes made low-level attacks around central areas
such as Friedrichstrasse and Halleches Tor.

"From noon on there were conferences almost without interrup-
tion. Paul Joseph Goebbels, as commander of the Berlin defense,
rushed in and out of headquarters many times.

"Subordinate commanders reported in a steady stream. Still no decision was made to remove us to the south."

Herrgeselle said the next day the Russian infantry began pressing steadily in toward the center of Berlin. One spearhead was moving along Brenzlauer Allee which ends at the Alexander Platz. Hitler's special company of SS escort men was sent to protect the chancellory from that direction.

"Various officers and government officials frantically rushed around trying to organize the remainder of the chancellory personnel into a volksturn unit," Herrgeselle said. "Finally, about five hundred such persons were armed with pistols and rifles.

"The first military conference that day was held between 12:15 and 1:45 P.M., but still no decision was made about leaving Berlin. But during the series of conferences—I cannot remember how many because things became quite confused—it was obvious that things were critical.

"Officers and officials continuously streamed into the conference room in groups anywhere from three or four to maybe up to thirty. During this period the first criticism was made of Hitler regarding remaining in Berlin. But Hitler seemed slightly hazy. He often failed to reply to questions. At other times he obviously was not paying any attention to questions.

"The big decision finally was made in a 15-minute conference beginning at 5:30 P.M. Those present were Hitler, Bormann, Keitel and Jodl. Hitler was dressed, as usual, in dark trousers, field gray jacket with the iron cross hanging from the left side and a brown shirt that had white collar and cuffs.

"In recent days he had not looked so fit. His face was rather puffy and he flushed easily. He seemed to become more stooped daily and when he walked his shoulders gave the impression almost of being a hunchback. His left arm shook considerably. His right hand, where he was wounded in the July 20 explosion, also shook."

Herrgeselle said that a steel door was closed for the 5:30 conference and then Hitler announced to Bormann, Keitel and Jodl: "It is lost. I shall remain in Berlin. I shall fall here in the Reichschancellory."

The conference, according to Herrgeselle, was confused and

heated. At times, everybody except Jodl was talking at the same time in loud voices. Keitel and Bormann opposed Hitler's decision to stay in the chancellory. Jodl appeared to be indifferent.

Both Keitel and Bormann, according to Herrgeselle, told Hitler: "My Fuehrer, that contradicts what you have taught us in past months."

They referred to Hitler's declaration that he would continue to fight so long as there was any German soil left to fight on.

"Jodl, who earlier had been the only one who dared to tell Hitler the truth, was quiet throughout most of the conference," Herrgeselle said. Bormann and Keitel, however, continued to try to persuade Hitler to change his mind and go to southern Germany or Norway.

"But Hitler would not be talked out of his decision. During the discussions he frequently tried to silence Bormann and Keitel, but usually they were shouting at once.

"Hitler ordered Keitel, Bormann and Jodl to leave Berlin—an order he must have repeated at least ten times. But Bormann and Keitel said: 'My Fuehrer, we will not leave you. We would be ashamed to appear before our wives and children if we did.' Then Bormann said: 'It is the first time that I will not obey you.' Keitel said: 'I will stay.'

"Jodl, however, calmly said: 'I will not stay in this mouse hole. Here one cannot work, fight or operate.'

"Keitel then tried to persuade Hitler that Germany still had much left with which to carry on the war, but Hitler did not seem to be impressed.

"Jodl asked: 'My Fuehrer, do you hereby yield complete leadership?' But Hitler never made a really clear reply to that question.

"Later in the conference he told the three others: 'Go to southern Germany. Goering should form a new government. In any case arising, Goering should form a new government.' But Hitler never explained whether he meant Goering should form a government immediately or should wait until after Hitler was dead."

The conference was adjourned temporarily at 5:45 P.M., Herrgeselle said, and then was resumed. This time the group was joined by Gen. Krebs.

"Everybody in the room except Hitler went out several times to telephone," Herrgeselle said.

"Later events indicated they telephoned various persons and ordered them to call Hitler and try to persuade him to leave Berlin. Admiral Doenitz telephoned Hitler and gave an optimistic picture of the situation. (Herrgeselle here explained that because Hitler's hearing had been impaired in the July 20 attempt on his life, a stenographer usually listened in on his telephone conversations.) Hitler listened to Doenitz for awhile and then said: 'Thank you, Herr grand admiral. Heil.'

"Then Foreign Minister Ribbentrop telephoned. He apparently was somewhere in Berlin and spoke excitedly. He claimed to have an authentic report of tension between the western Allies and Russia. Ribbentrop said: 'One of our best agents who traveled in the best British circles just arrived in Switzerland. He said the British cabinet already was split and that dissension between the Allies must come.'

"But Hitler merely said: 'Oh, that is what that man said; that is what you say.'

"Goebbels then appeared with his children. First he brought them into the conference room, but then took them into the next room. Goebbels argued about the Nazis' historic thesis of the fight against Bolshevism and said: 'I propose that we turn our backs to the western front and continue to fight Bolshevism.' Hitler replied: 'No, that is capitulation and I will not cooperate.'

"The argument continued until about 7:30 P.M. Keitel continued to say he would not leave Hitler and Hitler continued to order him and the others to leave.

"There also was an argument over whether the protocol (the notes Herrgeselle was taking on the conversations) should remain in the chancellory and be destroyed when the end came or whether another stenographer and I should fly south and transcribe our notes. Hitler suddenly decided in favor of the latter."

Herrgeselle said that when he left the room he saw Eva Braun playing with the Goebbels children and she asked whether he was flying south. When she learned that he was, she asked him to take along a package and said she would give it to him later.

"I had seen Eva Braun around several times," Herrgeselle said, "but I never paid any attention to her and did not know until later that she was the Fuehrer's sweetheart.

"I went up into the chancellory, ate, packed a suitcase and returned to the underground bunker to get Eva's package. She gave me a small, oblong box wrapped in paper and I was too anxious to get started to pay much attention to it. I suppose it contained some family jewelry or personal rings. She wanted to write a letter too, but I said I was in a hurry and she said she would give it to somebody else later when our party was leaving. At that time Eva and the Fuehrer were sitting by themselves in the reception room.

"We left the chancellory in automobiles after dark in a steady rain. There were some women with us and a fat professor named Morell, who was Hitler's personal physician. He was very nervous. We were surprised when we had no trouble driving west on the east-west axis to Gatow airport, northwest of Berlin. There was no artillery fire along the route and we were very happy.

"Gatow must have been the last airport in German hands, because when we arrived the soldiers already had abandoned it. But a pilot and crew were there with a big Condor transport plane. We took off about 1:45 A.M. and landed near Munich about 4:15 A.M. Russian ack-ack fired at us, but did not hit us."

Herrgeselle said that later that day (April 23) they drove to Berchtesgaden where he gave Eva Braun's package to a man named Mueller, who was one of Bormann's assistants.

Herrgeselle does not know what happened in Berlin after he left. The only person he saw from there was one of Hitler's adjutants, named Julius Scaub, who arrived at Berchtesgaden later on April 23, but had no fresh news.

Herrgeselle thought Keitel might have tried to remove Hitler from Berlin by force, but probably failed. He admits there is a "slight possibility" that Hitler still is alive, but is personally convinced the Fuehrer died in the underground fortress with Eva Braun, some SS retainers and probably Bormann.

Herrgeselle speculated that plans were made some time ago to prevent Hitler's body from falling into the hands of the Russians. He thought the bodies of Hitler and a few close associates may have been placed in a vault in the basement of some of the government buildings and then sealed by blasting debris down upon it.

. . . .

JACK FLEISCHER

Born in Luxembourg, in 1903, Jack Fleischer worked his way through the University of Missouri's School of Journalism as a Linotype operator on the Columbia *Tribune* and as campus correspondent of the St. Louis *Post-Dispatch*. In 1929 he joined the International News Service in Chicago, becoming its Berlin bureau chief in 1934. He received several awards for his coverage of the German military up to the fall of France. He joined the U.S. Army after Pearl Harbor but didn't see combat, and after the war he returned to journalism. He covered the Potsdam Conference, the Nuremberg trials, and the birth of the United Nations for the INS and subsequently joined the Hearst Headline Service as columnist and United Nations correspondent. He died at the U.N. Secretariat building in New York in 1966.

The Carrier That Wouldn't Be Sunk

· · · · · · · · · · · · ·

BY

JOHN G. ROGERS

NEW YORK *HERALD TRIBUNE*

[Editor's Note: The following dramatic story of the bombing of the American aircraft carrier *Franklin* is not strictly a frontline dispatch. It was written in New York on the basis of information released by the Navy, motion pictures, and the thrilling stories of survivors and is included in this book because it gives a vivid word picture of one of the great epics in the history of the U.S. Navy.]

May 18, 1945—The 27,000-ton American Aircraft Carrier Franklin suffered more than a thousand casualties and nearly fatal battle damage on March 19, 1945, off the Japanese coast, and was saved when her crew and escorts met the crisis with a heroism that still stands high in the annals of naval warfare, the Navy disclosed yesterday.

The saga of the big flattop, as it unfolded from Navy reports, motion pictures and the lips of survivors, formed an epic of disaster and death and valor on a ship that refused to accept doom even though she was under enemy attack and ablaze from bow to stern and ripped hideously by the internal shock of 200,000 pounds of her own explosives.

Now the charred and shattered Franklin is berthed in the Navy

Yard in Brooklyn, and her husky skipper, Capt. Leslie E. Gehres, said yesterday that only a miracle of bravery and sacrifice kept her from going down only fifty-eight days ago off Shikoku, one of Japan's home islands.

Of the 3,000 men aboard the Essex class carrier on that black Monday of March 19, there are 832 dead or missing today. A total of 270 were wounded, ninety of them very seriously.

The casualty toll was the biggest ever suffered by any American warship in a single engagement.

Despite the crippling punishment she absorbed, the Franklin sailed back alone with a skeleton crew of 704 and when she limped into Brooklyn on April 26, she was probably the most damaged warship ever to make any port.

A lone Japanese dive bomber, which was shot down two minutes afterward, smashed two direct 500-pound hits on the busy deck of the carrier at 7:07 A.M.

"It was an aviator's dream," Capt. Gehres said as he and thirty-one of his men and officers talked to this reporter at Third Naval District Headquarters at 99 Church Street.

"That Jap caught us the way any flyer dreams of catching an enemy carrier. He was a good pilot and a good bomber. He came down fast out of a low cloud and streaked a hundred feet over our flight deck.

"We had just sent up our first group of planes. Every one of the planes still aboard was ready for take-off and loaded with all the gasoline and bombs and rockets and bullets they could carry."

Exploding as they struck, one on the flight deck and the other down one level on the hangar deck, the two bombs caused terrific damage, killing scores of men and blasting to bits planes that were ready to attack Japan.

The 47-year-old Annapolis-trained Capt. Gehres remembered that "great sheets of flames shot up forward and starboard, and wrapped over the flight deck. Then the elevator disappeared and a few minutes later, things started to explode all over the ship."

Those two bombs were all that the Japanese ever were able to plant on the Franklin, though they kept trying. But the fires and explosions from the two direct hits caused a twelve-hour series of internal blasts when more than one hundred tons of the big carrier's own high-octane gasoline, rockets, bombs and ammunition blew up frightfully.

In that hell on water, big girders twisted like taffy and melted steel ran like ice cream in the sun. Two-ton bombs blasted great chunks from the flight deck. Detonated rockets swept the blazing deck at waist level. Aircraft engines were tossed aloft like [p]ing-[p]ong balls. Ammunition for the five-inch guns exploded, hurling gun mounts and gun crews out to sea.

Men and planes were thrown the length of the ship. Men were sealed into fiery tombs below the water line. Men were killed instantly by concussion. Heads bobbed in the water for miles behind the crippled ship as she was forced to turn and stagger toward Japan to lessen the wind's effect on the fires.

While Vice-Admiral Marc A. Mitscher's fast and lethal Carrier Task Force 58 threw up a big screen of planes to shield its stricken member, light cruisers and destroyers darted dangerously close to the Franklin to throw water streams onto her fires and to take off wounded.

Again and again the intrepid escorts risked destruction to help the crippled carrier and often were forced away by explosions. Among them were the destroyers Hunt, Marshall, Hickox and Miller, and the light cruiser Santa Fe.

The Santa Fe, commanded by Capt. H. C. Fitz, of Severna Park, Md., who has been recommended for the Navy Cross, was a hero ship. She came in so close to take off wounded in makeshift mail-bag breeches buoys that once she almost rammed the Franklin but managed to slide to a stop by reversing the engines and putting the rudder hard right.

Again she was so close that wounded were carried out onto the Franklin's horizontal antennae masts and lowered into the arms of seamen on the Santa Fe's deck.

Meanwhile, hundreds of frightened but resolute heroes on the carrier went into action in the Navy's best tradition to save the flattop they called "Big Ben."

For the work that they did that day, as the ship bucked from explosion and listed fourteen degrees to starboard and went down five feet astern, Capt. Gehres has recommended 184 decorations, including two for the Congressional Medal of Honor.

"But a lot of those acts of bravery will never be known," the square-jawed skipper said slowly. "I'd be looking down from the bridge, and I'd see men blackened and bleeding in the smoke, and doing things that . . . well, nobody knows who they were, a lot of them."

But some bravery was identified. There was a black-headed blue-eyed Irishman from Boston, Lieut. Commander Joseph T. O'Callahan, the ship's Roman Catholic chaplain.

"Father O'Callahan is the bravest man I've ever seen," Capt. Gehres said. "He functioned not only as a priest and first-aid man, but he organized the first dressing station on the flight deck when a doctor was trapped below. He organized hose crews and led them into the smoke and fire.

"Of course, lots of others were doing the same, but the point is that those things were not his job. By the middle of the morning, Father O'Callahan was down below helping lead a party of men who had to throw hot ammunition overboard. It was so hot they burned their hands on it, and it could have gone off any time, too."

In a motion picture display of scenes shot from both the Franklin and some of her escorts, Father O'Callahan was shown administering the last rites of his church to a curly-headed boy who lay dying on the deck while black smoke boiled and flames licked the air in the background.

Father O'Callahan is one of those recommended for the Congressional Medal. The other is Lieut. (j.g.) Donald A. Gary, an engineering officer, from Oakland, Calif.

"I began hearing about Gary within an hour," Capt. Gehres remembered. "If it wasn't for Gary and a doctor, Lieut. James L. Fuelling, we probably would have had another three hundred dead men aboard.

"They were trapped in a mess hall down below and the regular way out was blocked, both by smoke and damage. Fuelling kept them quiet and explained that they'd have to breathe as little air as possible. Gary somehow worked his way down there, and found an exit and then he went in and out about four times, leading long lines of men who held on to each other. They had to crawl through a vertical air intake beside the smokestack that had a ladder inside it.

"Later Gary fought fires, and checked on emergency fuel equipment and still later he was down working on the boilers."

Capt. Gehres, who lives in Coronado, Calif., and who took command of the Franklin on Nov. 1, told how five men were trapped four decks below at the after steering station in a compartment that measured twenty by twenty-five feet and was jammed with machinery and waist-deep in water.

"I had a communication line to them and they had one to my main engine station," he recalled. "I told them they'd have to stay there to keep me in touch with the engines and I promised them I'd get them out somehow.

"That was a reason that I never decided to abandon ship. I had promised those five kids I'd get them out. They were down there from the time we were hit until midnight and then finally Mr. Wassman helped get them out."

Mr. Wassman turned out to be Lieut. (j.g.) E. R. Wassman, 24 years old of New Rochelle, N.Y. An assistant navigator, Lieut. Wassman and several others crawled down to the trapped men through bomb holes and water and found the only possible exit through a compartment above flooded with ten feet of water.

After having a long job during which they had to retreat twice for air, they opened hatches to unflood water out of the compartment—enough so that the remainder wouldn't drown the trapped men when the proper hatch was opened.

One of the trapped men, 24-year-old Holbrook R. Davis, of Marstons Mills, Cape Cod, Mass., said yesterday:

"We had a slight mental strain when we would hear the explosions above us. But when we finally got out and saw what had happened above, we thought we were lucky."

Many men trapped below were not extricated until the next day, Capt. Gehres said, and they told of the mental torture when quiet set in by nightfall. They had no way of knowing whether the ship had been abandoned.

While fires fed by gasoline continued to start up for nearly twenty-four hours after the attack, survivors of the Franklin continued to turn up accounted for on rescue ships for many days. One case seemed to be a miracle. A pilot was in a bomber ready to take off when the first Japanese bomb blew his plane apart. A week later, the pilot turned up safe on a rescue ship. He had been blown overboard and soon picked up.

The lone civilian aboard, Donald Russell, an aircraft company technician, refused to leave when most of the carrier's air group boarded rescue vessels, and fought the destruction with the Navy. Negro stewards, led by one making his first sea trip, organized into hose gangs.

The worst of the Franklin's internal explosions was over by noon, five hours after the start of the holocaust, but ammunition kept buzzing about uncomfortably all night. By that time the Franklin was being towed by a cruiser. By morning the carrier was making three knots. As more boilers were repaired, she was making fourteen knots by noon, and told the cruiser she could make it alone.

Eventually, on the 13,400-mile trip to Brooklyn, the Franklin made twenty-three knots, manned by a skeleton crew, which since has organized "The 704 Club."

Commander Harry F. Hale, of Gary, Ind., the ship's air officer, told of the trip home.

"The only food locker we could get open for awhile held nothing but Spam. We got awful tired of Spam. Then we found one full of steaks. We ate so many steaks that we got tired of them, and wished we had some more Spam."

All the way home, the skeleton crew worked hard to clean up their ship. They did such a good job, Capt. Gehres said, that he thinks they saved about two months' work and $100,000 in labor charges for the government.

Whether the Franklin will be repaired to fight another day is a Navy secret, but even if she is lost, she will be avenged. Many of her survivors are being re-assigned to combat work in the Pacific, and presumably those left from her big flight group are already working on other carriers.

. . . .

JOHN G. ROGERS

John G. Rogers began at the New York *Herald Tribune* in 1937, working first as a general assignment writer, then as a foreign correspondent. Among other journalistic honors, Rogers won the New York State Bar Association media award for a series on student violence in 1969.

After the *Herald Tribune* closed in 1969, he was a free-lance writer and wrote articles and the annual "Police Officer of the Year" award series until 1979.

The First Atomic Bomb

· · · · · · · · · · · ·

BY

W. H. LAWRENCE

BY WIRELESS TO *THE NEW YORK TIMES*

GUAM, Wednesday, Aug. 8, 1945—The first atomic bomb wiped out 4.1 square miles of the Japanese city of Hiroshima on Monday, it was announced today. Gen. Carl A. Spaatz, commanding general of the Strategic Air Forces, made the disclosure that 60 per cent of the city had been destroyed.

Hiroshima, on the Inland Sea, had a built-up area of 6.9 square miles and a pre-war population of 343,000.

General Spaatz's announcement, based on a careful study of photographs taken a few hours after the bomb had been dropped, made clear the terrific destructive power of this weapon, which has harnessed the power of the universe and turned it against the Japanese.

General Spaatz said that the single bomb had "completely destroyed" the area cited, including five major industrial targets. The pictures made it clear that there was other damage in the area of the city that was not completely destroyed.

It was believed that much of this terrible destruction was executed in a split second and resulted from concussion rather than fire.

Thus, with a single bomb, we were able to destroy in a matter of seconds an area equivalent to one-eight of Manhattan.

The bomb was dropped at 9:15 A.M., Monday, from the Super Fortress Enola Gay, piloted by Col. Paul W. Tibbets, Jr. of Miami, Fla. The man who designed the new bomb, Capt. William S. Parsons of Chicago, went on the mission to see how the weapon worked. The bombardier was Major Thomas W. Ferrebee of Mocksville, N.C.

The missile, which crashed with the explosive power of 20,000 tons of TNT, covered the entire area of Hiroshima in two minutes with a black cloud which "looked like boiling dust" and climbed 40,000 feet.

That smoke cloud, visible as much as 160 miles at sea, still hung over the city at least four hours later.

[Crewmen of a reconnaissance Superfortress flying over Wakayama Prefecture at a point 170 miles from Hiroshima reported that they could see the flash of the bomb as well as the smoke, the United Press reported. "A tremendous flash like a ball of fire or a setting sun shone in the distance," the pilot said.]

That was the story told yesterday by the daring men who had charge of the first use of this tremendous agent of destruction. They were Captain Parsons, who is from Chicago and describes himself as the "weaponeer"—he is a naval ordnance expert who designed the bomb in which the energy of the split atom was channelized—and Colonel Tibbets, from Miami, Fla., the pilot of the Enola Gay, named for Col. Tibbets's 57-year-old mother, also a resident of Miami.

As they told their story to assembled newsmen at headquarters of the United States Army Strategic Air Forces, they were flanked by General Spaatz and his chief of staff, Maj. Gen. Curtis E. LeMay, who calmly announced that if the same weapon had been available to the American Air Force in England as late as February, 1943, there would have been no need for an invasion of the European Continent.

Although they would not, for obvious reasons, apply the same prediction to Japan, they left no doubt that they believed that the air forces could beat Japan into unconditional surrender with this new and terrible weapon, which General Spaatz said was the equivalent of 2,000 B-29's fully loaded with the standard type of incendiary and demolition bombs.

They told this, the greatest story of the war, with an air that was almost casual. They described simply the reaction they observed as the bomb was dropped, but they made no precise claims of damage resulting, preferring to let that wait for detailed photographic reconnaissance.

Captain Parsons, who had been working on the design of the bomb since June, 1943, and Colonel Tibbets, who had known a long time that he would pilot the plane to drop the first one, simply reported on a job that had been accomplished. They did so without heroic or unnecessary verbiage.

"When the bomb dropped we put as much distance between ourselves and the ball of fire as we could," Captain Parsons said. "In our desert experiments [in New Mexico] at about dawn there had been a blinding flash when the first one exploded, but yesterday, in the bright sunlight, the flash was not so great.

"I heaved a sigh of relief because I knew the bomb was a success. We felt the great concussion about one minute after the bomb hit and within another minute or two a great black cloud of boiling dust and churning debris was 1,000 feet off the ground, and above it smoke climbed like a mushroom to 20,000 feet. A few fires were visible around the edges of the smoke, but we could see nothing of the city except the dock area, where buildings were falling down."

Captain Parsons was asked for his reaction as the designer of the bomb, at the moment when its destructive terror was unleashed on the city and the people below. He said he had no particular reaction except that of relief that the bomb had exploded.

Until the bomb was released, only Captain Parsons, Colonel Tibbets and Major Ferrebee knew the exact purpose of the mission. The others of the crew, who had been selected carefully, knew that they were on an unusual mission of great importance, but not that the greatest contribution to the science of warfare since the invention of gunpowder was in the bomb bays below.

Some of them ejaculated, "My God" and few could believe their eyes when the great black cloud covered the city of 343,000 from the impact of a single bomb in a matter of seconds.

Captain Parsons remarked wryly that it probably was a good idea for the "weaponeer" to go along on the first battle mission on which his product was to be used because it gave him a great personal interest in making certain that the bomb he had designed could be used safely.

He recalled that the first laboratory experiment with the atomic bomb had been made on July 16 in New Mexico and remarked that the first bomb was dropped on the enemy on Aug. 6 (Japanese time), a date that the scientists and others concerned with this weapon had set as their goal more than a year ago. Although the technique of employing the bomb is not yet perfected, Captain Parsons said that it was important that the first one should be dropped as quickly as possible "because this weapon is worth so much in terms of shortening the war."

Colonel Tibbets said that the trip from the Marianas to the target city had been without incident. The weather was clear and a bright sun was shining. The target was clear below. There was no Japanese fighter or anti-aircraft fire to interfere with the big bomber as it settled on the bomb run from which it could not be deviated.

When the bomb was dropped, Colonel Tibbets said he banked sharply in a 270-degree turn, his motors turning over as fast as possible so the plane would be out of the area where the great blast would be felt.

Colonel Tibbets was asked what effect the concussion had on the plane. He said it was so slight that it seemed merely to be a burst of anti-aircraft fire that exploded near by. The airplane was not shaken as much by the blast as it would have been by thermal updrafts from an incendiary attack on a Japanese city at low level.

For his part in the mission Colonel Tibbets received the Distinguished Service Cross from General Spaatz as soon as he landed at his undisclosed base.

Two other men who played an important role in the development of this weapon, Rear Admiral William R. Purnell of Bowling Green, Mo., and Brig. Gen. Thomas F. Farrell of Albany, N.Y., were on hand for the first mission and at yesterday's conference.

. . . .

W. H. LAWRENCE

William Lawrence was *The New York Times'* chief Moscow correspondent from 1943 to 1945, and after the end of the war in Europe he reported on the last months of the Pacific war. Following war he covered the United Nations, the Balkans, and U.S. politics, before joining ABC News in 1961. A Nebraskan, born in 1916, Lawrence began his career with the Lincoln *Star* and was national affairs editor with ABC News when he died in 1972.

The Pit of Hell That Was Hiroshima

· · · · · · · · · · · ·

BY

JOHN R. HENRY

INTERNATIONAL NEWS SERVICE STAFF CORRESPONDENT

GUAM, Aug. 8, 1945—Of the Americans aboard the Superfortress, "Enola Gay" which shattered the Japanese city of Hiroshima, only three men in the crew of 11 knew the exact nature of the mission, and only one of these had ever before witnessed the devastating effects of the atomic bomb.

The attack on Hiroshima was summarized by the returning airmen in this way:

"The only way we could tell a city had been there was because we had seen it a moment before."

Later, a correspondent viewing photographic scenes of destruction said it was "a little like looking into a pit of hell."

Col. Paul W. Tibbets, Jr., of Miami, said even his co-pilot, Capt. Robert A Lewis, of 28 Hazelton St., Ridgefield Park, N.J., was uninformed concerning the terrifying aspects of the bomb the Enola Gay was carrying.

Tibbets, a veteran of the European air war, Capt. William Sterling Parsons of the Navy, a native of Chicago and resident of Santa Fe, N.M., and Maj. Thomas W. Ferrebee, bombardier from Mocksville, N.C., were the only men aboard the Enola Gay fully informed of the nature of the mission.

Parsons, who participated in development of the atomic bomb, was a witness to the first test in New Mexico on July 16 (1945).

The Enola Gay took off on its history-making mission sometime after midnight and saw Hiroshima virtually go up in smoke at 9:15 A.M. Monday, when the bomb was dropped.

Parsons was the least surprised man aboard the Superfort when the bomb exploded.

"We made a tight turn away from the target in order to get a maximum distance between us and the explosion," Parsons said.

"It was little more than a minute after we dropped the bomb that we felt the impact of the explosion."

Parsons described the men aboard the Enola Gay as "amazed and speechless" in the wake of the bombing.

"What had been Hiroshima was a mountain of white smoke mushrooming into the sky.

"I looked at this two or three minutes when the top of the mushroom broke off and floated into the sky.

"Another mushroom formed, the dust cloud spread and fires started at its edges, probably starting in buildings in which gas mains had broken or something like that."

As It Was When Japan Surrendered

. . . .

BY

WILLIAM B. DICKINSON

UNITED PRESS STAFF CORRESPONDENT

[Editor's Note: William B. Dickinson, former Southwest Pacific manager of the United Press, traveled with General Douglas MacArthur's headquarters from Australia to Tokyo. Dickinson recalls in the following dispatch, on the eve of the first anniversary, the formal surrender of the Japanese aboard the battleship USS Missouri in Tokyo Bay.]

NEW YORK, Aug. 31, 1946 (UP)—The distant thunder sounded in the east just as the little yellow man in the worn frock coat and the moth-eaten top hat reached the ladder which led down the grey steel side of the "mighty Mo'."

Mamoru Shigemitsu, foreign minister of beaten Japan, paused at the top of the ladder, balancing himself with his black cane.

He turned his face to look at the sky to the east, above the capital of the once proud Nipponese Empire, where the sun was breaking through scattered clouds. As he gazed, the thunder grew.

It was exactly 9:30 A.M. Tokyo time on Sept. 2, 1945 (Sept. 1 in the United States).

Only 30 minutes before, Shigemitsu had come up that ladder and on to the decks of the great American battleship Missouri anchored in Tokyo Bay, symbolizing by its very presence there the end perhaps for all time of his nation's dreams of empire in the Far East.

He had limped across the promenade deck to stand, awkwardly and yet not without dignity, and face the men who had sent Japan down to defeat. Her fleet was scattered, her air force decimated, her war industries and thousands upon thousands of her homes bombed to rubble, her army scattered in trackless jungles or bottled up in the home islands. The atom bomb had fallen.

There was proud, implacable MacArthur, white-haired Nimitz, strong-jawed Halsey, tough little George Kenney and lean Carl Spaatz. There, too, were representatives of the Chinese, who had fought Japan for eight long years; of Russia, which had come in late to stage a triumphant sweep through Manchuria; of Great Britain and Canada and Australia and New Zealand and France.

At 9:08 A.M. Shigemitsu heard MacArthur say, his voice quavering a little with the import of his words:
"The Japanese delegates now will sign the instrument of surrender."

The little man walked with downcast eyes those long 20 steps to the table where MacArthur stood, the surrender documents spread on the green felt before him.

He spoke no word as he lowered himself painfully into the chair before the table, his peg-leg sticking out grotesquely before him, picked up one of the new pens and signed his name to both copies of the document in which his nation admitted total defeat, and accepted unconditional surrender.

He rose and stood beside the table as ugly little Gen. Yoshijiro Umeju signed after him for the Japanese Imperial general staff.

Then he limped back to his place, and watched through lowered lids as the ceremony of surrender—suddenly and inexplicably relieved of its tenseness by the Japanese signing—continued on a note of almost jubilation.

MacArthur signed first for all the allied nations, using five pens to inscribe his bold signature—the last of them a little red fountain pen belonging to the Tennessee belle whom he had made his wife.

Then came Nimitz and the rest, one from each country, to write their names.

It was 9:30. Only 30 minutes had he stood on the decks of the

Missouri and already it was time for Shigemitsu to leave the ship, to return to the small boat that had brought him, and go back to share defeat with his people.

So he limped toward the ladder, and as he reached it he heard that thunder in the east. It grew to a tremendous roar, and then he saw the first wave of American B29s, with Navy fighters above and around them, break from the clouds and rush toward the ship.

They came in waves—a hundred of the mighty bombers, and hundreds of gull-winged Navy pursuits. Their thunder vibrated in the steel decks of the "mighty Mo'," it lifted the hair on the scalp, it filled the ears to bursting.

Shigemitsu turned away, his shoulders drooping in the ill-fitting old frock coat. Awkwardly he went down the ladder—a picture of defeat.

How the War Lords
Met Their Doom

· · · · · · · · · · · ·

BY
KINGSBURY SMITH

INTERNATIONAL NEWS SERVICE GENERAL MANAGER

[Editor's Note: As the sole representative of the combined American press Smith was eyewitness to the dramatic events he describes below. The two dispatches that follow were written only hours apart, under severe deadline pressure, as the historic events unfolded in rapid succession.]

NUREMBERG PALACE OF JUSTICE, Oct. 16, 1946—I saw through peepholes in prison cell doors today the grim resignation on the anguished faces of most of the eleven condemned Nazi leaders.

As the only representative of the world's press to enter the heavily guarded condemned block of the Nuremberg City jail, this International News Service correspondent walked down the death row of Nazidom and peered through cell door portholes at Hermann Wilhelm Goering and the rest of Hitler's doomed cohorts.

It was a sight never to be forgotten.

These men who played such leading roles in the greatest despotism the world has ever known since the Dark Ages were a miserable looking lot.

The power and the glory that was theirs when they dominated

379

most of Europe was nowhere to be seen, neither in their demeanor nor in the dismal surroundings of their last abode on earth.

The once-great Reichmarschal Goering, crown prince of Nazidom, sat slumped on a small iron cot which in the past had known only the weight of common criminals. His heavy shoulders sagged against the bare, white-washed wall of his small cell as he tried to drown thoughts of his impending fate by immersing himself in a book. It was a well-thumbed, soiled paper-covered ornithological volume entitled, "With the Passage of Birds to Africa."

I thought to myself that this successor to Baron Manfred von Richthofen as Germany's ace airman of World War I probably was wishing now that he had wings with which to fly out of his prison cage to take passage with the birds to Africa—or anywhere else he might escape the long, new arm of international law that has condemned him to a pirate's death.

Draped over the shoulders of his wrinkled pearl gray Luftwaffe uniform blouse was an ordinary khaki-colored U.S. Army blanket to help keep off the chill of the brisk October air that came through the tiny half-opened window along with rays of brilliant sunshine.

Unnoticed by Goering, I stood studying him over the shoulder of an American security guard, whose duty it was to keep the Nazi warlord under constant scrutiny.

The guard stood outside the locked cell door, peering through a small aperture and ready at an instant's notice to swing back the iron bolt and dash inside, should Goering attempt to cheat the gallows by trying to take his own life.

This constant night-and-day watch had been in effect since Robert Ley, the late Nazi labor leader, managed to hang himself in his cell.

I learned that his success in doing so was due, not only because the guard had several cells to watch on a patrol basis, but that when he saw Ley hanging from a toilet pipe and sounded the alarm, the warden who came running became so excited he jammed the lock.

The most striking feature about Hitler's one-time heir-apparent, as I watched him, was a grim, anguished look on his face.

It was not the face of a martyr.

There was no spark of ideological faith on that countenance; no sign of a fearless spirit who believed in his cause, right or wrong.

The mouth was drawn and the lips had a rat-trap tightness about them. I was struck by the deep, dark lines and the puffy pouches beneath the eyes, the jowl-like flabbiness of the cheeks. The thinning black hair, always so impeccably combed in the courtroom, was dishevelled as though Goering's pudgy hands had been nervously running through it.

The next porthole through which I peered disclosed the shriveled figure of the once arrogant foreign minister, Joachim von Ribbentrop.

He, too, was sitting on his bed, but no book was in his hand. Instead, the former diplomatic demon of Nazidom was staring vacantly into space with glassy eyes and a dazed look.

The once-dapper diplomat, who never wore a shirt unless it came from a leading Parisian shop and whose clothes were cut by the finest London tailors, was living up to his reputation as the DIRTIEST of all the Nazi prisoners at Nuremberg.

His suit was messy, his cell was disorderly, and strands of his gray hair were standing up in ruffled fashion.

The man who strutted around with an insolent air in the heyday of Hitlerism looked like a wornout, wretched human wreck.

There was a striking difference between Ribbentrop and the next figure I saw in an adjoining cell.

This figure was pacing up and down in an agitated manner over the 7-foot by 12-foot rubber-matted stone floor of the prison cage, his hands clenched tightly behind a ramrod-straight back.

Here was the soldier—Field Marshal Wilhelm Keitel, commander-in-chief of the Wehrmacht, symbol of the aristocracy of German militarism.

The papers on his frail little wooden table were in perfect arrangement, with the appearance of something that had known the touch of a member of the traditionally methodical German General Staff.

The most disturbed thing I noticed was the man's face. It looked as though he was being mentally crucified. The jaw was set grimly, as though he was making an effort to bear inward pain with stoicism.

That was to be expected of a proud Prussian officer, but the eyes were burning with a hurt, hate-filled look. It was obvious this military leader did not relish confinement in a prison cell, nor the imminence of a dishonorable, unsoldierly death at the end of a hangman's rope.

This man, who claimed he helped rearm Germany only "for peace," but who issued orders for the invasion of Poland five months before the event, did not appear to like the idea of being made a precedent for a great new concept of international law—the principle that professional soldiers cannot escape justice for waging aggressive war by claiming they were merely carrying out orders.

The inmate in the next cell was having lunch.

I saw the back of a bull neck, with a shining bald pate. A fat, slumpy body was huddled over an army tin cup filled with soup. The soup was being held close to a grisly chin, and a spoon was lapping the liquid impatiently into thick, vulgar lips. The man seemed more like an ape than a human.

This was Fritz Sauckel, boss of the foreign workers brought into Germany for forced labor, described by one of his judges as the "greatest and most cruel slave-maker since the days of the Pharaohs."

I moved away with a shudder.

As I turned and walked for the last time past the cells of the eleven condemned men, I thought how gratified would be the millions who suffered and died because of the wickedness of these Nazis, if they could file down the narrow corridor of death row with me and see that these evil figures finally had been brought to justice. The thought occurred to me that perhaps the spirits of the tortured victims of Hitlerian madness had already passed down the corridor, and that possibly that was the reason for the tormented look on the faces of those eleven about to face another great judgment day.

NUREMBERG, Oct. 16, 1946—Ex-Reichsmarschal Hermann Wilhelm Goering succeeded in cheating the gallows of Allied justice by committing suicide in his prison cell a short time before the ten other condemned remnants of the Nazi hierarchy were hanged today.

Despite the fact that an American security guard was supposed to be watching his every movement, the crown prince of Nazidom managed to place in his mouth and swallow a vial containing cyanide of potassium.

The vial of poison was hidden in a copper cartridge shell.

Goering swallowed the poison while Col. Burton C. Andrus, American security commandant, was walking across the prison yard to the death row block to read to him and the ten other condemned Nazi leaders the International Military Tribunal's sentence of death.

Goering had not previously been told he was going to die this morning, nor had any of the other condemned men.

How he guessed that this was to be his day of doom and how he managed to conceal the poison on his person are a mystery that has confounded the security forces.

With former Foreign Minister Joachim von Ribbentrop taking the place of Goering as the first to mount the scaffold, the ten other condemned princes of Nazidom were hanged one by one in the bright, electrically-lighted barn-like small gymnasium inside one of the prison yards of the Nuremberg city jail.

The execution of Von Ribbentrop and the others took approximately one hour and a half.

The once arrogant diplomatic double-crosser of Nazidom entered the execution hall at 1:11 this morning. The trap was sprung at 1:16 and he was pronounced dead at 1:20.

The last to walk up the 13 forbidding wooden steps to one of the two gallows used for the executions was Arthur Seyss-Inquart, Austrian traitor and Nazi gauleiter for Holland. He dropped to his death at 2:45 A.M. and was pronounced dead at 2:57.

All ten of the Nazis attempted to show bravery as they went to their deaths. Most of them were bitterly defiant, some grimly resigned, and others asked the Almighty for mercy.

All but Alfred Rosenberg, the pagan party theorist, made brief, last minute statements on the scaffold, nearly all of which were nationalistic expressions for the future welfare and greatness of Germany.

The only one, however, to make any reference to Hitler or Nazi ideology was Julius Streicher, the arch Jew-baiter. Displaying the most bitter and enraged defiance of any of the condemned, he screamed, "Heil Hitler" at the top of his voice as he was about to mount the steps to the gallows.

Streicher appeared in the execution hall, which had been used only last Saturday night for a basketball game by American security guards, at 12½ minutes after two o'clock.

As was the case of all the condemned, a warning knock by a guard outside preceded Streicher's entry.

An American lieutenant-colonel, sent to fetch the condemned from the nearby prison wing, entered first. He was followed by Streicher who was stopped immediately inside the door by two Army sergeants. They closed in on each side of him and held his arms while another sergeant who followed Streicher removed the manacles from his hands and replaced them with a leather cord.

The first person whom Streicher and the others saw upon entering the gruesome hall was an American lieutenant-colonel who stood directly in front of him while his hands were being tied behind his back as they had been manacled upon his entrance.

This ugly, dwarfish little man, wearing a threadbare suit and a well-worn bluish shirt buttoned to the neck but without a tie, glanced at the wooden scaffolds rising up menacingly in front of him. Two of these were used alternatively to execute the condemned while a third was kept in reserve.

After a quick glance at the gallows, Streicher glared around the room, his eyes resting momentarily upon the small group of American, British, French and Russian officers on hand to witness the executions.

By this time, Streicher's hands were tied securely behind his back. Two guards, one on each arm, directed him to No. 1 gallows on the left. He walked steadily the six feet to the first step, but his face was twitching nervously. As the guards stopped him at the bottom of the steps for official identification requests, he uttered his piercing scream: "Heil Hitler!"

His shriek sent a shiver down the back of this International News reporter who was witnessing the executions as the sole representative of the American press.

As its echo died away, another American colonel by the steps said sharply:

"Ask the man his name."

In response to the interpreter's query Streicher shouted:

"You know my name well."

The interpreter repeated his request and the condemned man yelled:

"Julius Streicher."

As he mounted to the platform Streicher cried out: "Now it goes to God," and after getting up the thirteen steps to the eight-foot high and eight-foot square black-painted wooden platform, Streicher was pushed two steps to the spot beneath the hangman's rope.

This was suspended from an iron ring attached to a crossbeam which rested on two posts. The rope was being held back against a wooden rail by the American Army sergeant hangman.

Streicher was swung around to face toward the front.

He glared again at the Allied officers and the eight Allied correspondents representing the world's press who were lined up against a wall behind small tables facing the gallows.

With burning hatred in his eyes, Streicher looked down upon the witnesses and then screamed:

"Purim fest 1946."

(Purim is a Jewish holiday celebrated in the Spring commemorating the hanging of Haman, Biblical oppressor of the Jews.)

The American officer at the scaffold said: "Ask the man if he has any last words."

When the interpreter had translated, Streicher shouted:

"The Bolsheviks will hang you one day."

As the black hood was being adjusted about his head Streicher was heard saying:

"Adele, my dear wife."

At that moment, the trap was sprung with a loud bang. When the rope snapped taut and the body swung wildly, a groan could be heard distinctly within the dark interior of the scaffold.

It was originally intended to permit the condemned to walk the 70-odd yards from the cells to the execution chamber with their hands free, but they were all manacled in their cells immediately following the discovery of Goering's suicide.

The weasel-faced Ribbentrop in his last appearance before mankind uttered his final words while waiting for the black hood to be placed over his head. Loudly, in firm tones, he said:

"God save Germany."

He then asked:

"May I say something else?"

The interpreter nodded. The former diplomatic wizard of Nazidom, who negotiated the secret German non-aggression pact with Soviet Russia on the eve of Germany's invasion of Poland and who approved orders to execute Allied airmen, then added:

"My last wish is that Germany realizes its entity and that an understanding be reached between the East and West. I wish peace to the world."

The ex-diplomat looked straight ahead as the hood was adjusted. His lips were set tight.

Next in line to the gallows was Field Marshal Wilhelm Keitel, symbol of Prussian Militarism.

Here came the first military leader to be executed under the new concept of Allied international law.

Keitel entered the death arena at 1:10, only two minutes after the trap was dropped beneath Ribbentrop and while the latter was still hanging at the end of the rope.

The field marshal could not of course see the ex-foreign minister whose body was concealed within the first scaffold and whose rope still hung taut.

Keitel did not appear as tense as Ribbentrop. He held his head high while his hands were being tied and walked with military bearing to the foot of the second scaffold although a guard on each side held his arms.

When asked his name, he answered in a loud sharp tone, "Wilhelm Keitel!"

He mounted the gallows steps as he might have climbed to a reviewing stand to take a salute of the German army. He certainly did not appear to need the help of the guards.

When turned around at the top, Keitel looked over the crowd with the traditional iron-jawed haughtiness of the proud Prussian officer. When asked if he had anything to say, he looked straight ahead and, in a loud voice, said:

"I call on God Almighty to have mercy on the German people. More than two million German soldiers went to their deaths for the Fatherland. I follow now my sons."

Then, while [he raised] his voice to shout, "All for Germany," Keitel's black-booted, uniformed body plunged down with a bang. Observers agreed he had showed more courage on the scaffold than he had in the courtroom where he had tried to hide his guilt behind Hitler's ghost. There he claimed it was all the Fuehrer's fault; that he merely carried out orders and had no responsibility.

This despite the fact that documentary evidence showed he "approved and backed" measures for branding Russian prisoners of war, directed "Draconian measures" to terrorize the Russian people and issued secret orders for invasion of Poland five months before the attack took place.

With both Ribbentrop and Keitel hanging at the end of their ropes, there was a pause in the grim proceedings.

The American colonel directing the executions asked the American general representing the United States on the Allied Control Commission if those present could smoke. An affirmative answer brought cigarets into the hands of almost every one of the 30-odd persons present.

Officers and GI's walked around nervously or spoke to one another in hushed voices while Allied correspondents scribbled furiously on this historic, ghastly event.

In a few minutes an American Army doctor, accompanied by a Russian Army doctor, and both carrying stethoscopes, walked to the first scaffold, lifted the curtain and disappeared within.

They emerged at 1:30 A.M. and spoke to an American colonel wearing combat boots. The colonel, facing official witnesses, snapped to attention to say:

"The man is dead."

Two GI's quickly appeared with a stretcher. The hangman, a sergeant, mounted the gallows steps, took a large commando type knife out of a sheath strapped to his side and cut the rope. Ribbentrop's limp body, with the black hood still over his head, was speedily removed to the far end of the room and placed behind a black canvas curtain. This all had taken less than ten minutes.

The directing colonel turned to the witnesses and said: "Cigarets out, please, gentlemen," and then, addressing another colonel, he called "Norman" and said, "Okay." The latter went out the door to fetch the next prisoner.

This creature was Ernst Kaltenbrunner, Gestapo chief and director of the greatest mass murders Europe has known since the Dark Ages.

Kaltenbrunner entered the chamber at 1:36 A.M. wearing a sweater beneath his blue double-breasted coat. With his lean, haggard face furrowed by old duelling scars, this terrible successor to Reinhard Heydrich had a frightening look as he glanced around the room.

He was nervous and wet his lips as he turned to mount the gallows, but he walked steadily. He answered his name in a calm, low voice. When he turned around on the gallows platform he first faced a U.S. Catholic Army chaplain attired in a Franciscan habit.

Asked for his last words, Kaltenbrunner answered quietly.

"I would like to say a word. I have loved my German people and my Fatherland with a warm heart. I have done my duty according to the laws of my people and I am sorry my people were led this time by men who were not soldiers and that crimes were committed of which I had no knowledge."

This sounded like strange talk from a man, one of whose agents—a man named Rudolf Hoess—confessed at a previous trial that under Kaltenbrunner's orders he gassed three million people at the Auschwitz concentration camp.

As the black hood was about to be placed over his head, Kaltenbrunner, still speaking in a calm, low voice, used a German phrase which translated means:

"Germany, good luck."

His trap was sprung at 1:39 A.M.

Field Marshal Keitel had been pronounced dead at 1:44 and three minutes later the guards had removed his body and the scaffold was made ready for Alfred Rosenberg, master mind behind the Nazi racial theories who sought to establish Nazism as a pagan religion.

Rosenberg was dull and sunken-cheeked. His complexion was

pasty-brown. But he did not appear nervous and walked with steady step to the gallows.

Apart from giving his name and replying, "No," to a question as to whether he had anything to say, this atheist did not utter a word. Despite his disbelief in God, he was accompanied by a Protestant chaplain to the gallows who stood beside him praying.

Rosenberg looked at the chaplain once, but said nothing. Ninety seconds after he entered the hall he was swinging from the end of a hangman's rope. His was the swiftest execution of all.

Then there was a brief pause in the morbid proceedings until Kaltenbrunner was pronounced dead at 1:52 A.M.

Hans Frank, the gauleiter of Poland and former SS general, was next in the parade of death. He was the only one of the condemned to enter the chamber with a smile on his lips.

Although nervous and swallowing frequently, this man, who was converted to Catholicism after his arrest, gave the appearance of being relieved at the prospect of atoning for his evil deeds.

He answered to his name quietly and when asked if he had a last statement replied in almost a whisper:

"I am thankful for the kind treatment during my captivity and I ask God to accept me with mercy."

The sixth man to walk with handcuffed wrists across the small yard separating the condemned block from the death house was 69-year-old Wilhelm Frick, former Nazi minister of the Interior.

He entered the execution chamber at 5½ minutes after two, 6½ minutes after Rosenberg had been pronounced dead. He seemed to be the least steady of any so far and stumbled on the 13th step of the gallows. His only words were "Long live Germany," before he was hooded and sprung through the trap.

Following Streicher's melodramatic exit and removal of Frick's corpse after he was pronounced dead at 2:20 A.M., Fritz Sauckel, the slave labor director and one of the worst of the blood-stained men, was brought in.

Wearing a sweater with no coat and looking wild-eyed, Sauckel proved to be the most defiant of any except Streicher.

Here was a man who drove millions into a land of bondage on a scale unknown since the pre-Christian era. Gazing around the room from the gallows platform, he suddenly screamed:

"I am dying innocent. The sentence is wrong. God protect Germany and make Germany great again. Long live Germany! God protect my family."

The trap was sprung at 2:26 A.M. and, like Streicher, the hatred-filled man groaned loudly as the noose snapped tightly under the weight of his body.

Ninth to come was Col. Gen. Alfred Jodl, Hitler's strategic adviser and close friend. With the black coat collar of his Wehrmacht uniform half turned up as though hurriedly put on, Jodl entered the death house with obvious nervousness.

He wet his lips constantly and his features were drawn and haggard as he walked, not nearly so steady as Keitel in mounting the steps. Yet his voice was calm as he uttered his last six words:

"My greetings to you, my Germany."

At 2:34 A.M. Jodl plunged into the black hole. Both he and Sauckel hung together in the execution chamber until the latter was pronounced dead six minutes later and removed.

The Czechoslovak-born Seyss-Inquart was the last actor to make his appearance in this ghastly scene. He entered the chamber at 2:38½ A.M. wearing the glasses which made his face a familiar and despised figure in all the years he ruled Holland with an iron hand and sent thousands of Dutchmen to Germany for forced labor.

Seiss-Inquart looked around with noticeable signs of unsteadiness and limped on his left club foot as he walked to the gallows. He mounted the steps slowly. When he spoke his last words, his voice was low but intense. He said:

"I hope this execution is the last act of the tragedy of the second World War and that the lesson taken from this World War will be that peace and understanding should exist between peoples. I believe in Germany."

. . . .

KINGSBURY SMITH

J. Kingsbury Smith had an accomplished career with Hearst papers, beginning as a copyboy for the International News Service and quickly becoming a correspondent and manager for the INS offices in the United States and Europe. In 1955 Smith won a Pulitzer Prize, along with colleagues W. R. Hearst, Jr., and Frank Conniff, for interviews with Khruschev and other Soviet leaders. After the United Press and INS merged, Smith became vice-president and general manager of United Press International for a year. He was then named publisher of the New York *Journal-American*. He ended his career as Hearst's Washington bureau chief.

The Honor Roll

· · · · · · · · · · · ·

AMERICAN CORRESPONDENTS WHO GAVE UP
THEIR LIVES BETWEEN THE START
OF WORLD WAR II AND V-E DAY

WEBB MILLER
  United Press

*Killed in London blackout mishap
May 8, 1940*

RALPH BARNES
  New York Herald Tribune

*Victim of bomber crash in
  Balkans
May 18, 1940*

HARRY L. PERCY
  United Press

*Died of malaria in Cairo
April 19, 1942*

MRS. LEAH BURDETT
  P.H.

*Slain by bandits in Iran
April 24, 1942*

MELVILLE JACOBS
  Time-Life Magazines

*Killed by plane in Australia
April 27, 1942*

EUGENE PETROV
  *North American Newspaper
  Alliance*

*Killed in Sevastopol
July 3,1942*

JACK SINGER
  International News Service

Killed on airraft carrier Wasp
September 15, 1942

BYRON DARNTON The New York Times	*Killed by shrapnel in New Guinea* *October 21, 1942*
HARRY E. CROCKETT *Associated Press*	*Killed by torpedoing in the* *Mediterranean* *February 5, 1943*
SAM ROBERTSON *New York* Herald Tribune	*Died in Clipper crash in Lisbon* *February 22, 1943*
FRANK J. CUMEL *MBS*	*Died in Clipper crash in Lisbon* *February 22, 1943*
ROBERT P. POST The New York Times	*Killed in bomber raid over* *Germany* *February 26, 1943*
CARL THUSGAARD *Acme Pictures*	*Killed in bomber raid over* *Dahang* *July 20, 1943*
LUCIEN A. LABAUDT Life *magazine*	*Killed in plane crash over Burma* *December 13, 1943*
BRYDEN TAVES *United Press*	*Died in plane crash in New* *Guinea* *December 27, 1943*
RAYMOND CLAPPER *Scripps-Howard* *Newspapers*	*Died in Marshall Islands plane* *crash* *February 3, 1944*
FREDERICK FAUST Harper's Magazine	*Killed in front lines in Italy* *May 11, 1944*
BEDE IRVIN *Associated Press*	*Killed by bomb in Normandy* *July 25, 1944*
TOM TREANOR Los Angeles Times	*Crushed by tank near Paris* *August 20, 1944*

HAROLD W. KULICK
  Popular Science Monthly

Killed in London plane crash
September 1944

DAMIEN PARKER
  Paramount News

Killed by machine gun on Pelekin
  Island
September 17, 1944

DAVID LARDNER
  The New Yorker

Killed by mine near Aachen,
  Germany
October 19, 1944

ASAHEL BUSH
  Associated Press

Killed by bomb on Leyte Island
October 25, 1944

STANLEY GUNN
  Fort Worth Telegram *and*
  Houston Chronicle

Killed by bomb on Leyte Island
October 29, 1944

JOHN B. TERRY
  Chicago Daily News

Killed by bomb on Leyte Island
October 31, 1944

FRANK PRIST
  Acme Newspapers

Killed by sniper on Leyte Island
November 13, 1944

JACK FRANKISH
  United Press

Killed by bomb in Belgium
December 23, 1944

WILLIAM CHICKERING
  Time-Life Magazines

Killed by Japanese plane in
  Lingayen Gulf
January 6, 1945

FREDERICK G. PAINTON
  Reader's Digest

Died of heart attack on Guam
March 31, 1945

ERNIE PYLE
  Scripps-Howard
  Newspapers

Killed by Japanese sniper on Iwo
  Jima
April 18, 1945

BILL STRINGER
  Reuters

Killed in Normandy, France

Permissions

. . . .